# THE GIRL AT THE FENCE

Carol Rowell Council

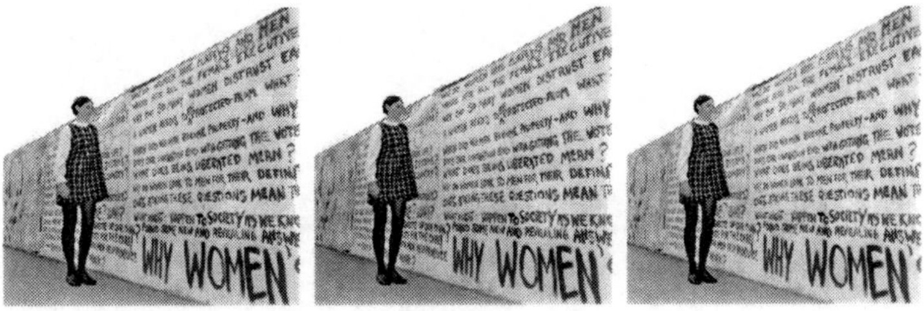

Published by
Bookstand Publishing
Morgan Hill, CA 95037
2184_10



ISBN 978-1-63498-046-3

Printed in the United States of America

Bookstand Publishing
www.BookstandPublishing.com

***DEDICATED TO***

# ***MOTHER***

***L'ALEEN JONES COUNCIL***

# I MOVE TOWARDS STILLNESS

By Joyce Nower

I move towards stillness
as if in a current
standing,
Sensing the moving waters,
the bobbing eyes,
and the soundless blue claw
scuttling.

Movement rings
my stillness, rings
it roughly, like water
ringing rock.
It is the rock I love.
With hermit hardness.
Withstanding.

But it is of the current too -
shaped by it,
shaping.
So I am -
There's no escaping -
shaped by it,
shaping.

## ACKNOWLEDGEMENTS

I would like to thank the following people for their invaluable support throughout the writing of these memoirs:

Trevor for his love, laughter, constant encouragement, relentless editing, and unwavering belief in me as a writer.

My son, Tim Council, and my cousin, Marie Collins, for their unconditional love and for editing portions of the book.

Joyce Nower, my mentor and co-founder of the Women's Studies Program at San Diego State University for BEING THERE THROUGH THICK AND THIN.

My dear friends and colleagues Cici Aguero, Nona Cannon, Jacqui Ceballos, Beryl Colvin, Ashley Gardner, Sue Gonda, Mary Maschal, Gracia Molina de Pick, and everyone at the San Diego Women's History Museum and Educational Center for reminding me that this book needed to be written. Nancy Yelverton for her sisterhood.

Margie Adam, Simone de Beauvoir, Rita Mae Brown, Riane Eisler, Juliet Mitchell, Robin Morgan, Ann Forfreedom, Betty Friedan, Pat Huckle, Ruth Rosen, Gloria Steinem, Charlotte Bunch Weeks, Laura X, and others I met early in the journey whose works have inspired me all of these years.

My nephew and author, D. Travers Scott, for his invaluable critique of the early manuscript.

The Baja Writers Workshop members, especially Marsh Cassady and Jim Kitchen, for their constructive criticism, teaching, and encouragement.

Melanie Bennett, a stranger/coworker on a charitable campaign who, back in 2002, said, "You have to write this book! Carol, you have to! This is too important. Don't let anyone or anything stop you now!"

The faculty of the 2007 Santa Barbara Writers Conference, especially Carolyn See, Leonard Tourney, and Ray Bradbury, who gave me the skills and motivation to write the ending.

A special thanks goes to Alice Donenfeld-Vernoux for being a brilliant wit, my writing buddy, and a true "girlfriend."

Kristen McDonald, the angel who arrived on our doorstep with inspiration, for the revolutionary image of the female centaur which adorns the cover of this book.

Most importantly the many volunteers and members of the Ad Hoc Committee for Women's Studies for their countless hours of work and dedication to reach our common goal, especially Rhetta Alexander, Mary Lynn Clemente, Maddie Farber, Patty House, Karen Howard, Teri Humphrey, Tracy King, Barbara Miles, Joyce Nower, Anne Nunez, Merilee Segade, Cristine Rofer, Chris Spaulding, and Mollie Stern.

# Table of Contents

# PROLOGUE

I became who I am today at the age of 13, on a hot sunny day in the summer of 1963. I remember the exact moment, peering past rows of church pews, between the stiff necks and bubble hairdos of Texas ladies and gentlemen. That was a very long time ago. I have never told the full story to anyone. I kept the moment fairly well buried until now. When the memory did rise to the surface, I referenced it in political terms of time and place, avoiding the guilt. Looking back, I realize I have been staring back into that red-carpeted foyer lit by the stained glass kaleidoscope window for the past 45 years.

In the kitchen of our San Diego home one night in 1999, my mother, who had been missing for over three years, called from somewhere in Northern California. She described a red Victorian farmhouse with two porches, a vegetable garden out front, and a scarecrow. Listening intently, I grabbed a pencil and scribbled notes. She talked on pleasantly; her captor was nearby. I memorized important words, listened for nuances, absorbed details, asked questions, and got no answers. Agonizing over a way to send her love and strength, I spotted the piano, set the receiver down next to the ivory keys, and played for her a Beethoven sonata she taught me as a child. A gruff voice in the background told her to get off the phone. "Lullaby and goodnight," I sang fervently, "May you sleep through the night, lullaby and…" A click, she was gone.

My dearest mother, who sat next to me in church patting my hand that Sunday, who sent letters of praise and saved all the news clippings about each successful step I made for the creation of Women's Studies at San Diego State, and told me she was proud of my work for victims of domestic violence and sexual assault at the Center for Women's Studies and Services for 20 years. The one who taught me right from wrong, who could not teach me to be strong, was beckoning me now.

When in my sophomore year at the University of Texas I announced to my parents that I was transferring to San Diego State to be with my anti-Vietnam War boyfriend, Daddy flew into a rage. He started with, "I will never give you another cent for college," and ended with, "You'll shack up with some guy, get pregnant, and become a waitress."

"Oh no I won't!" I countered. "Just watch me! And I don't want any more of your money!"

What I <u>did</u> do was to become a feminist on an unstoppable mission, dedicating my life's work to the cause of equality and liberation for women. I became the student founder of the first Women's Studies Program in the United States. That was a great achievement for the Women's Movement, but the victory — both personal and political — was soon stolen. I could never tell my parents the painful part of the story and how it changed me. It has haunted me since. "Victim" or "victor" wouldn't sum it up. "Wounded heroine" might be a closer depiction.

As a child I was not courageous enough to save the people in the back of the church that Sunday. The Women's Movement made me stronger, strong enough to fight many battles — sometimes sister against sister. But when I heard my mother's plea for life, I wondered if I now possessed the courage to face real danger full on.

# 1
# THE IRONING BOARD STORY

It was a long roller coaster ride, one that started when I was a 19-year-old college student. From that time I learned how to speak before a crowd of 2,000 students, negotiate with administrators, impress faculty members, debate hostile men, overcome sabotaging women, endure insults, hide my fear and aching stomach, cope with insecurity, and jump off a diving board naked. Now I was a 21-year-old seasoned student leader with a huge responsibility as Coordinator of the first Women's Studies Program in the world.

We didn't know if it was possible to change our world. A small group of students and one faculty member at San Diego State College (SDSC) toiled in every conceivable way to educate administrators, husbands, boyfriends, sorority women and anyone we could, including ourselves, about the new roles and potential for women which could be just over the horizon. It could not be left a dream. This was our conviction. We must create a permanent institution to keep on educating generations to come. And, somehow, we did.

That whole year I came up against many people who thought it was impossible or unnecessary to start a Women's Studies Program. And many more thought it was a good idea, but not something we could pull off. Who was going to listen to a group of students and one radical instructor? Especially at a conservative campus in a city everyone still considered a military town. East Coast academics with money would have a much better chance of being successful at this.

All along the way, I was determined, but when I was afraid or had doubts, my good friend and co-founder Joyce Nower urged me on. Joyce, a poet and English lecturer, really wanted to shun public life, and when she'd had enough, I encouraged her to go on. There were dinners at the Nowers when both Joyce and I had been so frustrated and worried that we wanted out. Then her husband Leon, a professor, sage, and activist, would start with a pep talk. We complained and resisted until he would come forth with an eloquent speech that convinced us that what we were doing was critical to changing the world, and that our partnership combined skills that were formidable. The bottom line was that without the two of us as mainstays, it would never get done.

My feminist passion had been sparked by a conference up north where I had met "radical feminists." This contact reignited flames from the previous year spent protesting the Vietnam war and sent me out to search for a feminist at SDSC. Looking back on it now, I know that it goes back further to that Sunday morning in Texas when I watched helplessly as a family of black people was turned away from the church doors. That's when I first got angry.

Today, though, it was a sunny California day, and I was happy. After all, we were now victorious. A small group of young women and one faculty member, called the Ad Hoc Committee for Women's Studies, had succeeded in climbing the "Seven Steps" of the SDSC pyramid, all the while fending off attackers, and had finally won approval for the Women's Studies Program to begin in the fall of 1970. On May 21 (three weeks after four students protesting the war were shot dead at Kent State University in Ohio and hundreds of campuses were shut down), we reached the summit and won the final battle, at the Faculty Senate. The Birthing was over and now we could get on to the *Creation*. I was 22 years old and elated at what the Women's Movement had accomplished for the world. We were making history.

I was dancing on air. The next day I phoned the man at Campus Operations to find out about getting our office space. We were going to have a home, a center for women!

"There is no unoccupied space on the campus for an office."

"No way!" I thought. My heart began pounding.

The sound on the other end of the phone was of papers being flipped through one after another. "No. Nothing. The only unoccupied space is an old house next to the campus which is being held for researchers coming this summer."

"Would you mind if I just looked at it?"

"Well, I have to be across the street from there anyway in a half-hour."

"Good, I'll meet you there."

Not bothering to dress up for this man, I grabbed my briefcase, hopped into the '59 VW Beetle that had made it all the way around Canada, through the streets of Chicago during the police riot at the Democratic Convention in 1968, and was still rumbling. I was enjoying the idea of taking a drive. Blue skies and sunshine everywhere. Morning-glory vines made giant blue bouquets of happy flowers along the fence-tops near our commune in the suburb of La Mesa. And it was a Saturday! Like Saturdays used to be. I felt giddy.

Once on the freeway I turned on the radio. The news was all about the rising death toll of our boys in Vietnam and how the parents of the kids killed at Kent State were demanding an apology from the National Guard and the governor of Ohio. I switched to my favorite music channel. Ah. The Beatles were rejoicing to the tune of "Good Day Sunshine, Good Day Sunshine!" I sang along. "I'm in love and it's a sunny day."

"I still love Lonnie," I admitted to myself. "I miss him. Those fun days together." A memory returned to me of the wonderful night of our blind date, the night we fell in love under a tree, looking up at the sparkling stars, of that innocent Texas time.

Oops. My exit was coming up, the College Street Exit I took so many times I could roll down its long curve blindfolded. The radio announcer mentioned Buffalo Springfield, and the slow notes of a warning song began: "Paranoia strikes deep." A funeral dirge.

Oh, my God. There was no way of avoiding the fresh horror of Kent State. The image came again, her agonizing scream, arms reaching skyward as she sunk to her knees by the body of a student lying dead on a campus sidewalk. This photo of the girl, a student like me, haunts me always. Her long dark hair and blue jeans reminded me of myself, and I felt her inside of me. How could *our* parents give orders to kill their children? Had this ever happened in the history of the world? How could boys who couldn't become college students or avoid the Draft, take up army rifles and be ordered to shoot students? Who was the enemy?

That silent scream now the cover photo of *Life* magazine, like Edvard Munch's painting of that skull of a man screaming against a swirling holocaust in the sky.

Next, I saw the TV image of Robert Kennedy's limp body being carried through the would-be victory party Lonnie attended while I stayed home to finish plans for our wedding. *No! Stop! Can't we rewind?*

*Get those pictures out of my head. Got to push them away.*

Just that short drive to campus had wrung me out, another roller coaster ride. As I swung the car onto Linda Paseo

Avenue, a cloud passed over the street of little houses. I saw the plain, heavyset, middle-aged man I was to meet.

Getting out of the car, I strolled towards the man from Campus Operations, said "Hello" and stuck out my right hand. I could feel his surprise that I was so young, only a student. Jeez, not again, but I was getting used to this reaction, so I smiled and joked to put him at ease. I turned and saw a small, plain, green stucco house of the 1950s post-war suburban variety. As we entered, I noticed the man held large blueprints with penciled notations. Once inside, my hopes began to fade when I saw only two bedrooms and a living room. He rolled out the blueprint and pointed to the evidence: All the rooms were marked with names of professors.

My instinct or feminine intuition made me not want to give up. Down the hallway, I spied a Dutch door that drew me like a magnet.

"What's in there?" I asked.

"Nothing, really," he responded. "Nothing worth seeing."

Faded light-green paint covered both halves of the Dutch door. I pushed on the top half. It was nailed tight. Seeing a doorknob on the lower half of the door, I tried it. It gave. I bent my slight body down and crawled under all in one swift motion, before the large man could utter a further objection.

"I don't have a key to it, and it's not to be allocated," I heard him say as his backbone scraped the upper half of the door as he followed me in.

Dusty green tiles covered the counters on three sides. Great for mimeographing and collating documents. A back door inset with a curtain-less window faced the campus. "Hmmm. not even room for a desk in here," I thought.

*Stall for time,* an inner voice told me.

"You see, no office space here," he said, standing directly in front of me.

I knew if I agreed with him now, it was all over. We hadn't come all this way to be left in the gutter. *Don't say anything, Carol.* I averted my eyes from his, turned, and locked in on the wall to my left. Then I recognized it, a slender wall cabinet. Lightning was striking! A magnetic pull came over me again — stronger this time.

I remembered when I had been a very small child looking up at Mother's ironing board, one that came out from the wall. Opening the cabinet door, I reached for the ironing board, pulled it down, hoisted my briefcase up and slung it on the ironing board. Our new desk.

"This will do just fine," I stated with a combination of the firm Southern politeness I'd learned from Mother and my newfound authority gained from the still-fresh victorious moment at the Faculty Senate.

I floor-boarded the accelerator to push that VW Beetle home as fast as it could go (about 58 mph), rushed to the phone, and called Vice-President Walker's office at the administration building. The secretary put me right through. I told him I found a location, but it wasn't quite on the map. He said he'd make a phone call. Next I called Joyce, told her of my tour of the tiny kitchen, and screamed, "I think we've got a place!"

"Maybe we can finally move out of the trunks of our cars!" she exclaimed. We both laughed uproariously. "Just in time for a baby stroller," Joyce added. *Huh? Oh, my God, Joyce's due date was in just three weeks.*

"Right." Oh, right. She was almost in another world, and I was oblivious to it. *Get a grip, Carol.*

The next day I got the keys to the castle. The press release announcing the beginning of the nation's first Women's Studies Program was written on that ironing board, letters recruiting faculty were drafted there, and the brochure for the first official 10-course program was designed and laid out on that ironing board. No shirts or skirts were ironed there again.

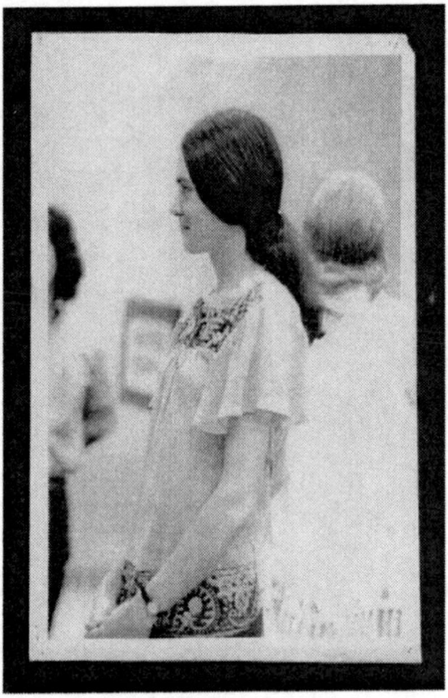

And that is the story of how the first Women's Studies Program got its desk and office on a university campus. Little did they know what we women would cook up from that tiny kitchen.

6

# 2
# BABY DAYS

As I stood alone in the kitchen office at SDSC (soon it became San Diego State University, or SDSU), my mind turned to the bottom opening of the old Dutch door. I saw myself as a little girl crawling under that door to find Mommy. Where was she? What was going on in her cheery kitchen? Did she already know I was there? When her eyes met mine, Mommy would break out in a big proud smile, lean down, and whisk me up. Everything I did was wonderful to her. Life was fun in this little playhouse.

Daddy and Mother did everything to make this modest two-bedroom house a nice home. In spite of the hard times brought on by World War II, my father, Frank, and mother, L'Aleen, worked at making the house "middle class" by working odd jobs, taking in piano students, and making things at home. My father, a telegraph repeater man for Southwestern Bell in Corpus Christi, Texas, also made honey in jars they labeled "C.F. Council Honey Company" and sold to the H.E.B. grocery store for their customers who had used up all their sugar rations.

Daddy made friends with kindly ranchers and farmers who let him keep his hives on their land in exchange for a few jars of honey when he came around. Years later, he still dropped by to see these men, and they'd swap tall tales or reminisce about some flood, drought, or crooked evangelist. Sometimes he took my older sister, Kay, and me with him, but we mostly stayed in the car, far away from the bees. I remember how alien he looked when he put on the bee hat with its hood and netted window in front of his eyes, and covered every speck of his freckled flesh with the protective material of the beekeeper's suit. You couldn't tell if he was a man or a woman, especially when he got farther down in the chaparral where he was looking to spot the wooden boxes in which the bees made their honey. It was a very solitary task, something like a communion between bee and man. I was to learn later how extremely solitary a person he was.

Mother was a second-grade schoolteacher who knew she would have to quit teaching upon getting married. Married women were not allowed to teach school in Texas then. The policy was based on the idea that women with families wouldn't devote full time to their work and would quit when they got pregnant. When this sexist rule was finally eliminated, she no longer had to put off her marriage, she told me. That was her version of their courtship that I grew up with.

When she was in her late eighties and hospitalized, though, she gave her husband's "love letters" to me to take home for safekeeping. They were scathing! He urged her to quit teaching and get a skill such as stenography so she could move to wherever his work was. Many years later my cousin Marie told me Grandpa tried to get Mother to break it off with Frank by sending her to spend a summer with her Aunt Helen in Houston.

In the 10 letters postmarked July of 1935 and addressed to "Miss L'Aleen Jones, Premont, Texas," he harassed her incessantly for withholding sex, attacked her parents as hypocritical evangelicals, and did it all with grand rhetoric, a vast vocabulary, and nasty sarcasm that ended in a sweet tease. He should have been a writer.

Mother had her first daughter at age 33 and her second at 36, making her older than most moms with young kids. She also taught chorus and rhythm band, and sang in the huge choir of the First Baptist Church of Corpus Christi. People I met around town praised her, and I basked in her glory, too. I knew that if I grew up to be like her, people would like me too. To help make ends meet, she gave piano lessons in the afternoons, sewed our own dresses, and cooked fresh vegetables from our Victory Garden.

For me it was a happy time, but my sister Kay was trouble, Daddy was moody, and Mother put the best face on everything.

When we moved to a house in a brand new subdivision, things changed. I started school and began to realize how busy everyone was. Kay stayed clear of Daddy until he grabbed her, threw her over his knees, and spanked her. Mother caught up and begged him to stop. Next he'd yell at Mother for being "a goody two shoes." She would try to arbitrate, but Kay would run to our room, and Daddy would go back to the garage; other times he'd slam the door to his bedroom, and she'd run outside. When I asked Mother what happened, she'd say Daddy worked too late and Kay needed to learn to hold her tongue. Looking back on those days later, I realized that Mother never left us alone with him.

I always wished I had something to do. There were a couple of kids on the block that I played with, but they were boys, and I couldn't throw or hit a ball, something which I tried to hide by pretending disinterest. Sometimes I'd try to practice in the backyard with my sister, but I was always afraid I'd get hit in the face. I don't remember my father ever trying to teach me to play. The only yard game we played was croquet. I watched Daddy at his workbench in the garage. He preferred to nurse his ulcers in privacy and often sent me away when he saw I spotted his forbidden bottles of cold beer.

By second grade I was dying to take any kind of lessons at the Linda Vista Recreation Center. Mother insisted on treating us girls as equals in everything, so we were given an equal number of lessons. I took ballet, tap, and pottery. Ballet lessons were trying. I couldn't get my long legs to stretch or bend as far as the others could, but I had great fun performing in a final recital before hundreds of people. Tap was too tricky. I couldn't find (or was it keep?) the beat. So that was that. In pottery I got to use the kiln and made a lizard green ashtray shaped like a leaf and a pale blue bowl that was crooked. Mother loved them both and kept them on display in our den.

Naturally both of us girls took piano lessons, given that our mother was a music teacher. I took my lessons from Mother in the living room, but Kay refused to follow her instructions. Eventually Mother took her to a private teacher who was very strict. We both studied for four or five years, performed in annual recitals, and received a statuette of a composer each time we completed a section. I loved to line them up on top of the piano, rearranging them and imagining what things were like during their lifetimes. Beethoven, Schubert, Hayden, Handel, Mozart, Liszt, Brahms, Mendelssohn, Bach. No women lined the piano top, though. Mother told me Clara Schumann was a great composer and taught me one of her works, but there weren't any statues of her to play with.

Other favorite toys were Lincoln Logs and Tinker Toys, which I could play with by myself, and Pick-up Sticks, which really needed another person. I'd play on the chartreuse green carpet on the living-room floor, hoping someone would come along and join me. Usually, Mother was grading papers or ironing, and Kay was nowhere in sight. I don't know what she did or where she went. I think she mainly just hid places or wandered down the street a bit. I can never remember much about her. It was like I had a sister, but there was a secret. She lived in another world. We both attended Fisher Elementary, a school close by the house, although I remember my mother driving or walking us to school in the first year. When I was in second grade, Kay was in sixth grade with the big kids in the main part of the building. We had separate lunch and recess times, so I never saw her. One day someone told me my sister was in the principal's office, but I never found out if it was true. She never told me anything, and Mother was the soul of discretion.

Mother took off time from teaching so she could be with us when we came home from school, which I thought was really a nice thing for her to do. She put notes in our brown lunch bags that said, "I love you," or "keep smiling," and I read them while sitting in the dirt on the playground. She would have a snack ready to eat on the kitchen table soon after we got home. She always wanted "to hear about your day," so I'd tell her everything. Kay would make a face or look sullen and be restless to move. Sometimes I wondered if she could be jealous of me. Or was it because Daddy was coming into the room? Maybe there was a change in the wind.

First and second grades were fun, but in third grade things got complicated. I was self-conscious on the playground. All girls wore skirts, so we weren't supposed to hang on the chin-up bars upside down, and climbing over the jungle gym wasn't wise unless it was after school when there were no boys around. I was no good at baseball, so I focused on tetherball. This I could do with either sex. Because of my height, I was better at it than all but the most powerful opponents.

In third grade two big events happened. Dickie gave me his older brother's cleat to wear on a chain around my neck. Dickie was a friend. I didn't know he had a crush on me. But that was okay. Most people liked him, and I liked him too. He looked a little like Beaver Cleaver and always had a smile. I started thinking a lot about how I looked. Was I pretty? Maybe I should cut my hair. I couldn't walk down the hall without wondering who was watching me or how I should be looking. I started getting stomachaches regularly, and when the pain got too bad I ran to the nurse's room to lie down until they sent me back.

One afternoon Miss Appleby left the room briefly, putting someone in the front row in charge. Debbie, who was sometimes my friend and sometimes turned cruel, said something mean to me, and the other kids laughed. I never felt so bad in my entire life. When the teacher returned, she found me with my head on my desk, sobbing.

"What's the matter Carol? You can tell me, what's wrong, honey?"

"Nobody likes me," I cried out.

"Well, now, that's just not true. You are one of the best students in the class, you treat everyone nicely and anyone who says differently is just plain wrong. You get up and go to the bathroom and wash your face. Then hold your head high when you come back. We'll find that smile again." I don't know what she did or said when I left the room. Like many things about feelings, they were not spoken about again. I acted like that moment never happened, but I was mortified. From that day on, I was on guard. I learned that I was what they called "sensitive," and decided to hide it with a smile and a calm veneer.

I still didn't have a close friend. I needed a girlfriend, and I tried really hard to find one. Sometimes I was invited to spend the night with a friend, but I was nervous. At this time in my life I did not know how to have fun, but I made up for it later.

# 3
# MORNING GLORIES (1961)

When I was 13, I lay in my bed and wondered who I would be when I grew up. I gazed up at the arching drape of the cornflower-blue cotton canopy and lost myself in the dots of eyelets and tiny embroidered white flowers. A row of ruffles in the same fabric flounced from the canopy top, and two tiers of ruffles fell from the bedspread. I loved my bedroom. It was the safest place to be other than in Premont, the small south Texas town where Grandma's house was, a house full of love and joy. I painted three of my walls pale blue, and Mother let me splurge by buying will-o'-the-wisp wallpaper for the other wall where my vanity stood. I could spend hours losing myself in the fantasy of plantation life the wallpaper depicted. I was reading *Gone with the Wind* and I liked to imagine was living at Tara.

My room was definitely the prettiest in the house. All the furniture matched — white French provincial — the dream of any southern girl in 1961. The other rooms had end tables, bookshelves, magazine racks, and bric-a-brac bought with S&H Green Stamps. My mother, sister, and I collected them with a vengeance. We got them every time we went to H.E.B.' s grocery store near our house in Corpus Christi, and the biggest excitement in our house was on the days when sat around the table counting them up. We pasted them into Green Stamp books while looking at pictures in the latest catalogue of what we could get with them next. Usually we could only get to the point of filling five or six books before we were unable to contain ourselves any longer. Someone would shout, "Let's get the lazy Susan and the TV stand! Come on, let's go!" and we were off.

Arriving there was another delight. In the window were new items not in the catalogue, causing us to huddle and discuss new strategies. In the store, black, Mexican, and white women mingled together exclaiming over their prizes or giving advice to the undecided. I guess the S&H Green Stamp store gave me my first taste of "diversity" and "sisterhood."

It was summertime, and there was nothing to do except listen again to my new 45 rpm record of Elvis singing "I Can't Help Falling in Love with You." I could not wait for that to happen to me. *Breakfast at Tiffany's* was showing downtown, and maybe Kay would take us in the new Chevy Impala. Nevertheless, I knew Kay didn't want to have anything to do with her younger sister. She was three years older than me and skipped first grade because she was so tall my mother felt it would be embarrassing for her. Besides, the second grade teacher said she covered first grade in her kindergarten year. She was smart as a whip. So she was always four years ahead of me in school, which meant we weren't at the same schools or Bible camps. Her friends were two or three years older than her and talking about existentialism and beatniks.

Kay thought Corpus Christi was boring and wanted to get away from Daddy, so she took extra classes and tests in high school, skipped the 12th grade, and enrolled in college in Missouri in a flash. I never really knew her. At least that was the way I explained it away. The truth is, I can't remember my childhood days with her, even though we shared a bedroom. The relatives referred to her as "a handful" or "restless." I do remember that she never sat on anyone's lap as I often did. She didn't like to be touched.

Funny, the college she chose in Springfield, Missouri, was just miles from the spot Daddy identified for us to move to and build a bomb shelter if it looked like the Russians might start a nuclear war. He showed us the location of military facilities, ports, major cities, etc., and explained that this looked like the safest place in the United States. I couldn't imagine moving for that reason. He was paranoid, it seemed.

Outside the day was heating up. Morning glories were steaming, and the weeping willow tree outside my window was gently swaying. Mother was doing laundry — she didn't teach in the summer — and planning our trip to historic sites in Goliad, Nacogdoches, Austin, Natchez, Vicksburg, Oxford, and New Orleans. We were going to see Texas history, Civil War sites, homes of famous authors, and plantations.

Daddy was sleeping as late as possible before going to work at 3:00 p.m. at the telephone company. He got home after we went to bed, and, since he was an insomniac, he had his own room where he would play his record player into the wee hours. Mother and he had an agreement that there was no alcohol in the house; so, he drank his beer in the garage. Later he put a door in his bedroom, which opened into the backyard, giving him direct access to the garage and an escape route if he didn't want to run into any of us in the house.

My grandfather, a west Texas judge, died when Daddy was 12 years old, and Daddy never got over it. *"O, my papa…*

*To me you were so wonderful..."* came the mournful cries of his favorite Eddie Fisher song, over and over. It choked me up to listen to the lament coming from his bedroom. Where was my papa? He had lost his father, but why couldn't he love me?

Besides music, Daddy's only source of consolation was gardening. Our corner lot on Stirman Street provided him with endless opportunities for creating beauty. He must have done similar things with the first house where we lived until I was five. I remember sky-blue hydrangeas all along the front of the house and gigantic, purplish-blue morning glories along the fence. All my life I would want to be near morning glories because they made me feel happy. There were gardenias and night-blooming jasmine on the north side of the new house. Roses of all colors lined the backyard fence, with a backdrop of purple bougainvillea filling the spaces in between the bushes. Red hibiscus plants and a low-trimmed hedge of boxwood flanked by purple and yellow lantanas ran below the big glass picture window all the way to the porch. They framed the graceful front yard of a 1950s ranch-style house, which I slowly began to learn we could not really afford. Daddy said Uncle Charles "helped us" to buy the house, but not to tell anyone. The neighbors had newer cars and "fine furniture" that my mother admired.

Below the south porch leading to the driveway were the only shade plants that could survive the heat and humidity. These elephant ears were so tall and wide they towered over me as I hurried down the red cement steps. For some reason I didn't like them very much. Maybe it was because of the loud buzzing of giant black bumblebees, which swarmed around the vines hanging from the latticework above. When the family was getting ready to go somewhere, Daddy would tell us to meet him next to the driveway. I hated this because it meant I had to run through these terrible shiny black bumblebees and then stand still like a waiting target until the car backed out and someone went to pull down the heavy garage door. He didn't want us in the garage. There were secrets in there — near the long, green workbench that was his headquarters. When no one was looking, I would run through the garage and out the raised door before Daddy started up the motor, so I could make it safely past the bees. Bees liked me. That's what everybody said. Years later, I would tell my young son the same thing.

I could lie in bed as long as I wanted. So, I did. I thought about which shorts set to wear today and rolled back over.

Maybe the pink seersucker shorts and matching button-up sleeveless blouse. I loved seersucker, and I felt good in that cool, comfy outfit. A door closed down the hallway. My father was awake.

As he padded down the carpeted hallway, I could hear a muffled scratching sound. Once I saw him running his hands on the walls as he walked through the narrow hall. Why? Why did he walk that way?

Mother came into my room a few minutes later and cheerfully sang her wake-up song, "Good Morning to You." It was hokey, but I always loved it. I loved it, too, when she tucked me in bed and sang "Lullaby and Good Night." She didn't do that much anymore. At 13, I was too old for that. "Breakfast is almost ready, and Daddy is already having his coffee."

"Okay, I'll get up."

Daddy made it clear to us that he would not talk to anyone until he had his coffee. So it was best to avoid him until after I heard the water kettle whistling.

I went down the hall into the knotty pine kitchen and silently slid into one of the turquoise plastic kitchen table chairs.

"Hello, kiddo."

"Morning, Daddy."

Mother took a skillet full of scrambled eggs and dished them onto our plates while the bread popped out of the toaster. "Oh, we are almost out of bread!" she exclaimed as she rushed over to her kitchen desk to add it neatly to one of her many lists. The washing machine, piled high with clothes to be ironed, was rumbling and jiggling behind us. "Tell me what you want to wear to church tomorrow, Carol, and I'll iron it tonight," she added. Daddy was an atheist, so she didn't need to ask him.

"Soooo, whad ya gonna do todaaaaay? Huh?" he slurred. His tongue sounded thick, and he swayed back in his chair a bit.

Embarrassed, I answered, "Not much."

"Whaz a madder? Cat got your tongue?" He sounded out the words slowly and sarcastically.

"Daddy had a bad night last night," Mother interjected. "We'll make sure everything is nice and quiet, Honey, and maybe you can get a nap before you go to work," she said, giving him a placating look. His eyes twinkled faintly.

"Now wouldn't *that* be nice," he drawled sarcastically.

I held my breath.

It was always too quiet at our house. Nobody ever came over except Mother's piano students. Friends never came to visit here. I wondered if my parents had any real friends. When I went places with them, we always ran into "friends of theirs," and my parents were always proud to introduce me. Mother said Daddy didn't want people at the house because of his odd sleeping hours.

We passed newspaper pages from the *Corpus Christi Caller Times* around the table and fell silent. The news was about the construction of the Berlin Wall, Gus Grissom becoming the second man to go into space, a hurricane off the Gulf Coast, the high surf on Padre Island, debutante balls, and summer garden parties. Daddy sighed loudly, shifted in his chair, and we waited. My stomach tightened as I gulped my orange juice. Why did he have to be this way? I didn't feel like eating anymore. A sunny-side egg was staring up at me, and I hadn't finished my biscuit. My stomach began cramping miserably. Even if I finished eating, I wasn't allowed to leave the table until Daddy was through with his meal.

Why did we have to go through this?

If I didn't say something soon, he would notice. I stirred the little pile of egg pieces around with my fork the way he did.

If I ate the last bit, he would start in on that lecture about not gobbling your food and how it was bad for your digestion. That would get him going on some other criticism, which might rile him up to the point of spoiling the day for everyone.

"What are we having for Sunday lunch?" I asked Mother quickly.

"Well, let's see, I could thaw out that roast, cut up some vegetables and put it in the pressure cooker before we leave for Sunday School, and it should be about ready when we get home, say about one o'clock. All we'd need to do is put some hot rolls in the oven. How does that sound, Frank?"

Daddy eyes stared out window somewhere over the fence top. "Boy, I needed that coffee. I'm beginning to perk up a bit. What did you say? Oh, yeah, pot roast? We haven't had that around here in a good while. Sounds all right to me. What do you say, kiddo?"

"I love pot roast."

I checked his plate. *Good. He was getting to the end now.*

"L'Aleen, you know, I'm working up a good appetite. I think I could eat some more eggs."

"Sure thing, I'll just crack open some more eggs and have them ready in a jiffy."

My stomach sank. *Now I really had to think of something he liked to keep us occupied.*

"Maybe we could take a drive tomorrow," I began.

*But where? We'd recently been to Rockport, Aransas Pass, Ingleside and the other seaside towns. He wouldn't want to visit the old library mansion that used a dumbwaiter to carry books upstairs this soon again either. If he began to nod his head, I should have the perfect suggestion ready. One that would make us all happy. Mathis Lake? The Nueces River? Definitely not Padre Island. No more mosquitoes and sunburns!*

"You know, I ran into a fella I hadn't seen in years the other day. He told me old Mr. Dickerson still has one or two of my original bee hives out on his ranch. I'd kind of like to go see for myself. Maybe afterwards, if I'm feeling up to it, we can drive on up to Mathis Lake. We'll see how I'm feeling after you two get back from church tomorrow, okay?"

We nodded our heads in unison.

"I can make up some tuna fish sandwiches to pack in the picnic basket and bring along some deviled eggs too."

"Have we got any Fritos?"

"How about chocolate chip cookies, and watermelon slices?"

"Or, we could stop and get fudgecicles..."

Finally, Daddy was eagerly finishing his eggs.

# 4
# SANCTUARY, NO SANCTUARY

The next morning, Mother and I ate breakfast quietly in the kitchen and then went to our rooms to dress for church. There was no talking between rooms, and, when we did speak, it was in hushed tones, so we didn't wake the bear in his cave.

Today I would get to wear my new high heels. I bought them soon after I turned 13. It was a major rite of passage. After all, I would be in the eighth grade and be old enough to have a date to the school dance. Oh. Those heels were dreamy. Such beautifully pointed toes, solid bone color, a classic look, and did they ever make my legs look gorgeous! I liked to wear them while I dressed at my vanity table, my legs crossed, doing my hair. Occasionally I swung my foot so I could gaze down at the beauty I saw below. Too early to play my record player or I would have put on Bobby Darin's "Oh, Venus. Venus if you will, please send a little girl for me to thrill, a girl with all the kisses and the charms ... make my wish come true."

The fabulous high heels and flirting with tall, handsome Bob were the only reasons I wanted to go to church. Bob was two years older than me and mainly hung out with his own age group. Lately he'd stop and tease me, and I just loved it. I tried hard, well, not real hard, to feel religious, but it just didn't come, and I accepted that when I was 12. Now I was content to enjoy the music. Mother sang alto in the huge choir of the First Baptist Church of Corpus Christi, and I loved listening to them rehearse for their special performances of Handel, Bach, and Beethoven. Sometimes they would bring in a small orchestra. With trumpets, violins, cellos, and cymbals added to the grand piano, and golden harp and pipe organ always on stage, the counterpoint, harmonies, diminuendos, crescendos, and final climax carried me away. When guest soloists performed, it was almost operatic.

I still loved standing up en masse to sing the familiar hymns, but, to be honest, the high point nowadays was parading in high heels and tight skirts from the parking lot down the curving hallway to the double doors opening into the beautiful sanctuary, stepping prettily inside to show myself off. Today I was wearing a midnight blue dress that zipped up the back with a fitted bodice and darts that accentuated my bust line. The tight short sleeves were slightly gathered at the top, as was the waistband, giving me curves I ordinarily didn't have. At the neckline was a tiny band of a collar which stood upright and set off my small chin and high cheekbones. My sleek auburn hair parted on the side and flowed down below the ears, then turned up gracefully in a soft flip. From every angle my silhouette was perfect. I clutched the bone handbag, which matched my heels, and scanned the congregation for someone to sit with. I already knew by then how to make an entrance. As usual, there was no one sitting alone I could join. My friends were sitting with their parents.

I began to lose my nerve. Did I look silly? Why didn't I have any friends to sit with? Oh, there he was, Bob! On the opposite side of the sanctuary. So handsome in his navy blue suit, and two years older than me. He looked my way, and even from that distance I could feel his eyes looking me up and down like Rhett did to Scarlet as she went up that winding staircase. He obviously noticed my size three figure, taking in the full effect of my dark blue fitted dress with its tiny waistline and tight skirt. Then he turned away to meet friends his age, and I was crushed. Someone said that plain girl there was his girlfriend. Was she?

When you were a teenager you didn't have to sit with your family all the time. I didn't have a family to sit with. Of course Daddy never set foot in the church. Kay and I used to sit on either side of Mother, but my sister had stopped coming to church a while back, and Mother was sitting up in the choir loft. I chose a pew up front where I could see her well, and placed my handkerchief on the aisle seat next to me so she could join me for the sermon.

Sigh. Nobody to talk to, nothing to do but look pretty. This was boring. I browsed through today's program. It began with a reading from Ecclesiastes. The assistant preacher said, "Everyone will please turn to Ecclesiastes Chapter Three, Verse One, in your King James Version of the Bible and read along with me." I looked down at the Bible in my lap and saw that I had brought my little black leather New Testament copy with the name "Carol Diane Council" engraved on the cover. It was a gift from Grandma. I turned it over and gazed at the familiar imprint of a horny toad outlined on its back cover. In my childhood I used to bring small objects to play with during the sermon. One day, riding home from church, I left my Bible on the shelf of the car's back seat and set my rubber horny toad on top. The next time I saw my Bible I was shocked. The toad was stuck to the cover and I had to pull it off. Hot sunshine melted it just enough to make a gray engraving of the ancient reptile, like a fossil print on the back cover. It was a nice distraction. Besides, I knew the verses by heart. Over 200 voices rose and fell in unison:

> To everything there is a season,
> And a time to every purpose under the heaven:
> A time to be born, and a time to die;
> A time to plant, and a time to pluck up that which is planted;
> A time to kill, and a time to heal; a time to break down, and a time to build up;
> A time to weep, and a time to laugh; a time to mourn, and a time to dance.

I loved those words. So consoling, so unifying. Something even an atheist like Daddy could agree with.

Suddenly Mother was next to me taking her seat. As I asked her why she wasn't in the choir loft, I heard men's anxious voices in the otherwise hushed church. The organist stopped playing her interlude, turned on her bench and stared at the back of the sanctuary. I saw the deacons leaving their posts and converging at the front and sides of the room. "Mother, what's the matter?" She turned backwards, looked over the pews, and whispered tersely. "We'll have to let the deacons take care of it."

Craning my neck to peer between the heads into the far back of the room, I was afraid I would see a medical emergency. Or maybe a drunken man? I was lucky, I guess, to have never witnessed anything awful. Not even a fight.

I was relieved when I didn't see anything wrong. No blood. Not a fight. So where was the problem?

I noticed two women in navy blue dresses and matching hats and veils who came in the door and were standing inside waiting. Then four men in black suits and black hats entered. No, they were not wearing hats. Those were black faces!

"Oh, good," I said softly. It would be nice to have black families in our church. In a flash I remembered the scene on television when James Meredith had walked alone into the all-white Old Mississippi University last year. Daddy, Mother, Kay, and I had all gathered in front of the TV to watch as he made his heroic march up the steps of the administration building. Soldiers carrying rifles were lined up on either side to protect him from racists. Surely *we* would welcome these people today.

More deacons walked toward the doorway. Then something went terribly wrong. They ushered the visitors not to a pew — but back out the door!

*Wait! No! How could they? They don't speak for me!* I wanted to jump out of my seat. To cry out. To say, "Those people are welcome here, we are not bigots!" Instead I sat still. I said nothing. Silence is a decision, I learned.

Later, as a student leader, I would state, "Not to decide is to decide." Now, though, I was paralyzed. I was aware that I was too young for anyone to listen to me. I turned to look toward my teachers for help. They sat looking straight ahead like statues, like the busts of Beethoven, Brahms, Schubert, and Bach on my shelf at home; they were immovable, dead. The stoic looks on the faces of four of my former elementary school teachers in the congregation were saying, "Pretend nothing is happening. Don't move." But those sweet women couldn't possibly believe this was right! They taught fairness and righteousness every day.

I can still see their faces 40 years later. Miss Appleby, her sister Miss Appleby, Mrs. Williams, and Mrs. Horne sat stoned-faced — like the little white busts of famous composers I lined up on my shelf at home. Evidently, they agreed with the preacher. Or else they thought it was a matter only the men could decide. The last shred of respect I had for our preacher dropped away as he softly reassured us that the deacons were "taking care of our visitors." He told the organist to resume playing. "Jesus, Jesus, Jesus, Sweetest Name I Know. Fills my every longing, Keeps me singing as I go" came the usually soothing notes. They sounded hollow now.

My throat was tight. I held my breath. My stomach bubbled. A fire was building up within me. I had never felt like this before. I wanted someone to stop the show. I wanted to go home to tell Daddy, but if I did, I knew that he would rail at Mother again that all her church friends were bigots, snobs, and hypocrites. Racists. That's what they were!

I forced the rage back down. *Be a good girl.* I had always been a good girl. I should never humiliate my mother. She had suffered enough already. When the shortened service ended, I walked over to my friends from my youth group to express my dismay. Before I could say anything, Bob spoke for the group, siding with the adults and saying "The deacons will be having a meeting about it." Oh, yeah. I forgot. His father was a deacon.

Shock and shame hit me again in waves. Then came despair, another new feeling. Tall handsome Bob, my dreamboat, was never going to be my boyfriend. He wasn't even a friend. I backed off quickly, saying I'd see them later. How could I have lost so much in a few moments' time?

I found Mother in the parking lot walking quickly to the car, and I joined her grimly in the front seat. We pulled away from the church, taking the long way home, down Ocean View Drive where the blue-green waters of the Gulf Coast rose and crashed over and over again as if nothing had changed.

I felt like I had been kicked in my stomach, and it ached so hard I needed to lie down or throw up. I could barely speak.

"But Mother, they taught us to love everyone, didn't they? Didn't they? Remember the Sunday school song? 'Brown and yellow black and white, they are precious in his sight.'"

"Yes, I do. And some of them need to be reminded of this, but now is not the time. I just don't know what will happen…"

"But this is <u>not</u> the Deep South. We don't have signs on drinking fountains that say, 'Colored' or 'White'! That's in Mississippi and East Texas, not here! And how could my elementary teachers just sit there? You saw them. And my Sunday School teachers too!"

"I wish it hadn't happened that way," she said grimly. "We'll see. We'll see." Then she added, "Carol?"

"Yes?"

"<u>Please</u> don't say anything to your father about it."

I examined her face. It was tense. I could see that she was afraid.

"It will only spoil our day."

Of course I didn't want to cause her pain! She was my only real ally. I loved her dearly. Reluctantly I said, "Okay."

My first lie. I was lying to my mother now. When I promised not to tell, I had already decided I would tell him on another day. *Maybe he won't tell her, and then it will be our secret. My heart raced at the thought. Could it be that I now had a bond with him?*

Looking back on it now, I know the events of that day changed me. I did not know it then, but nothing would ever be the same. I think I have been peering into the back of that sanctuary all these years.

Even today people ask me what made me so determined to found the first Women's Studies Program. All I know is that when I saw those black people kicked out of my church, a fire ignited in my soul that would burn to this day. It seems to me now that was the first lightning strike that led toward the creation of the first Women's Studies Program in the world.

# 5
# ANGRY

Never had I wanted to feel anger, and now I was angry. As a child, I was taught that it wasn't ladylike to show anger. The implication was that girls were not only forbidden to show anger, we weren't supposed to feel it, either. But I was angry. No, mad!

I felt like exploding. But if I did, then I would be acting like Daddy, not Mother. Angry that those people were insulted, rejected, thrown out like garbage because the color of their skin was black.

How could <u>we</u> treat them this way? I felt guilty. Did any of our church leaders feel guilty? Those church leaders, schoolteachers, Sunday School teachers, and deacons had betrayed me. My friends had betrayed me too.

I was so angry that I felt just like my father. My only example of anger was him, and I sure didn't want to *be* like him. He wasn't happy or lovable like Mother, or her mother and father, or Aunt Josie and Uncle Leamon in Premont. You never heard a voice raised in anger there. Mother was proud of that. They were good people. They seemed happy all the time. They cracked jokes, teased, praised each other, and hugged everybody. But, Uncle Leamon — wasn't he a Baptist deacon? Were they bigots too?

Men got angry. When a woman got angry in the movies, men put her down and grinned, "You're beautiful when you are angry."

I was struck by a question churning within me. Was I going to be like my mother or like my father? Never like him. He was disgusting when he was sarcastic, and no one could predict when it was coming. I was scared of him. Embarrassed by him. What made him so angry? He had a good enough job, a loving wife, a pretty house, and two girls.

Maybe he had wanted a boy. If he had a son, would he throw a football to him? Daddy didn't care for football. He wasn't athletic. He had not gone off to war, discharged from the army for some minor health reason. Measles or something. He didn't talk about it. He was ashamed of it. Or maybe he was angry about it. Like he was ashamed (or angry?) about having dropped out of high school to take care of the women — his mother and sister — after his father died. Was it shame or resentment that made him grow up angry?

He was also angry at the rich. Howard Fast, a prominent author and an outspoken socialist in New York, was his friend, and they wrote to each other now and then. Once when I was little, Howard and Betty visited our home. After dinner in the dining room, Daddy recited Omar Khayyám, Kipling, Shakespeare, and they all had a grand time, talking like I never heard them talk to anyone else. Late into the night I heard laughter and excited voices coming from the dining room. My mother, L'Aleen, and Betty hit it off when they first met in Mexico, and they remained long-distance friends.

When I was little, Daddy instructed Mother what to do if any men in suits came to the house asking for Frank Council. They would show a badge, but it would not be from the police. Maybe the FBI or somebody else. They would want to harass us. "We haven't done anything illegal. Don't let them in. Don't talk to them." This was my first lesson in standing up to people. I committed my father's instructions to memory. "You don't have to talk to anyone, even people in authority, if you don't want to." An example of American freedom in action. Silence can be powerful.

"We have a right to our privacy. We don't have to tell them anything." A few weeks later, they came to our house when Daddy wasn't home, and Mother stepped out onto the porch and politely told them when he would be back. A year later the men in suits came back. Daddy saw them walking up the driveway and went outside to talk to them. They questioned him about Howard Fast, called him a "communist," and asked Daddy why he would want to associate with communists. Daddy told him that Howard was a friend, someone he had met when he and his wife were on a road trip in Mexico in the 1930s. They enjoyed talking about literature and traveled together. That was all.

I remember his righteous indignation coupled with sarcasm when he talked about the stupidity of the House Un-American Activities Committee. I also remember that when, as a college student, I began learning about Frieda Kahlo, Trotsky, Diego Rivera, Orozco, and socialist realism in Mexico, I thought my father and I must have had more in common than we realized. By then, he and I we were angry at each other and couldn't talk. I missed that. I had to take a new father image and learn from him.

When we got back to the house, Daddy was still sleeping. No drive today. I went to my room and shut the door.

The blue canopy bed didn't look as inviting as it did yesterday. Everything had changed.

All I could think about was those black people. What had been said to them? Were they physically pushed away? How were they feeling right now? They looked so sweet. What were they feeling now? Were they hurt? Maybe they were very angry now. Would it be reported in the newspaper or hushed up?

My stomach felt sick. Another revelation came. Mother *was* a passive person. I didn't want to be like that. I wanted to speak out. I used to feel ashamed for thinking of her like that, but I had known it was the truth for a long time. Kay was always disgusted with her passivity. I couldn't ignore it any longer. I did not want to be like Mother, or like my "good" elementary schoolteachers at the church. They had been my role models. Now I had lost them. I put my head on the pillow and cried softly so no one could hear. I cried and I didn't know why. Looking back on it now, I lost so very much that was precious to me.

The full extent of my loss didn't come to me until many years later. I lost my sense of community, the church family, that day. And I lost my only teenage friends. I gave up on making friends at school after my best friend became a cheerleader and dropped me to hang out with the popular crowd. I turned to being active in the youth group as my last alternative, and now I had no respect for them.

My teachers had betrayed me. I had lost my role models. I had lost my community. I had lost respect for Mother.

# 6
# THE SUNDAY DRIVE

I moped around the house for days. Each day I checked the morning newspaper. There was nothing about the incident in it! Mother came back from choir practice on Wednesday night, and told me there was talk about it in the ladies' robe room. Some men held a meeting, and the preacher met with some families. The deacons would hold a special meeting, but we wouldn't hear anything because they met in secret. They did not have to give a report. They were in total control, and the women could only speculate. I felt powerless.

The next Sunday I said I wasn't feeling well and didn't go with Mother to church. I watered Daddy's rose beds and sat on a stool out by the hot, white sidewalk, pulling weeds from the edge of the grass as he'd been asking me to do for weeks. When Mother came back from church, he politely asked how the sermon was. She answered that it was okay, but the preacher's delivery was rambling this time. Had they talked?

"Why don't we take that drive out to the lake now?" he suggested.

Soon we were rolling past cotton fields and cattle pastures. You could hear only the hum of the Chevrolet engine and a "whisk" sound when a car passed us on the two-lane highway. It was hot, and we had the windows rolled down. I didn't know what to say or think. So I just watched the loopy loops made by passing telephone wires strung from one brown pole to the next. In fast motion, it was mesmerizing.

Daddy said he wanted to check out the old beehive and pulled off onto a winding dirt road, then turned into an empty field by a row of mesquite trees by a dried-up old creek bed. He stopped and got out, striding toward an old white box on a stand that used to be a beehive. Normally I waited with Mother in the car. This time I grabbed my sunhat and hopped out to join him in this slightly dangerous investigation. His eyebrow came up, surprised, and then he smiled because I was interested. Bending over the box, he peered into the darkness of the hive with the confidence of a man familiar with his territory.

"Well, would you look at that? They were here not too long ago, even though the queen must have left before that." I wondered how he could tell so much by a quick glance, and then remembered the two-inch-thick book always on his desk, *The Life of Bees*. I guess it was his Bible.

He looked happy. This was a world he enjoyed. A child's fascination animated his face.

"I used to have over 60 hives out here. They were part of my regular rounds when you were just a baby. Take a deep breath. The air is good here."

I took a gulp and smiled.

"Yes, I kind of miss coming out here."

I could tell things were better for him back then. He had a bond with these bees that a wife and two girls didn't share. We only knew the outcome of his labors, the jars of honey with the label "C.F. Council Honey Bee Company." He knew their lives. It was almost like they were a big family, and he knew the members by name. His kind of church almost. He was in awe of them and proud of his communion with them.

I felt closer to him, as if we could be friends somehow. I wanted to blurt out what had happened last Sunday at church. Mother sat patiently in the steaming car fanning herself and waving to us. *Better let it be.*

"This heat is beastly. Let's head back and get a drink from the water jug." Our moment had ended.

Back in the car, he told us stories of the beehives and the people who owned the land. I wished he could still have his world of honey. Not owning any land, he thought it was not possible. He could put some on Grandma's farm, but that was over 60 miles away, near the King Ranch. Besides, after the War was over, there was no sugar shortage and people didn't need to buy honey as much.

We drove on lazily to the lake, found a nice spot under a grove of trees where the afternoon shadows reflected in the waters, and Daddy brought out a fishing pole I didn't even know he had with him.

"Here, kiddo," he called. "Hold this for me."

It was a round plastic container filled with brown stuff. I took it and saw the brown stuff was moving. I gasped. Daddy grinned. "Now, you going to hand me one of those worms, or am I going to have to do it myself?"

In that second I wished I was a boy. He must have wished I were a boy sometimes. A boy would have grabbed a worm, taken the fishhook, and skewered it all in one motion. But me, I hesitated. And the moment was gone. Daddy's gnarled and freckled fingers had helped themselves to the diamonds that might lead to a treasure. He drew back, flinging the rod high in the air and throwing the line far out in the lake expertly. I could never do that. I could not even catch a baseball. But that was because he never taught me or I was just too afraid.

Mother must have known something I didn't know, because she set up a small Coleman stove on the picnic table, lit the pilot light, and put a pot of water on it. Oh, she was just making coffee to fortify him for the drive home after dark.

"Whoopee! I got one!" he yelled within minutes.

Like magic! It seemed like that big earthworm was a magnet to the first fish anywhere near it! Daddy went to clean it, Mother put grease in a frying pan, and, at twilight, we looked out over the glassy lake as we savored every last bite of that fish. If only it could be like this always.

It was dark when we drove back home together. Stars twinkled everywhere, and there was a cozy feeling between us. I asked Daddy to tell me more about what he did at the Robert L. Moore Community Center on the other side of town. I knew that he was the only white member of their board of directors. Once he took me there. I was the only white kid on the premises, and I began to feel that I was an oddity, like any one of them would feel in my classroom. There was a difference, though. They would feel despised in my world. In their world, I was respected either because I had the power of a member of the white class, or because my daddy earned their respect.

He said he wanted to spend more time there, and now he would be able to since the phone company was putting him on temporary disability for treatment of his ulcers and other things.

"I want you to remember this. It is very important. When you fill out your registration form at school, on the line where it asks for your father's employer, put 'Self-Employed.' Got that? 'Self-Employed.'"

Yeah. I got it, but I didn't know what it would mean.

For as long as I can remember, Daddy was always sick. He had his good days and his bad days. A bad day was usually followed by a bad night. If you asked him, he had "a lousy night" or he "didn't get a wink of sleep — not a wink." If he wasn't talking, and had a mean look on his face, I'd ask Mother why, and she'd say, "He is not feeling well." As I grew older, it seemed he was not feeling well every day.

I can still see him standing in front of the refrigerator when he thought no one was around, glugging milk down right out of the bottle. When he saw me watching, he said it helped his stomachache. He said the doctor thought it would be good for ulcers. I felt sorry for him. I had stomachaches too. Kay said he had stomachaches because he drank too much.

He worked the 3-to-11 shift at the telephone company. Although the building was less than 15 minutes away in downtown Corpus Christi, he came in after midnight. Stopping for a drink? I knew this because when I got up to go to the bathroom, I could see that the lights were still on in the kitchen and everything was quiet. Mother heard me, and came down the hall to lead me back to bed and tuck me under the covers. Kay was asleep in her twin bed on the other side of the room. Often I'd hear him bellowing about something that happened at work. Mother pleaded loudly "Frank, Frank, lower your voice. The girls are asleep." Things would quiet down; I'd fall asleep and wake up with a start.

"Don't tell me what I can and cannot do! You're so goddamn critical. Where do you get off criticizing me, you, and your goddamn relatives, hypocrites, all of them. Oh, they act nice all right, but it's all a big act. They'd sell their souls to the devil if they got a chance. You betcha! Churchgoing bigots. Think they're better than me. Well, they're your family, but they're not mine, and I don't want them in my house. You understand? They are nothing but stupid, holier than thou idiots giving all their money to those goddamn crooked evangelical bastards!"

Kay was awake, sitting up now, listening to his tirade.

Mother's voice came in between outbursts, "Hush, hush, you'll wake the girls."

"Yeah, that's exactly right. So what? That's all you care about. Kay and Carol. Everything you do is for them, isn't it? Isn't it? Answer me!"

"Frank, you know I love you…"

"Well, do you now?"

"Of course, that's why I married you…"

"That would never have happened if your father had his way…"

"Shhhh. Shhhh. You promised not to be this way."

I heard a door slam.

Kay said, "He's gone to the garage to get his booze. I hope he rots in it."

I thought my mother's thoughts. *His ulcers hurt badly, and that's what makes him angry. He wouldn't talk that way about Grandpa and Grandma if I were in the room. Maybe I should go in there… it would help Mommy… but I'm sleepy…*

The next morning we all walked on tippy toes, fearful of waking the monster in his cave.

I hate remembering the bad stuff. It was bad enough then; it was worse that I let it repeat itself later, and for that, a thousand times over, I was ashamed.

Kay, I suppose, reacted differently, blaming her father, cursing her mother, hating her family, becoming her father — only worse.

# 7
# END OF SUMMER

Summer began to fade away. The newspaper declared it with giant back-to-school ads. Mother took all the clothes out of my closet and did an inventory of how many school dresses I had. She asked me to try on some of last year's dresses to prove to me that they still fit, but we both knew I was going to get some of the latest fashions. Maybe we could take the train again to Houston and go to the finer stores there like we did last year? That was the year cranberry was featured everywhere, and I got a gorgeous cranberry suede two-piece suit.

Kay came back from her summer school session in Missouri. She seemed very mature — calm, too. We went to the opening of the first shopping mall, and she asked me how Daddy was, and how Daddy and Mother were. I didn't really know, and I didn't want to talk about it. She used to say that they should get a divorce. That evening, when Kay left on a date with a Mexican boy, Daddy came in from the garage with a beer bottle in his hand, yelling at Mother. He stood by the refrigerator flailing his arms and shouting in her face. When I came in he yelled, "What are you looking at?"

"Stop it," I said flatly. *Now he's being a hypocrite!* He didn't want his daughter dating anyone who wasn't white. Or was he just drunk?

At the moment, he whirled around and raised his arm towards me. Mother raised her arm fast and blocked the blow, saying, "You don't want to do this. Frank, you never want to do this, you know that." He dropped his arm, turned and walked slowly down the hall. "It's all right, Carol," she said, loud enough that he could hear her. "It won't happen again." It never did.

Now I was scared for Mother. He was acting crazy. When Kay came home, I told her all about it. She looked pensive, like a doctor.

"I was afraid of something like this happening," she said. "We've got to convince her to leave him, Carol. Things are getting worse. He is becoming a maniac. All those pills they give him are drugs. They are barbiturates! Who knows how many he is taking? He's addicted to them. I've talked to Mother before, and she is just so passive. All she says is she'll think about it. She won't do anything. I think she will have to listen if we both talk to her."

The next day we found Mother alone in the kitchen, after Daddy had driven away, and told her we needed to talk about Daddy. She nodded and sat down heavily at the kitchen table. She held her arm, rubbing the spot where his arm had met hers.

"I am so sorry, Carol," she said. Tears welled up, and she hung her head.

"It's not your fault, Mother, but something must be done."

"I have gone over and over it so many times in my mind. I know he is addicted to those pills. I've tried everything to get him to stop taking them. That's when he yells at me and says it's none of my business. I can't talk to his doctors because he won't let me go to the appointments with him. He needs to go somewhere and deter from medicine and alcohol. I took him up to a hospital on our last trip, but he wouldn't finish the treatment. Just walked out. What can I do? Leave him to stay in some cabin in the woods and try to quit cold turkey? He'd die."

*How could we pass judgment over him?*

We both nodded our heads. We were in agreement, and it was terrible. I said the "divorce" word to spare Kay from saying it, and I also said I knew how much she loved him. That she wanted to do right by her kids and her husband, but she had to do right for herself. She couldn't go on like this forever. *She was sacrificing her life.*

Mother cried and hugged us. She said it was good to get it out in the open at last. We told her we would help her if she made a decision, but that it was her decision to make.

In that moment, we became the parents, and she was the child.

Soon I was back in school. The eighth grade promised to be a better year for me since I had weathered the shock and nervousness of seventh grade. Now it was someone else's turn to be harassed by the smart-ass art teacher, someone else's embarrassment to undress in P.E. class while trying to hide a size AA-cup bra. I was a size A now and had a new softly padded white cotton bra for added confidence.

I chose to take a Spanish class and was excited to meet my teacher, Mrs. Ramirez. At the first part of class, she seemed strict and demanding as she took attendance and recited the rules. Next, she taught us to say, "Hola," "Adios," and "Mucho gusto." Then she assigned everyone a Mexican name. "Me llama Carolina," I repeated proudly. A whole new world was opening up to me.

It turned out that Mrs. Ramirez was Señorita Ramirez. Not married! And she was so attractive. Black wavy hair flowed down to her large shoulders, and her broad smile (when she let loose) lit up the room. She had strength, confidence, and beauty.

She was intelligent, modern, and younger than all of the other middle-aged teachers. She was the only Mexican-American teacher I had ever had.

Ms. Ramirez had a twinkle in her eye that said, "There is more fun to life than you know about now." At that moment, I felt I wanted to grow up to be like her.

One day, while sitting in her classroom, my frequent stomachache grew into unbearable pain. That morning I put on my new waist cincher in an effort to draw in my natural bulge and look sexy. It pulled my stomach muscles and intestines in and was getting tighter and tighter. By now, it was fourth period. I had been wearing it since 7 a.m., and the hamburger and fries I ate in the cafeteria were getting squeezed as they tried to poke out above the waist cincher and below my ribs.

My face must have turned white because, when I finally asked Ms. Ramirez if I could go to the bathroom, her look of concern said, *Go! I know how you feel — we are both women, and we get cramps!*

I rushed down the outside walkway and scurried into the main hall to the nearest bathroom. Slamming the metal stall door behind me, I began ripping the thing off me, but it was a tedious job. I had to find, pull, and release tiny metal hooks out of their metal eyes. Since the worst pain was now in my belly, I started with the lowest one. One by one, flesh burst forth. With each hook I released, I breathed a little easier. With a final gasp, I tore the thing off of me and collapsed onto the toilet seat. All the pain left me in a rush. My head reeled, and I leaned it on the wall of the stall.

I thought of Scarlet O'Hara. That morning I wanted a tiny waist like hers dearly. Now I wanted to burn that thing. I was so glad to be free of the torture of a corset. Maybe that is part of the explanation of why I joined "the bra burning" Women's Liberation Movement when I got to college. Looking down at the little thing, I thought of throwing it in the trashcan. Out of the question. Someone would see it! But what <u>was</u> I going to do now? I had to get back to class, and I didn't have anything to carry it in. If only I had taken my purse. Of course I did not, because the boys would have whispered that I was going to put a tampon in. God, this was misery.

I considered waiting until the bell rang and then trying to sneak back, holding the cincher rolled up in my hand or covered by paper towels. But it was impossible to hide it. I had no choice. I had to put it back on and bear the pain.

I stayed on the toilet seat as long as I could, savoring each moment of relaxed breathing. Better get back or they'll send someone to look for me, and the looks on the boys' faces would be unbearable. Carefully I hooked the top eye, then one below, then one more. The pains began again. I couldn't hook them all up, or I'd faint. I decided to leave the rest of the waist cincher open around my stomach and hope no one noticed the strange bulges and points coming from my tight skirt. Walk straight and tall; look them in the eye with confidence, and you can fool them all, I told myself. So I opened the door, acted my way back into my chair, and sat down as if nothing had happened. Below my chair on the wire shelf was my paperback copy of *Gone With the Wind*. I felt like I now knew Scarlet's secret pain, and I was going to have none of it ever again. A well-rounded Señorita Ramirez smiled a knowing smile.

# 8
# OVERDOSE

It was Thursday night, a school night, and I was writing an essay for English class on the white French provincial desk in my bedroom. I glanced at the clock. It was 8:45. That would leave me enough time to do my math assignment, roll up my hair, and make it to the living room to watch Johnny Carson. It was the only TV show Daddy watched, and Mother brought her students' papers to grade while she watched with him.

*I stared at the wallpaper. The slender, graceful woman in a long billowing dress and wide brimmed bonnet was under the plantation tree that was dripping with Spanish moss. What was it like for her when she had her period? There was no Kotex, much less tampons, back then. Mother told me she and Grandma had used rags and, since they could never really get the blood completely washed out, it was embarrassing to hang them out on the backyard clotheslines along with Grandpa's and Uncle Leamon's underwear and overalls. When they lived in Oklahoma City, they sent dirty clothes to a woman who took in washing. Here in this "hick" town they had to do with less and did so cheerfully.*

"Carol! Carol!" Mother shouted. "Come quickly! I'm in Daddy's bedroom!"

Shocked out of my reverie, I recognized panic in her voice and rushed down the hallway. The door to his room was open. I didn't know what to expect because I went in there rarely. Mother bent downward, then leaned out the doorway and beckoned me in. I stepped in looking for my tall daddy. One step more and I was almost on top of him! He lay on the floor on his back jerking. His eyes rolled back, glazed over, and around his open mouth was white frothy stuff like a horse that had been run too hard.

"Daddy?" He didn't answer. Mother said, "He is out of it; he was conscious but.... You stay here. He told me to call his doctor. It's all the pills he has been taking. Stay here."

Call his doctor? We should call an ambulance, I thought. Oh, I got it. She was following his orders!

She was gone. The phone was at the other end of the hall. I stared at her and looked down at him. He is going to die, I thought. We had to call an ambulance, not a doctor. There was nothing I could do for him. He was shaking now and turning his body in a circle. I tried to touch his shoulder, but his arm struck out at me!

I made sure there was nothing nearby that he could knock over, and then walked calmly but quickly down the hall to Mother. I knew it was crucial to stay calm. I also knew I was going to have to be in charge now.

"Mother," I said firmly, "We have to call an ambulance. A doctor will take too long."

Her faced contorted, and she moaned, "Oh, no!" She looked away, stricken like a statue. "I can't do it. I promised him."

"I can do it."

"No! He wouldn't want the neighbors to know!"

I couldn't believe my ears. Would he not want the neighbors to know if he died? Oh, maybe *she* didn't want the neighbors to know. To know he was sick. She was ashamed.

"Mother, if we don't call an ambulance, he may die right here!"

We both stared at each other. For a fleeting second I thought she might want it that way. I almost did, too. It would all be over. Quietly. He had already paid for his cemetery plot at Seaside Memorial.

Strange gurgling sounds came from down the hall. As Mother rushed back to him, I picked up the receiver, but waited for her to reappear. When she did, it was to say, "I told Frank we have to call an ambulance. He said, 'Tell them no sirens!'"

I dialed "O" for operator. "We need an ambulance at 624 Stirman Street."

"I'll connect you with the police," she said flatly.

The police officer asked me what was wrong. I told him my father was on the floor. He asked me if he had fallen or been shot. He told me to stay on the line. A woman came on. She asked me what had happened and if I could lift him. I wanted to cry. "He's throwing his arms around, and he is heavy."

Mother whispered, "Tell them not to turn the sirens on."

The woman said, "You have to keep him from swallowing his tongue. Try to put a ruler or a stick above his tongue. Then cover him with blankets and stay with him until the ambulance gets there. They are on their way now."

"Okay," I said. "My mother wants you to tell them not to turn the sirens on."

"Just go back to him now, you hear?"

"Yes!" I hung up and ran back down the hall.

What was I going to do? He was calmer now, his eyes closed halfway, and he nodded his head. Mother handed me an army blanket, and we snuggled him up inside it. He said, "Okay."

I heard a siren on the thoroughfare nearby. My stomach lurched, but my brain said, "Good."

I went outside to make sure they found the right house. I saw the swirling red lights of the ambulance coming down our street. They had turned off the sirens.

The doctors pumped his stomach, began running tests, put him on oxygen, and told us the critical period was over because he got to Thomas Spahn Hospital quickly enough. They said he would be there for a week, and advised us to go home and get some rest. It was the wee hours of the morning, and all I cared about was sleeping.

My homework lay where I left it, unfinished. Mother said I didn't have to go to school the next day. "I've already called and told them to get a substitute for me," she added. "I said Frank had to go to the hospital with stomach problems. I think since you have been up so late it won't be too much of a fib for me to call your school tomorrow and tell them you are sick."

I felt sick. Sick and disgusted. What a mess with my father. All the hell he had caused, and now this.

The next day Mother kept the blinds drawn tight so no neighbors would come over asking questions. She didn't believe in lying, and felt guilty about telling a half-lie. She would wait until the doctors gave him a word to seize upon before deciding what we should say to people.

I did not care. I figured no one at school would know anything. It was not really my shame. If there was shame in this, it would be my Mother's and Father's shame, and they could deal with it any way they wanted. They were going to have to work everything out. Maybe he would go away now. Maybe he would get better. Maybe he would die.

Mother went to the hospital each day. She said I didn't need to come. She wanted to spare me, I know. Besides, the hospital had a policy of only admitting adult visitors.

I was aware that I was feeling more and more like an adult now. At 14, I felt 10 years older. If only I could drive a car. Then I could do as I wanted. That's what Kay had done. Later I learned this would become her pattern. She moved around a lot, and couldn't be counted on to be at family events. She didn't like us; she didn't like herself.

Things after that were a blur. Bob Newby surprised me by asking me to the spring dance at his school. I thought he had forgotten me. I had pretty much forgotten him. Last summer I would have been elated. Now it was nice, but I wondered if he called me because he had trouble finding a date from his own school.

His parents picked me up and dropped us at the dance, saying we could walk back to their house, since it was only two blocks away. I found it ironic that his father, a deacon in a church known not to condone dancing for decades since the writing of its founding bylaws, was driving us to a dance. ("Don't ask, don't tell," I guess.) I didn't know a single person at his school so my opening line of "Hi!" was scratched.

I made a few trips to the girls' bathroom, nervously waiting out the fast dances. I didn't know the steps to "Swing" or "Jitterbug" or whatever they were doing, and I sure as hell wasn't going to learn in one night. I got more and more tense. Ahhh, I heard the slow soothing sounds and came out quickly to dance to "Blue Velvet."

I knew Bob was wondering why I wasn't flirting with him like usual. I guess I didn't find him so desirable anymore. I looked around at all the other boys to see if there was anyone gorgeous to fix on. No, just little boys. A couple of hunks, but they were with bouncy, beautiful, curvy-and-smiling girls. Probably cheerleaders. What a shame. Dating wasn't fun either. There was nothing romantic in this for me. I needed the lovers in *Oklahoma* or *South Pacific*, but they weren't at this small-town dance in Corpus Christi.

My dress was a pale blue strapless one covered in blue net. At the bust line, the net was crinkled and gathered in a way that accentuated the positive. Below the waist, it billowed out in a big wide skirt of blue net that fell to below the calf line. Mother had let me buy white linen shoes and have them dyed pale blue to match. It was lovely. But not my colors. It was Kay's dress. A stunning black-haired Elizabeth Taylor she was then. I had brown hair, freckles, and bones. Trips to the bathroom to pull up my strapless bra were essential, since I had nothing "upstairs" to hold it in place.

After the dance ended, we walked out into the starlight and headed to Bob's home. I covered my shoulders with the matching blue net shawl. I was freezing.

When we got to his porch, he asked me to sit on the porch swing, went inside, and brought out his varsity football jacket.

"Here. Put this on. It's very warm, and I don't need it. You can keep it for a while, if you want to."

I grabbed it, covered myself, and let him put his arm around me to warm up. Did this mean we were going steady? I felt it was too stupid to ask, and besides, maybe he didn't really know either! My chest puffed out with pride at the thought that I could wear it to school next week. Nobody there knew how popular or unpopular Bob Newby was, so they would really be impressed!

He began talking to me, getting to know me. This was the first time we had been alone. Talking I could do. I started talking about my school, the upcoming summer, the Civil Rights Movement...

*Oh no!* He was pulling me toward him gently. I moved back, gently. I tried to keep talking. He tried again. I tried to keep talking.

"Why won't you let me kiss you?" Bob asked.

I couldn't tell him I'd never been kissed before and I didn't know how to do it.

"Oh, no reason."

Bob, my dreamboat, was holding me finally, but I did not feel dreamy like I did at home in front of my mirror. What was the matter with me? I was blowing my only chance. I would feel the same way six years later when I would consent to break my hymen with the guy I was to marry a few days later. Today, thanks to the Women's Movement, we have *The Vagina Monologues* theatrical presentation to express our needs for foreplay. There was no Women's Movement then, and nice mothers and sisters didn't teach you how to kiss, so I had no cues or guidelines to go by.

I froze up. Thought, *I'm frigid.* Next, I tried to relax, snuggling into his armpit. He turned my head up, and I let him kiss me. I didn't feel anything except nervous.

Bob tried again. I was horrified. Humiliated. I can't do this. But I have to! I held my breath. His lips touched my tightly closed lips again. I relaxed a little.

His tongue was washing my lips!!! Disgusting. He was trying to open my lips to stick his tongue inside!

The front door opened slowly. Bob's father cleared his throat. "It's about time to take Carol home. I'll bring the car out of the garage."

Whew! It was over. Thank God for Bob's dad. I chattered with him on the way home and relaxed totally. Bob looked at me forlornly. I smiled, thanked his dad, and Bob walked me up my porch steps. We were under the porch light, so nothing could happen now. He rang the doorbell. Mother answered. I told him I'd had a nice evening, smiled, and said "Good night." Mother asked how it went, and I said that I'd had a very nice time. Then I raced down the hall. She unzipped my dance dress; I kissed her goodnight, closed my door, and released the hooks of the stupid strapless bra. Ah! Freedom. I wished I'd had a sister to come home and talk with on nights like this.

*Next year I would be in the ninth grade, the last year of junior high. Bob would be in his freshman year at a different high school district. Not much to worry about, especially since I did not go to church much anymore. I could play the field and play hard-to-get at the same time. If only there was another playing field.*

*Oh, no, why did I sign up for church camp? Mother had already paid the deposit. I would have to be with him for a whole week this summer. Oh, well. It could be interesting.*

Bob. I dreamed about him all my life. Wanted him. If I had never seen the other world, could I have married him? Could I have been a teacher and a deacon's wife? No. I didn't believe it. But it would have been a safer journey to take.

God, I hated being in my body. My mind was a much safer place. Growing into the teenage years was a true ordeal.

The scene of my father's body writhing on the bedroom floor, his gray cotton underwear revealing his pubic hair and penis, made me sick. I just wanted to go away or be alone.

I got my wish. My best friend, Susan, had dropped me like a hot potato when she was elected cheerleader. She was too busy practicing. When I did come over, I sat on the grass and watched since I was the only one uncoordinated enough to do any cheers. I wasn't invited anywhere to slumber parties. I had no other friends.

Grandma's house, 60 miles away, was a refuge. I went there several times and hid out for a week or two. Now I was too old to run and play on the lawns with my younger cousins Ruth Marie and Clyde David, and, besides, they didn't live in the little house out back any more. Uncle Leamon worked for Mobile Oil Company. He and Aunt Josie had bought a large mobile home and moved it out onto my grandparents' farm about six miles away. It was south of Premont, a little ways off a long road, with nothing but three or four other farmhouses in between. We used to chase the chickens around there. When Kay was younger, she had taunted a bull, and it had come after her. Those days were gone.

Grandpa still wanted to make me hotcakes when I was there, but I began sleeping later and later. I wouldn't get up until Grandma called to me some time after 10:00 in the morning. By then Grandpa had been long gone to his office.

I gave up going to church on Sundays. What was the point? Instead I'd go at night to my youth group. I suggested we study other religions and, to my surprise, they agreed. Islam and Buddhism were interesting, especially because of the exotic cultures. I checked out library books with pictures of mosques, temples, palaces, cathedrals, and synagogues; I looked at the costumes they wore in ancient times. Studying about these faraway cities, cultures, and histories became more interesting than their religions.

# 9
# THE DAY JFK DIED

Between second and third periods, I stopped at my locker to change books. One of the advantages of high school was that we each had our own locker — a little personal space. That was before the days of guns brought to school and lockers ripped out for security reasons. Although you could only linger there for a minute or two at the most, it was a private time and a nice break from the cattle herd routine. I was lucky enough to have an upper locker, which, with the metal louvered door halfway open, provided me with a good viewpoint for the Who's Who of the Hallway at W.B. Ray High School, the mainstream high school in Corpus Christi. I wanted a boyfriend badly and dreamed of someone coming up to ask me out on a date. The three boys I liked only flirted with me inside a classroom. In the hallway they were always with the popular girls.

Looking out over a sea of faces moving in both directions, I spotted only members of the ordinary crowd doing ordinary things. *What's that? A streak of white?* Silver white hair meant Farrah Fawcett was here. There she was! I wanted a closer glimpse and wished for her not to turn into the other hallways. I had heard people speak her name many times, like the way someone would say "diamonds." Everyone said she was a real knockout — with movie star qualities. Some said she looked too sexy and might be "loose." In 1963, she was already a legend in Corpus Christi, simply for her looks.

That day she was wearing a black-knit dress that hugged her slight curves, a black belt around her tiny waist and black high heels. (I had already given up wearing high heels to school in exchange for loafers or flats. The pain was too severe.) She swayed slightly as she carefully placed one high heel in front of the other — just as they had taught in the modeling class my sister had taken. The goddess/whore practically floated above the sea of students jostling, bumping, and darting around each other in a mad dash to get to class on time.

Tall, slender, and sensual, Farrah had pheromones that would not quit. She was sophisticated and seemed bored with immature high school kids. They said she only dated college men and barely knew anyone to say hello to in the hallway.

As she came closer, I involuntarily smiled at her. She smiled back.

A few years later in California, I was a feminist leader, and she was one of the three leads in the first TV show featuring female (very sexy, young) detectives, the hit series *Charlie's Angels*. Large posters featuring a provocative Farrah were plastered on fences, tacked up in auto mechanics' bathrooms, and hung in men's bedrooms around the world. A decade later, after we had organized a crisis center for rape victims, she starred in a powerful movie feminists loved in which a rape victim imprisoned and tortured her intruder, *The Burning Bed*.

The first bell rang loudly, reminding everyone that we had one minute to get to class. Slamming the locker door, I clamped the padlock on it and raced for the wide stairway. People were still streaming down the stairs as I pushed my way up, rounded the corner, and found the door to Dr. Steiner's class still open. He shot me a pretend frown, raised one eyebrow, and then lowered it as I slid into my seat at the precise second the final bell rang. He liked to use his authority to tease.

Steiner began lecturing his honor students. He strolled up and down each aisle, turned dramatically, tossed a question over his back, considered the reply with furrowed brows, nodded tentatively, reeled back with a feigned look of horror, and laughed aloud.

"Very clever but not too wise, Mr. Johnson. I'll let it go as acceptable."

He walked back to the front of the room and sat down at the big brown wooden teacher's desk to begin the portion of the class where he read aloud. I loved this part, and everyone else did, too.

Nobody knew who he was. Why was a man with a Ph.D. teaching in a public school in South Texas? When did he come to Corpus Christi? Was he a bachelor or what? Never referring to his personal life, he was brilliant, arrogant, and entertaining. Probably he was a radical who had been fired from some Eastern University. (Maybe he was gay, but that thought never occurred to me until now. In 1963, I had never heard homosexuality even discussed. Therefore, it didn't exist.)

Putting on his brown-rimmed glasses and leaning down into the book before him, he opened his mouth, sighed, took a deep breath, and began. "The quality of mercy is not strained. It droppeth as the gentle rain from heaven. Upon the place beneath."

His moving delivery of Portia's courtroom speech in Shakespeare's *The Merchant of Venice* made it understandable to us. His passionate portrayal of the desperate Jewish merchant made me wonder where he was during the War. Dr. Steiner, was that a German name? Was he Jewish? Had he been persecuted? Could he have been a persecutor?

A jolting screech accompanied by static caused us all to jump. It came from the loudspeaker on the wall behind him. You never heard it used except in first period when the principal would start the day with announcements. Dr. Steiner scowled at the interruption. (Did he not get along with the administration?)

"May I have your...attention...one moment please." Then nothing. Silence, except for muffled voices in the background. Steiner made a face that said, *Come on you idiots, we're waiting*. We grinned. He drummed his fingernails on the desktop, crossed his legs, and searched the sunny skies through the row of windows. Next a woman's voice came on. "Students and teachers, your principal has something to tell you." Steiner's face fell. He closed his book, folded his hands on top of it, and looked straight out at us.

"We have received word from a news broadcast..." (Was it the atomic bomb we feared?) "...that, while President Kennedy was riding in the motorcade in Dallas this morning, he was shot. He has been taken to a hospital in Dallas," said the principal, his voice cracking slightly.

"This is grave news," he continued, "but our President is being well taken care of, and we are listening to the news on a radio we have in the office. Please resume your classes. I will inform you when there is anything else to report. Teachers, remain in your rooms with your students."

I was stunned. *How? Who shot him? Would the Russians try to assassinate our President? Oh, my God, the Secret Service had warned that Kennedy shouldn't ride in an open convertible when he goes to Dallas....*

Two girls on the other side of the room began crying. One said her grandparents were there now at the parade. I looked at the faces nearest me. They looked scared. An outspoken Republican boy who disliked Kennedy stared at his feet.

Dr. Steiner cleared his throat, pushed back his chair. He looked from one face to another to see what shape each of us was in. I stared back wondering what was going through his mind. He stood up, walked over to the windows and looked down at the street, then turned back to the class. He just let us react.

People started sentences and stopped them unfinished.

"Who would do such…"

"He was coming to Texas to show…"

"Oh, poor Jackie…"

"Who else was there?"

"The Governor was there."

"Connolly?"

"My older brother is in Dallas at SMU, and he said he might go to see Kennedy."

Presently, Dr. Steiner said, "Okay, ladies and gentlemen, let's not panic."

"What if he dies?" someone asked.

"Lyndon Johnson would become President and…" Dr. Steiner started to reply but was cut short when the loudspeaker crackled again. "The news report is that the President was shot in the head and is being taken into surgery. Mrs. Kennedy is by his side. There is a report that a bullet also hit Governor Connolly."

*Oh, no!*

We were all horrified; you could feel the fear pulsing through our collective veins.

"Stay in your seats. We'll get through this together." Dr. Steiner picked up a Kleenex box and passed it down a row of sobbing girls. I asked a boy nearby what was wrong with the girl sitting next to him.

"Her uncle works in the Governor's office."

"Dr. Steiner, if they shot Johnson, too, who would become President?"

"As you know from your Civics class, the Speaker of the House would be the next in line…and after that…there is a chain of succession that would be followed."

We were acting like intellectuals in a normal classroom. This was surreal.

"It's too early to speculate. He is in surgery now. He may be just fine. School is still in session. So, we'll continue with the reading in a little while."

His tall figure sunk down heavily into his wooden teacher's chair. Oh, my, did he look weary. Steiner knew so much more about the world than we did. What was he feeling?

Suddenly I was scared. *Something is happening here. Something none of us can understand.* There was no source of strength anywhere in this room, in this building. My brain told me not to be scared. *How do I do that? If I think he will come out of surgery fine, then I will not be so scared. Nothing will change then. It would be a false alarm. Like yesterday's fire drill. No need to feel anything.*

The principal came back on the loudspeaker. "I have decided to let school out early today. If you need to make a phone call to arrange a ride home, come to my office. If not, please go home directly and be with your families. You don't need to go to your lockers or take any homework home with you today."

I stood up and thought of walking the eight blocks home. Mother usually picked me up after she got off teaching at her elementary school. I would walk alone since the only girl who lived near me had not come to school that day. What would I do there? Mother would not be home, and I could not call her since she stayed with her second graders constantly.

I went down the stairs, down the hall, out the triple set of double doors and into the sunshine. I felt numb. My knees wobbled, so I headed to the low wall where I usually sat to wait for Mother. Directly in front of me, parked at the curb, was a car like ours. I looked inside and saw my father leaning across the steering wheel staring at me! *How could that be? He was here? Now? Why?*

Walking towards the car, I realized he must be worried to have come out to pick me up. I opened the car door and did not know what to say.

"Did you hear the news?" he asked. I stared at him in a daze."President Kennedy is dead." I felt his anguish, heard the sorrow in his voice.

Daddy had come here out of instinct, to be near to me now. I looked out the car window at the other students waiting for parents, and stifled a sob. My father was here for me. We were bonded together again.

I had an overwhelming feeling that I was becoming an adult at 15.

"He died? That fast? The principal just said he was in surgery..."

"The news came out on TV about ten minutes ago."

"Maybe it's a mistake, you know..."

"Walter Cronkite announced it. It's true."

"Oh, no. How horrible."

"It is a sad day for the nation."

We drove the short distance in silence, pulled in the driveway, and went into the den where he had left the TV on. He had never done that before. We had to save on electricity. Things had changed already.

We pulled up chairs and sat close together with our hearts pounding as we watched live coverage from Dallas. They repeated the part when the doctor announced the time of the President's death due to massive injury to the brain caused by a bullet. He said Governor Connolly was in good condition, and they were treating him for a bullet wound in the shoulder. Vice President Johnson was flying to Dallas to be sworn in as President.

I couldn't believe it. I could not believe the horror. It was all happening too fast. I had the same feeling many years later when my high-school-age son came running up the stairs to our bedroom saying, "Turn on the TV. A plane has flown into the World Trade Building." We had stood close together, the three of us, in front of the TV, horrified as we watched the burning skyscraper, then stunned beyond belief as we saw another airplane aim straight for the second tower, disappear inside it. Our hearts had pounded fiercely.

I will never forget what Trevor said at that moment: "This means war."

I had dropped down on the edge of the bed. We had averted war ever since the Anti-War Movement ended the war in Vietnam. Ever since the time of JFK and Lyndon Johnson. Now what my father had feared was happening. We were being attacked? Should we look out the window? There could be a nuclear war coming soon. As I write this, President Bush is threatening to drop bombs on Iran because of their nuclear program. The paranoia that spiked after Kennedy was assassinated, and peaked after Martin Luther King, Jr., and Robert F. Kennedy were assassinated within two months of each other (April 4, 1968 and June 6, 1968), returned on September 11, 2001. Bush used it to rule the country with an iron hand and stir up the boiling pot that was the Arab countries of the Middle East. We cannot trust our leaders. Democracy has been at the mercy of a series of aristocrats and imperialists ever since the day JFK died. I would come to live under Nixon's rule of lies and insanity, and thousands of American boys would die because of him. Hundreds of thousands of Vietnamese soldiers, women, and children would be tortured, raped, and killed. As I write, it is happening all over again. One man's patriarchal regime massacring thousands of Iraqis and Americans in outrageous war.

# 10
# THE RELUCTANT MADONNA

It was going to be Christmas soon. Temperatures dropped to close to freezing. Daddy watched the news each night for frost warnings. When the weatherman said it was going to dip down close to 32, we grabbed rags and sheets, bundled up in our coats, and took flashlights outside. Mother and Daddy ran to the exposed plumbing pipes in the backyard and wrapped them round and round with rags to insulate them throughout the night and keep them from breaking. Then Daddy began giving orders about how to spread the sheets over long flowerbeds and vulnerable shrubbery to protect them from the frost. It was exciting, exhilarating.

As we rushed back in, the phone rang, and Mother picked it up. She smiled. "Oh hello, Bob. How are you? Well, that's good. And how are your parents?" I looked at her with a question mark on my face.

"Carol, Bob Newby is on the phone for you."

I couldn't believe it. My heart started pounding faster. *Why was he calling me now? Didn't he have a girlfriend? Was he going to ask me to the Christmas Dance?*

"Hi. How are you?"

"Fine, thanks. You?"

"Fine. Listen, you know, we are making plans for Christmas."

"Yeah, we are too. We've still got to get the tree. We haven't decided whether to get a flocked white one again this year or go back to a Douglas fir. They smell like real pine trees, you know."

"Yeah. We're going to be setting up the Living Nativity Scene on the lawn in front of the church. They have me to play Joseph."

I pictured him standing there, tall and handsome, looking down at Baby Jesus. I would get to pull up the car and sit there looking at him all I wanted to for a week.

"Emily Thomas is Mary again this year. Her Grandma is sick and they've decided to drive up to Oklahoma for Christmas."

"Oh, that's too bad." Emily was a quiet, short, dull, pious girl who played the part proudly as her personal calling from God.

"So we need someone else. Would you do it?"

Me play Mary? I wasn't even religious anymore. I didn't look the part, either. My auburn hair and dark eyebrows didn't fit the pale, blue-eye, blonde-haired, virgin image. It would be a sacrilege almost. At best, it was poor casting.

And yet — Bob and I would be playing a man and a woman with a newborn baby! That was titillating, scandalous. I got excited thinking that we would pretend we were in love with each other but couldn't really show it. Was that why he was asking me? The devil! What a perfect flirtation. Even if he did have a girlfriend, we would be making eyes at each other, for hours on end.

"Sure, I can do it. I don't have to learn any lines do I?"

"No, the whole thing is narrated on the loudspeaker. All you have to do is, when he says 'and when it was time that Mary should give birth, she.... uh, did... and wrapped the babe in swaddling clothes and laid him in a manger.' That's when you pick up the baby..."

"It's a doll isn't it?" I didn't want to be responsible for a real baby!

"Yes, so that's when you pick it up from under your skirt and hold it in your arms."

*Oh, my God.* This was so embarrassing. Bob was telling me I was supposed to act as if I pulled it from my vagina. I was turning red. He was silent on the other end of the phone. He was thinking the same thing! The sexual tension was ramping up. Did anyone know this about us? How were we going to control our feelings doing this every night?

"Can you do it?"

"Can I or will I? Of course, I want to, but this is going to be scandalous..."

"Can you?"

"Oh, sure. Okay."

"Good. Thanks. I'm going to call the committee chair now and tell him we got our Virgin Mary."

"Virgin." I cringed at the word. I had never said it in mixed company. It was so explicitly sexual. I was going to play a virgin. In my mind, I was acting as Bob's wife. And, I had the hots for him. Dangerous play. What a Christmas this was going to be.

# 11
# BLIND DATE

"Carol, Betty is on the phone."

Betty, my good friend in my senior year of high school in 1966, had been talking a lot lately about a new guy in town. Her boyfriend, John, was home from college for the summer and working at the best men's shoe store downtown. John was tall, handsome, polite, and smart, and they were a serious couple. My curiosity was up about the new boy from California who was working with John now. John liked him a lot, and was introducing him to his friends. Betty wanted me to meet him. I picked up the princess phone in my blue bedroom.

"Hi there."

"Hi. What's up?"

"I just talked to John, and he told Lonnie about you."

I couldn't believe it. "Really?"

"Sure, he told him how great you are."

"Really?"

"Yes, I said so, didn't I? Listen, there is a party at Duane's house Saturday night. Lonnie wants to take you!"

"You mean a blind date?" A bad feeling came over me.

"Well, yeah, but John and I will be there, so it won't be like you'll be alone with him all the time."

"Gee, Betty, I don't know. I thought I could just meet him at the shoe store or somewhere. Then see what happens."

"Don't worry. You're going to like him. He's real cute and easy to talk to. John's told him how cute you are, and he really wants to meet you! Don't chicken out on me."

"Well..."

"I know what. We'll make it a double date. John will pick Lonnie and me up, and then we'll come get you."

That made me feel a lot better. John and Betty were both very talkative and funny, and that would help put me at ease with the stranger.

"Okay. Yeah, okay!"

"I'm gonna call John now. Bye bye now."

"'Bye bye. And thank you!"

My last blind date had ended in catastrophe on prom night with my drunken date. Why should I go out with some stranger named Lonnie when thoughts of my earlier blind date came screaming to my mind?

I remembered the evening with Gary had started out fine. I dressed to look sexy and sophisticated. My black satin dress was sleeveless with a scoop neckline and an empire waist that cupped my breasts high up, then slid tightly down my torso, hugged my hips and stopped daringly above the knees. It was shiny and mysterious. Right below the bust line was a wide-open blood red rose blossom like the one Carmen taunted men with in Bizet's opera. The beauty salon took my thick auburn hair, teased it, swept it up high off my neck and wound it into a shiny French twist like Farrah Fawcett's. My parents stood side by side admiring us and taking photographs.

The dance was disappointing because the school chose a band that wasn't with it. So we went over to Gary's apartment to drink Jack Daniel's and Coke. After awhile Betty and John went into the next room. I didn't want to be alone with Gary. He was a drunken college guy pawing at me. So I tried to keep up a complicated conversation as long as I could.

After about an hour, Gary steered me into his bedroom, pushed me on the bed, and got on top of me. I asked him to get off, and he would not. I yelled at him to get off, and he pushed down on me harder. It was 4 o'clock in the morning. I was afraid that Betty and John might be asleep.

Gary said, "Don't be a prude. Come on. You know you want it. It will feel sooooo good." He held my wrists down. "Come on Carol. I've got a rubber."

"No!" I cried out for help. "John!"

The bedroom door was closed. What chance was there that he could hear me?

"John, come here!" I yelled.

Gary was getting pissed now. John was his fraternity brother! He kissed me to shut me up.

I turned my head and yelled as loud as I could, "Betteeeeee!"

The door came open, and I saw John's silhouette in the light.

"Hey Gary, take it easy now."

"You get out of here!"

"Now listen, buddy…"

"Don't 'buddy' me, you bastard." He was still on top of me. Betty came in the room.

"Gary, get up. Now!" He rolled off, tried to sit up, and fell back. John took his elbow, lifted him up, and escorted him from the room, saying, "You're drunk. You need to come out here and go to sleep." Gary was mumbling angrily.

I gasped for breath and filled my lungs with relief. I just wanted to go to sleep. Betty came over and touched my shoulder. She sat on the bed next to me.

"Carol, are you okay?"

I nodded. I still had all my clothes on, and he hadn't hurt me. I was in shock, though.

"I'm so sorry. He can be a real asshole when he is drunk. I didn't know he'd go this far though. What a shit. John is going to be really pissed at him."

I lay there thinking that I was so lucky Betty was there. She had saved me. Thank God she and John were protecting me. They were true friends. They didn't think I was a prude. They took my side.

I knew Betty was in control. John had Gary restrained for now. But we couldn't go home until at least 8:00 in the morning because our parents thought we were at another girl's house sleeping there overnight, and Betty would drive me home then.

I lay awake listening for stirrings from Gary and worrying about what he would be like if he returned. I tried to think of ways out of there. I could try to call a taxi. That wouldn't work. I had no place to go and no money. I wished I had an old brother who would come pick me up. I thought I heard the refrigerator door close. When I heard the sound of shuffling feet I knew it was Gary. Where could I hide? The creaking of the bathroom door gave me my chance. I grabbed my purse and shoes and headed out to the long glassed-in porch. Once inside I saw there was no exit. I knew Gary would go back to his bedroom and hoped he wouldn't notice I was gone and just pass out. But he didn't. Footsteps came shuffling towards the porch.

"Carol, where are you?"

I was trapped. I sat down on the couch and held my purse close. Nowadays, Veronica Mars just picks up her cell phone and calls a friend for help. No such technology then. All I could do was to sit stoically, giving him the message not to try it again. Gary had a beer bottle in his hand. He slouched down next to me.

"What are you doing out here?"

"I like it out here better."

"Oh, come on, this is ridiculous."

"Just leave me alone."

"I won't do anything, just come back to the bed."

"I'm fine right here. It's cooler on the porch."

He put one arm around me and set the beer bottle on the floor.

"Just lie down with me, then."

He pulled me down, and I gave in. He was behind me on his side. I lay on my side with my back towards him. I hoped he would fall asleep. Gary's big hairy arm came over my shoulder, and I felt trapped again. I listened to his breathing get heavier. Then his hand came down over my breast, and he stroked it. I picked his arm up and put it back where it belonged. He kissed the back of my neck, and I began to panic again. If only he would fall asleep. I could feel his hard-on pressed against my buttocks. Should I shout for help again? Could they hear me way out on the porch? A muffled sound. I couldn't identify it. I held my breath. It came again. It was a snore! Thank God. If I lay perfectly still with the monster behind me I would be safe for a while. The urge to go the bathroom was strong, but I didn't dare. Neck, arms, and stomach muscles so tight they hurt. Breathing was difficult. I had to wait until he got into a deep sleep before I could move an inch. After many minutes passed, I shifted slightly toward the edge. He didn't move. I waited, and then shifted again. Now there was air between our bodies. How many more breaths until sunrise?

Gary's big muscular body rolled over onto his back. I waited some more to see if he would wake up, then slowly crept to a sitting position. As I bent to get up, the couch springs screeched.

"Hey, where are you going?"

"Nowhere. Just across from you on the cot so I can stretch out."

"Don't leave me..."

The snoring started up again, and I made my escape to the cot four feet away. There I lay down and let out a deep breath. I could breathe safely here, and I could hear his snores. Light was coming through the window like a ray of hope. I heard a car start up nearby. The nightmare would soon be over. I fell asleep.

Someone was shaking me gently.

"It's 8:00 a.m.," said John. Betty motioned to me that Gary was asleep.

"Let's go."

I don't know exactly how I got home. All I know is that I did. It was a terrible night.

# 12
# LOVE AND WAR

I was 18. It was a warm summer night, my last summer before I would go away to college at the University of Texas. I ran the comb through strands of hair that fell to my shoulder and then flipped up in a saucy but casual hairdo. Looking into the mirror of my vanity table, I was pleased with my looks. I stood up, walked to the full-length mirror and checked my dress. The red cotton sundress was belted at the waist and had an A-line skirt hemmed right above the knees. My shoes were simple: white open-toe pumps with a slight heel, and I carried a matching white purse. Was everything right? My hem was straight, slip not showing, and my curves looked good. I was ready. He'd better come soon while I was still confident. He did.

When Lonnie rang the bell of our front door, my father and mother were dressed up and already waiting in the living room to meet the newcomer from California. John and Betty came in first, shaking hands with Daddy and hugging Mother. Next came a nice-looking, bright-eyed fellow with shiny, light-brown hair parted down the middle and a slight mustache. He wore a freshly ironed, yellow, short-sleeve cotton shirt with khaki pants and polished brown shoes. On a closer glance, I saw that his straight hair fell to chin-length and was combed behind his ears. We'd never seen a boy with long hair before, but no one seemed to care. He was clean, neat, and smart looking.

Daddy asked him what he was studying and what he wanted to do after college. "So, what are you studying out there in California besides surfing?" he teased.

Lonnie laughed. "I admit that I do surf a little, but I don't own a surfboard, so it isn't too serious." We all laughed. "I like American history and took a couple of classes in European history, so I've decided to be a history major."

Daddy loved history. I could see his eyes light up. "History is an enjoyable subject. I've always found it intriguing. I am re-reading some Civil War stories now. Of course, I prefer literature and especially poetry. Ever read any of Edna Saint Vincent Millay's works?"

Mother cut in to ask what had brought him to Corpus Christi. He explained that his parents had just moved to Corpus because Lonnie's dad, a retired chief petty officer, had just gotten his M.A. and been hired to teach English at the junior high school on the other side of town. He had come to visit them for the summer.

Daddy seemed intrigued and asked Lonnie to have a seat. That would mean a half-hour conversation at least. Fortunately John was quick to say others were waiting for us. I looked at Mother's face. Her eyes sparkled. She liked Lonnie. She talked with him about teaching being a rewarding career field. After a while, Betty reminded us we had to leave for the party, and soon I was in the back seat, listening to Lonnie answer my questions about California. It was easy, and Lonnie was very interesting.

At the party he was introduced around. Lonnie brought up the subject of the Vietnam War, something we all knew you didn't talk about. Corpus Christi had a major navy base. It was understood that everyone supported the military. Some boys who had dropped out of high school or didn't go on to college were headed for boot camp or Vietnam right now.

"It is important to talk about it, and it is okay if we have different opinions, you know, it's a democracy."

"I never understood why we went to Vietnam anyway. I don't think it's because of the oil, but I don't think it's because of communism either."

OUT OF THE KITCHEN! – Women United Against the War, a women's liberation group, leads Saturday's antiwar march through the streets of downtown San Diego. Some 12,000 persons participated in the demonstrations, including a rally in Balboa Park. There were no violent confrontations, although one seemed imminent as a splinter group staged an unscheduled march back to Horton Plaza, the march's origin, after the rally. The business district echoed with shouts of "Peace Now!" and "F--k War!" photo by Harry Meyer

"Historically we are in a period of great social change. We've seen a big Civil Rights Movement develop in the U.S. and now there is a growing Anti-War Movement."

"Anti-war! That's stupid," said a guy with a crew cut. "How can anybody be against all war?"

"Well, there are some people who are pacifists, who don't believe in any war, like the Quakers and the Amish. I'm not against all war."

"Nobody could have been against World War Two! The Japanese attacked us at Pearl Harbor."

"Right, but that's different. It was a defensive war."

""We had to fight Hitler or he would have taken over the whole world. That would have been the end of democracy."

"Well, isn't that what it's all about in Vietnam?"

"We have to fight communism wherever it is. Cuba, Russia. Vietnam is just the beginning. If we let it go on, there will be a domino effect, and then we will be under communism."

I listened to Lonnie with rapt attention. He had told me the "domino effect" was a destructive fantasy and that countless lives of good men were being lost in Vietnam. I liked the way he encouraged people to talk, not to take sides necessarily. It was a good dialogue and he was leading it.

He looked over at me, saw me nodding, then excused himself from the conversation and joined me. We went out onto the patio and sat in lawn chairs while chatting and joking with others. Lonnie was funny, too. He told stories and people laughed! He was a talker, and he was charming.

Mostly what I remember about that night was us lying on the grass together looking up at the sparkling eyes of Texas. It was a magnificent summer night. Magical. I felt light, happy all over for the first time since the fireflies drew us children outside. Back then we took their individual magic, captured it in a glass jars and multiplied it to make magic lanterns.

Lonnie and I studied the constellations, moved closer to each other, and kissed. The linger of the kiss promised many, many more to come.

About 1:00 a.m. they took me home. Lonnie came up the porch steps with me, and we kissed. It was a kiss that said, "I can't wait to kiss you again."

When I got inside, I changed into a white cotton nightgown and lay down under the cornflower blue canopy; I knew the world was changing for me. I had a real boyfriend. Not just any old boyfriend. I had an intellectual, progressive guy. Someone who I could trust, learn from, and share lots and lots of fun.

That summer, the summer of 1966, was a joyous time. Lonnie and I spent all of our free time together. Drive-in movies, water-skiing on the Corpus Christi bay, miniature golf, picnics, barbecues, and beach parties on Padre Island kept us busy all the time. The sweet smell of honeysuckle vines, star jasmine, and gardenias, and the bright colors of red hibiscus blossoms, pink oleanders, yellow roses, and fuchsia bougainvillea accented our happy days and wonderful nights. After long nights out, I slept in late and then went to my part-time job at a trendy women's clothing store just down the street from my house. I snagged good discounts on cute outfits to delight my boyfriend and dreamily felt the soft nylon of negligees sold to brides-to-be. Betty was already talking of marrying John and was collecting heirlooms from relatives and silverware to put in her mahogany hope chest. When my room was painted blue, Mother found a chest, painted it the same shade of blue and put it at the foot of my bed. It was piled with games, paper dolls, old toys, rags, and bedding, but I began to secretly call it my hope chest. The inside was cedar, unpainted, and full of that woody aroma. When my sister brought home her fiancé, the son of a Baptist preacher, whom she had met at Baylor University, she took me downtown to the best department store to set up her bridal registry. After pouring over each brand and style of sterling silverware, she chose a pattern that was sleek, modern, and graceful. While the clerk prepared the paperwork, Kay came over to me and suggested I pick out mine, too. I thought this was a bold idea, but when she said, "You can start a hope chest early, you know," I was thrilled. I had studied all the patterns, too, and already knew my favorite. The handle was thin and different, but the pattern of a climbing rose vine was traditional. It was me. I bought one fork that day and tucked the slender white box under the rags in the cedar chest. I loved indulging in this fantasy. Months later I had enough money to buy the knife and spoon.

The whole summer was a dream. I pushed far back into my mind the knowledge that Lonnie would go back to San Diego State in September, and I would move away to Austin for my first year of college at the University of Texas.

Looking back on it later, I knew I had fallen in love, and so did he. Little did I know how it would change everything in my life.

# 13
# BULLETS FROM ABOVE

"He was like our initiation into a terrible time."
Guadalupe Street Austin merchant, Austin, Texas.

In the fall of 1966 I began my freshman year at the University of Texas at Austin. I arrived in late July to take a summer session class and get oriented to campus life. Saying goodbye to Lonnie had been hard; but this was my college, and his was San Diego State. My new routine was comfortable for the time being. Kensolving dormitory was my new home, shared with my roommate Sissy. The only thing we had in common was that we were both from Corpus Christi. She arrived ready to hit the ground running in order to get into the right sorority. Day and night, Sissy was busy with tea parties, dances, mixers, and luncheons, leaving her precious little time to find the right color shoes and handbag for tomorrow's occasion. Every time she returned to our little room, she dumped shopping bags on her bed. She had hit every shop in Austin and was beginning to frequent the nooks and crannies of the University Coop daily. The Coop was a cornucopia of linens, clothes, notebooks, and hats, many of which bore the famous "Hook 'Em Horns" logo. Orange and white shouted out gaily, "We are the Texas Longhorns." Football season was starting up soon, and plans were already underway for the state's most famous rivals, the Texas Aggies, and the Long Horns to face off in the biggest fight of the year.

I was writing a letter to Lonnie when Sissy came bustling in with news of who she saw where, the cranberry shoes she bought, and a party invitation in her hand. She switched the radio on without asking if it was okay. From her top drawer she drew out a bag of hair bows, spread them on the bed, and gasped with relief when she saw there was indeed a cranberry one to match the new Mary Janes. Then she ran back to the mirror to check her short bubble hairdo, adjusting a curl and straightening today's blue hair bow. Her plump lips got a touchup of pink lipstick while she adjusted her pale blue pantyhose. She hadn't cracked a book. She knew I was serious about Lonnie, but kept trying to convince me to join a sorority. She had connections because she was a "legacy"; her mother was a Chi Omega, and that gave her instant status as well as priority consideration when formal Rush Week began.

Sissy pestered me to set me up with a blind date. The thought made me shiver. My last experiences were too fresh. I could do a party, maybe, but not a blind date. I told her if I did go out, it would be to have fun, because I already had a boyfriend. She went along with this and took me to two parties. Both resulted in drunken "men" pawing over me, followed by a mad rush to get back to the dorm before curfew. It was exhausting. Lonnie and I devised a plan. He sent me his Honor Society pin so I could wear it on my blouse. This was a sign that you were not available for dating. It was something like a stage higher than going steady and right in line for getting engaged. Engagement meant you were ready for your "M-R-S Degree." That is what Sissy was here to get.

One particularly hot and muggy morning, August 1, I left the dorm and headed south down the long sidewalk to the center of the huge campus to my British Literature class. There was a steady stream of students headed in each direction like on a two-lane highway. I kept to the right; those walking north kept to the left, and no one spoke because no one knew anyone, especially on dormitory row. I passed the modern Academic Center with its glass walls, wondering how soon I would have to start studying there for peace and quiet. It looked unfriendly, like a place you could not breathe in.

The sun was beating down, and the humidity was stifling. I hovered under a shade tree, but could not linger. I was approaching the Administration Building from which the Tower arose. The imposing sandstone structure was tall and narrow, 23 stories high and surrounded by a blinding white stone plaza. It felt 10 degrees hotter now.

I wondered who had designed the Tower. Visitors often took the elevator up to the observation deck, and I should, too, one of these days. I had heard that from there you could get a beautiful view of the Texas State Capitol and grounds. Its dome rose south of there on the same axis as the UT Tower. The Tower stood as a beloved symbol of Texas pride and greatness, the heart of the City and campus. What a beautiful sunny day! Even if it was hot. The familiar buzzing sound of cicadas and the sweet scent of jasmine reminded me of home. What a lovely campus to inhabit.

Crossing the plaza below the Tower, I peered up at the big clock face high in the sky, and quickened my pace to get to class on time. The red brick English building was a two-story rectangular building. I walked on down the wide, short steps. It was spacious, and I loved the feeling of descending from a grand monument.

I crossed the east mall, entered the air-conditioned building, took a seat in the classroom, and prepared to concentrate hard on the lecture. There was so much to hear, understand, and write down. I wished I knew shorthand. The class was an advanced one, and I was the only freshman in it. The language of *Beowulf* was hard to understand.

Soon the bell rang, and class was over. My fingers were tired from bearing down hard with the pen on my notebook. It was time for lunch in the dorm cafeteria. Passing down the hall with a trickle of other students, I noticed people stopping in front on the doorway. I walked up and someone said, "We can't get the door open."

We all turned and walked to the solid metal doors at the other end of the hall. Someone said, "The doors are locked." As one student stood on tiptoe to look out the small square window set inside a door, we heard our professor's voice saying, "Come back into the classroom."

Now we were all very curious. We stood holding our books in front of the teacher's lectern.

"There is a sniper on the Tower."

"A what?"

"A sniper. A man with a rifle. Maybe more than one man. The campus police chained the doors. We are right within shooting distance, so no one can leave now. Stay away from the windows."

The windows were at the west end of the building. How could a bullet come through there? It would have to curve. Oh, maybe they didn't know where he was. He could be in the bushes. This was truly bizarre. Why would anyone be shooting from the Tower? Maybe he is drunk. Or maybe it is not true. We had not heard any gunshots.

"How do you know?"

"I got a phone call," said the professor. He pointed to a black phone behind the lectern. "The campus police. They said it is on local TV stations."

I was stunned. Nothing had ever happened like this before. Yes, it had. Three years ago, I had been trapped inside my high school classroom when the principal announced over the loudspeaker that John F. Kennedy had just been shot at a parade in Dallas, and they did not know where the sniper was. Sniper? Someone else said "shooter." Shooter. Was there such a word in the English dictionary? Shooter. Not "killer." Not "assassin." Not a "hunter." *Shooter.* Shooting at what?

The whole world was changing again. My head was spinning. *Can't they get him? Is there going to be a shootout by our classroom? Is Texas still the Wild West? I wish I had a friend. I want my father to come get me out of here!*

Some guy said, "They have no right to lock us in here." He sounded rough. Wide shoulders, a thick neck, and a blonde crew cut gave him the look of a farm boy turned jock. "I'd run over to those bushes and be out of here before he saw me."

"That's why they locked the doors. They don't want anyone else getting killed."

A deadly silence struck us all. Slowly it dawned on us. Someone was shot and killed practically in front of us. Just for walking in front of the Tower? Like I just did.

Killed? Maybe it was a worker at the Tower. The man's wife maybe.

"At least three students have been shot on the quad or on the steps."

*Pop! Pop! Pop!*

"Did you hear that?"

"That sounded like gunshots."

My heart was pounding beyond belief. It must be true. Over the hum of the air conditioning I heard a series of gunshots. I sat down. Everyone else sat down. The professor plopped in his chair, his terrible announcement completed.

*Pop! Pop! Pa-pa-pa-pa-pa-pa-pop!*

An automatic rifle!

*Oh my God! He wants to kill us. Why? Why? Because...we are...because we are students?* He might have killed me, if I had walked out that door five minutes earlier. The sniper had picked the busiest time of day, right around lunchtime, to crouch up there, aim through the crosshair, and shoot. Kill students? That has never been a motive in all of history.

Now I wanted to run. I stood up and starting pacing the classroom floor. *What can be done?* I was alone. I had no friend in that building. If only I could talk to Lonnie. Or Mother, or Daddy. But, I would just scare them and, of course, I could not use the professor's phone line.

Scare them? Oh, my God. If it were on the Austin TV channels, it would probably be on national TV, too! They were already scared to death for me!

The telephone rang. *It must be over. They'll unlock the doors, and we'll be safe. Did they kill him?*

The professor listened closely. We waited, unable to breathe. "Yes. All right." He hung up the phone. "The State Troopers spotted the man by helicopter. He is on the observation level at the top of the Tower. He can move around all four sides of the balcony without being seen, and he shoots at anything that moves. He is out of range for any police on the ground. There are more bodies on the quad and on the lawn. The police can't get to them or they will be shot. All we can do is stay put."

I thought about my life. I had always been safe until now. *What have I done to deserve this? Be born in 1948? Left Corpus Christi for Austin? Could I have avoided this? Not unless I had cut class. Where is Sissy? Is she hysterical, obliviously shopping, or dead?*

It just could not be about killing students. Something else was going on here. We were so close to the Capitol Building. Maybe President Johnson was in town. Was there a connection with the assassination of Kennedy in Dallas in 1963? Was there a conspiracy? They wounded Governor Connolly then. Were they after Johnson now? He had been a Governor of Texas, too. Was this related to the Vietnam War somehow? No. We barely had a handful of protestors on this campus. It could not be that.

A student from a classroom across the hall came in and said they had a closed circuit TV in their room. We could watch it from there.

Watch it on TV? A choice had to be made. Did I want to see people dying? I had to know what was happening. My survival instinct drew me across the hall to view the snowy, black-and-white picture. There was no sound, no newscaster. The camera was aimed on the top of the Tower. No sign of the shooter. No movement. We stood and waited. Then sat and waited. I couldn't take the tension anymore. Some people lit up cigarettes. I wished I knew how to smoke.

"There he is! Over by the corner. I saw something move." I ran back to the TV, but couldn't see anything. It was quiet, it seemed. I left and then paced my way back towards the TV. Now the scene was totally different. No Tower. It was hard to make out anything. Someone's finger touched the lower-right screen. I made out the lines of the steps I had taken down from under the Tower. There was a body lying on its stomach. A boy, judging from the dark pants and light shirt.

"He's dead. He has been lying still like that since the beginning," someone said.

"And look over there by the edge of the lawn, there is someone crumpled up. Oh, my God. Look, the police are in the bushes. They are trying to crawl towards her. You could see the outline of her skirt and bare legs."

This could have been me. I was there only minutes ago. Or was it hours now? My stomach clenched. *How long was this going to go on? Help me!*

An eternity went by. I figured I was safe in this brick building if I didn't go outside, but I wanted out badly. I looked at my professor's face for news. He sat still by the phone.

A professor from down the hall came in and talked to him. Then they told us we could leave by the west door and follow the motions of the police to be safe behind buildings. They had cordoned off much of the area with yellow tape. Walk quickly and quietly.

"But did they get him?"

"All I know is what the police are telling us. That it is safe to come out and to follow their routes."

Some comfort.

Would we see bleeding students?

Could I help? No.

All right. When it was my turn at the door, I spotted a police officer across the lawn motioning me to come ahead. There was a yellow ribbon to follow. I decided not to look left or right. I put my faith in that police officer and went. Soon I was on the other side. Another police officer asked me where I lived. "Kinsolving."

"Follow that policeman over there, he will show you the detour to get to Kinsolving." I nodded and did what I was told.

Now I was back on the sidewalk that led past the library and down to the dorms. There was no steady line of walkers going south and north. Instead, there were a few dazed students wondering who knew what.

"Have you seen so and so?"

"Were you at the Tower?"

"Did you hear what happened?"

"What happened?"

I passed by them in a stupor. My only thought was to make it to the dorm safely. I did. As I entered the glass doorways, I saw looks of horror on people's faces. Girls crying. I walked up the dorm mother's window. The clerk said, "You are Carol Council?"

"Yes. What?"

"Your parents are on the way here. They started driving from Corpus when they heard the news, so they should be here soon."

My knees grew shaky. Mother. Daddy. They had come running. *I love you sooo much.*

"What about my roommate? Sissy?"

"She came in just a little while ago. She is okay."

"And, uh, others here?"

"We don't know yet. I have to help the next person."

I moved over, watching the faces of the girls wandering the lobby. I didn't know any of them. Some were standing in line to use the pay phone to call home. Another girl was telling how her friend was shot. Looking at the glass doors of the lobby, I saw my mother and father enter, searching the room. They could not see me; they must have been wondering if I was alive or dead.

I rushed towards them, they both hugged me. I was their baby again. The three of us all held each other, for the first and last time I can remember.

I was still in control, but I wanted to be alone with them. Daddy told me we were going to stay in a hotel together. A warming, comforting feeling flowed over me. I was alive. They were my refuge; they had sped over 300 miles to find me.

Two years later, in the police riot of the Chicago Democratic Convention, my parents had stared at the TV, hoping to catch sight of my face as others were shot. Now, I have my own son in college; I feel sorry for how much I worried them.

What happened after that? Life went on. News reports came in that a man name Charles Whitman was killed atop the Tower, finally cornered by heroic officers who had risked their lives to save hundreds. They said he was crazy. No one could have predicted it. Nothing made sense. He killed 14 people and injured dozens more that August day, and life had to just go on.

For me, it was a warning of violence to come. Terrorism had started.

After the Tower was cleaned up and spaces marked off for investigation, it was supposed to be over. Classes resumed. Football games became important news. But, only two years later, Martin Luther King, Jr., and Robert F. Kennedy were assassinated. Soon after that, the National Guard killed Vietnam War protestors on the campus lawn at Kent State University. Today, my son told me terrorism began for him when he experienced the explosion of the Oklahoma City Federal Building. For me it began at the UT Tower.

After the shootings, the Tower was closed to tourists. Later they erected a barrier to keep anyone from doing that again.

I remember houses that didn't have fences between them in Grandma's small town. Since those days, I've seen many barriers erected everywhere in the U.S. to prevent violence from returning. The fences still aren't working.

Fourteen unique individuals died that day. People often tell me I made a difference in this world by leaving the University of Texas and struggling to create Women's Studies. I am fortunate to have escaped death that day. I often wonder what those 14 souls might have done had they escaped the bullets from above.

# 14
# COMING TO SAN DIEGO

At the end of the first semester of my sophomore year at the University of Texas, I boarded an airplane for San Diego and left my old life behind. No more parental oversight, no more loneliness. Only excitement — adventure, romance, and powerful opportunities lay ahead. In spades. Thrilled to see Lonnie's grin and sexy mustache again, I wrapped my arms around him and squeezed hard. He was so excited he could barely stand still. Lonnie whisked me off, first to meet his roommates, and then to meet his childhood friends. Dropping my bags at the house of his newly wed friends, I knew we had hit it off immediately.

Next he gave me the tour of beautiful San Diego, starting with its gem, Balboa Park. I drank in the magnificent fountains, curving colonnades, organ pavilion, international houses of hospitality, the Old Globe Theater, and amphitheater for musicals called the Starlight Theater, a riot of colors and intoxicating aromas in the hundreds of blossoms in the rose gardens. The lush, exotic plants of the arboretum and a tranquil lily pond drenched me in hues of blue and green. I was immersed in European beauty — in a living and moving world of Monet's brushstrokes.

I fell in love with the Spanish/Moorish architecture from the 1913 International Exposition, with its arches, arcades, towers, friezes, and statues on the façade of the art museum and adjacent buildings along the promenade called the Prado. Inside the San Diego Museum of Art, I discovered lovely paintings from Italy, France, Germany, sculpture and ceramic wonders from China, and modern pieces too abstract for me to understand or relate to at the time. Next door at the smaller Timkin Museum was a huge glimmering painting of the waterways, gondolas and magical edifices of Venice and smaller darkly colorful wooden panels of Russian-style Madonnas — icons, I learned. I found myself a frequent visitor to the sacred sanctuary of the Timken galleries.

Lonnie took me on a historical tour of San Diego, starting with Spanish Landing, the Mission San Diego de Alcala, and the Mexican hacienda, western and Indian stores in Old Town. I could almost feel myself living back in those times until I pictured myself in either the rough clothes of a maid and felt my back hurting or saw myself in the corseted taffeta of a rich man's wife and felt trapped. No place for an independent woman like me here.

Next we toured the beautiful, Spanish-style mission almost hidden downstream from the massive Mission Valley Shopping Center. This was where, in addition to building a cathedral graced by a campanile with bells hanging from romantic arches, Father Junipero Serra created vegetable gardens and taught the Indians agricultural methods. Lonnie embarrassed me in front of the nuns by explaining that the happy natives rose up and murdered a priest. They'd had enough of Catholic slavery, and the ruining of their precious, peaceful culture between the valley and the sea.

He told me that many Mexicans had their land stolen by gold digger Anglos who came west to make their fortunes ultimately on the backs of Mexicans, Native American Indians, and Asians. I wondered what life was like for women under the Anglo "padron." "Minorities" clearly weren't the only people oppressed by men because of their Biology!

Mexican Americans were organizing under the adept leadership of migrant farm workers' advocate Cesar Chavez and others. I watched the movie *The Grapes of Wrath* and recognized the parallel — white bosses beating and starving the inferior Okies driven west by the ravages of weather in the Dust Bowl. Wasn't this when Daddy rode the rails, hitchhiked and sought any kind of work to help support his mother and sister?

I remember the night I lost my virginity to Lonnie. It was a week before our wedding. I had gone to the doctor a few weeks back and gotten a pink plastic dial-a-day circle filled with birth control pills for one month. I was happy to have taken that step. It made me feel grown up to carry them in my purse. But I wasn't feeling like "doing it" yet. I didn't know when that feeling would come.

I was staying overnight in Lonnie's tiny apartment above a liquor store on University Avenue. The huge neon light of the store blinked pink and green all night long into our bedroom where the TV was.

I was becoming an insomniac.

We were on the double bed watching the continuing coverage of the California primary election, praying Robert Kennedy would win. It was looking good. Lonnie wanted to go down and join the crowd at the Kennedy headquarters. I didn't. I had wedding plans to finish up, and I never liked crowds. I wanted time alone.

Lonnie started to fool around with me. Stroking my small breasts and grinning, he said, "You know we don't have to wait until the wedding."

I said, "I know we don't."

"Besides the first time is just going to be breaking the hymen, you know. It probably won't be that comfortable. Might as well get it over with before the honeymoon trip, you know?"

His rationale was acceptable, but ...

He undressed, and I saw his hard-on. God. How was that big thing ever going to get inside of me? I pulled off my panties and kissed him. I wanted him to kiss me more to get me into the mood for making out and wanting more. He stroked my thighs, and then spread my legs. He suggested that I bend my knees, so I did. He was on top of me and this big dry thing was poking up against the inside of my leg, then against the outside of my vagina. Each time he rubbed it against my flesh, I thought it was in the wrong place. Nothing was opening up. He must have the wrong hole. Or the hole was too small.

I didn't know my genitals well. I never rubbed them with my fingers so I wasn't sure where my clitoris was exactly. Was it at the top? In the middle? How small was it? Was it true that it got bigger during sex? A year later, I would be looking up close at a big vagina, one spread on the top of an upright piano at an educational forum inspired by the infamous feminist handbook *Our Bodies, Ourselves*.

When I masturbated, I squeezed my wrist hard between my legs and pulsated on it. (I had discovered that sensation as a young girl sitting on my bicycle seat looking out the garage on a rainy day.) That would get me horny and after 15 minutes or more I'd come. But he wasn't doing that.

Lonnie licked his fingers then wiped them on the opening to the hole, my secret place. Again he poked with his penis. It was a little easier. I sighed. Maybe we should have been drinking. Or smoking. But there was nothing in the house. We kissed again. He kissed my neck and gave me a hickey. I thought, "People will see this tomorrow at school." He thrust again and was inside.

I don't remember feeling anything dramatic. He shuddered and heaved a great sigh, leaned over me and almost collapsed. I could feel perspiration on his neck. “Did you break it?” I asked.

“I think so,” he mumbled, unable to speak. I motioned him to get off me so I could breathe better, and then got up to look at the sheet. There was no blood on it. I went to the bathroom to clean up. There was still no blood. I had read that some women’s hymens broke naturally before they had intercourse. From riding a horse or doing exercises in P.E.

Oh, well. Neither of us cared about that. For a liberated woman, I wasn’t very. This was the time of the Sexual Revolution. What was wrong with me? I wished I had a girlfriend. If only I had a girlfriend I could talk to about what happened tonight. But I had never been close to my three roommates or any other girls in college.

When I was a kid, I had two girlfriends. My best friend, Kathy, lived one street away from me. She was smart and pretty, and lived in a lower-middle-class house like we did. Kathy and I always saw things the same way. We read the same books and saw the same movies. We didn’t hang out with the popular kids, but we were on friendly terms with them. We got invited to the same birthday parties and shared the same perspective on kids at school. We didn’t get invited to the country club or the exclusive ballroom dancing lessons, so we took some inexpensive dancing lessons together. She had an older brother, and once she told me that she knew he read *Playboy*, but we never got to see the pictures.

Looking back on it, I really wished we had found his magazines. I needed to see a vagina for myself. Since those magazines were not politically correct now, I still was ignorant. It occurred to me that they sold them at the liquor store next door, but….

Hell. I was such a prude. I had flipped through the pages of *The Joy of Sex,* but the drawings of all those positions intimidated me. And what about Masters and Johnson?

I was tense and needed to be alone. The TV was showing an excited crowd gathering at the Kennedy headquarters at the Ambassador Hotel in Los Angeles, and then switched to a similar, smaller scene at the U.S. Grant Hotel in San Diego. Lonnie was beside himself with joy. “Let’s go! I want to go!”

“Oh, nooo. No way. I don’t feel like going out.”

“Well, I am not going to leave you here, sweetheart.”

"You know, if I had a bottle of Southern Comfort to celebrate with, I would love to just stay here in my nightgown and finish this list for the wedding. It is only four days away, you know. "

"I don't know. Well, if you're sure?"

"Do you have enough money for a half-pint?"

He pulled on his jeans, fished some dollars out of his pocket, and then counted up coins for gas money.

"I'll be right back," he said, all the while keeping his eyes on the TV like it was the biggest game in football history. I knew it was the most important political campaign of the 20$^{th}$ century. *If Kennedy wins this, we could return to the good days of the John F. Kennedy administration.* Social change would abound.

I snuggled into the blankets, propped up the pillows, and reached for my notebook. The green spiral school notebook was entitled "Wedding Plans, June 10, 1968" in my handwriting. I flipped through the pages, crossing out things that had been done, underlining things still to do, and started a list of things I hadn't thought of yet. The virginal white wedding dress, full length and lacy, already hung in the closet. My friend in the campus library where I worked had lent it to me complete with a plain, short, white-net veil. A bouquet of yellow and white daisies with baby's breath and ivy, and wedding cake to be topped with the same flowers, were on order.

I worked more on the wedding plans, made a motel reservation for my parents, and savored a Milky Way bar. The wedding would be really sweet. Lonnie planned to quote from Kahlil Gibran, and there would be a traditional wedding march with Daddy giving me away. At the reception in the basement, we would dance to Simon and Garfunkel and the Beatles. Things were going to be good. Except for the long camping trip of a honeymoon across Canada. I needed motel comfort, but we couldn't afford it.

The phone rang.

"Hello?"

"Hi."

"Lonnie, is that you?"

"Have you heard the news?"

"No. What?"

"Kennedy was just shot."

"What?"

"Turn on the news. Someone shot him at the victory party about five minutes ago."

"Is he dead?

"I think so. I'm coming home now."

Our second hope, JFK's brother, was assassinated that night. The world was spinning out of control.

# 15
# THE PASSION OF THE WOMEN'S MOVEMENT

One day Lonnie and Ron told me about an upcoming teach-in on sex roles in Reno, Nevada. Ron said there would be some strong women there like myself who I might want to meet. John wanted to go, too. Soon I found myself in a marathon weekend with people who looked like hippies and called themselves radicals and feminists. The topic was something like sexuality and sex role stereotyping. One after another strong, outspoken women, radical women, taught us about patriarchy, discrimination, sexual domination, and reproductive freedom.

Michael Rossman and his wife Karen Rossman, from Berkeley, looked like hippies, but were passionate and eloquent intellectuals who called themselves feminists and made an enormous impact on Lonnie and me. Michael's shaggy black hair and beard made him look like a wild man. Karen, wearing no makeup and a full-length dress made of Indian madras, was a mature hippie. They lived in a commune they had started called Dragon's House. Karen worked as a teacher when she could and Michael, who was well known as a free speech leader at Berkeley, was an organizer and writer trying to make a little money from speaking events and consultant work. They were in their thirties, as were the other workshop leaders.

Lack of child care centers, the need for equal pay for equal work, the right of women to control their own bodies, the omission of women from history, and many more problems added up to one thing: The problem of the oppression of women due to centuries-old, world-wide, multi-layered systems of government, church, and reproduction. Patriarchy was the problem. The solution: Radical change of the economic, cultural, social, and political institutions, and self-transformation at the individual level.

Is it possible? Could it be that western society in all its intelligence and wisdom gained from past civilizations, geniuses, and scholars, is in some kind of dark ages in the way it views/treats half the population of the world today? Women. Could the need for change and the cause of the status quo be based on centuries of bias and oppression in all institutions, all societies? Obviously, World War II's demands upon the female population had shown that women could do men's work, and that the German mantra "Kinder, Kurche, Kirchen" was not the correct prescription for the role of women. Obviously, too, the Industrial Revolution had created jobs with machines that employers needed anyone to do, even children. So when modern society needed women to work, it recruited them, but most men and many women still believed "a woman's place was in the home." This wasn't rational.

But why had the role of women even been a question? Weren't women the same as men, but with the additional power of giving birth? Many people had assumed that women, being burdened by annual childbearing before the time of the birth control pill, were incapable of both manual and intellectual work, and fit only to tend to the nest. Schools, churches, boyfriends, and parents were still teaching us this.

How deep-rooted was this thinking? Was it a belief system entrenched over thousands of years but now archaic? And what of the goddess-worshipping cultures? Was that a time when women were not only revered but in power? Had there been a Matriarchy before there was Patriarchy? What was fact or fiction? Truth or unexamined assumptions? And, if things had been different or could be different, was there any evidence out there to support the need for women's revolution and, thus, men's revolution?

I became hungry to study feverishly. Not for my college classes, but for answers to world questions about women past and present. I had to know the truth. The objective truth, not fantasies or dogmas spawned from emotion. If we had been deceived, like blacks had been, enslaved, not allowed to learn to read, to travel, to write opinions, someone was benefiting from this. It was not just ignorant thinking.

I had already read Marx and Engels during my initial orientation to the Anti-Vietnam War Movement and concluded that their analysis of the world's power imbalances as oppression along socioeconomic class lines did not address the treatment of blacks and women as inferior. As much as I liked the idea of redistribution of the wealth from the rich to the poor, history showed their theories had little practical application. Socialism and communism ushered in cruel dictatorships, not people's freedom from oppression. Of course, all revolutions had been undertaken under patriarchy with male assumptions, male leadership, and male violence predominant. Now women were going to try to free themselves, and in so doing humanize the whole world.

We would have to proceed carefully in order to get it right. How exciting! What we do in America can benefit women in other countries. The ripple effect will be tremendous. This work would take a lifetime. I had found my purpose! Remembering the conviction the Baptist preacher asked for, to give myself wholly to Jesus, I decided instead to dedicate my life, unconditionally, to the cause of women's liberation. Lightning had struck me.

I didn't have time anymore for the Anti-War Movement. The Women's Movement consumed my every waking moment with a passion. To be honest, I didn't have time for men. I had so much to learn. So much to study. And very little of it was in books. I had been told by the feminists I had met from up north to look for the underground self-published pamphlets that were circulating, and that a woman named Lucinda Cisler had typed up a Women's Liberation bibliography! I was going to have to figure out how to get my hands on these things. There was a women's bookstore starting up in Berkeley, "A Woman's Place," and I longed to make a pilgrimage there to examine their treasures. What a wonderful time that would be! Soon I was shopping there every few months.

Meanwhile I had to content myself with starting at the beginning with Betty Friedan's book, *The Feminine Mystique*, because it was the easiest to get a hold of, having been in bookstores and libraries for years since it came out in 1963. I already knew that it was out of date, and that it spoke to the generation of "Leave It To Beaver" suburban housewives that preceded my own. That was my mother's generation, but Mother was never a housewife. She was an elementary school teacher and a music teacher. Of course, there weren't many professions open to women then. And why was that?

I knew the Rosie the Riveter image of women during World War II had been replaced with advertisements of women (white women only) bending over their shiny new white ovens. Why couldn't they keep working when their men, who had seen them working for years, were through fighting the War?

I needed to know what had sparked the Second Wave of the Women's Movement. Of course the publishing of *The Feminine Mystique* was a watershed event, so I soaked up every word. It was now acceptable mainstream reading as well as a feminist classic, and I could cite it with professors without the risk of ridicule. Betty's work was invaluable because it uncovered the "problem without a name." You see, there is no problem until it has been given a name. The power of Naming is immeasurable.

Next, I devoured Simone de Beauvoir's *The Second Sex*, published in 1948, the year I was born. The famous French writer minced no words in declaring that women continued to be considered chattel, property to be used, sold or dispensed, and had suffered generations of not having an identity. She taught me to see how we were viewed not as men, not as women, but as "the Other." The advent of birth control and the longer life spans of women in the 20th century had allowed women to not have to spend their entire adult lives in childrearing.

French women had been less puritanical about sex because they had had access to birth control sooner than we did. Diaphragms and other methods were openly discussed amongst women, and centuries of treatments and medicines had been handed down since ancient times. Abortion was a part of women's knowledge. Midwives, healers, and medicine women were in charge of women's healthcare. Not men.

The same Catholics who said abortion was a sin practiced it as birth control when abstinence was impractical. And in various cultures female babies were thrown away because males were valued more highly as potential moneymakers.

How much of this had to do with religion? How much with culture? When did the change take place from women controlling medicine to men controlling it? Is this the basis of patriarchy or just one pillar? What exactly is patriarchy? Its scope? Its history?

Not men = women, but women don't have identities without their men; therefore, they are really neither, but the Other. The Other was unknown, invisible, even untouchable, dirty. The Bible taught me that man was made in God's image, and woman was made from man. I knew then that we were secondary (if not inferior) in the ideas of Christianity.

Had there ever been a feminist writer before them? Joyce Nower pointed me to *A Vindication of the Rights of Women* by Mary Wollstonecraft, written in 1792. Now there was a radical document written a long time ago by someone who already understood what we were just discovering now! Had it been suppressed? And what about Margaret Mead? Did male scientists praise her for her anthropological fieldwork that proved not all cultures were male-dominated? No, some were female-dominated or matriarchal. How had the entire modern (civilized) world changed from matriarchy to patriarchy? When and why?

There had been a time of women-led female societies. It must have been before recorded history. Right? On the surface, this seemed true, because no historians had written about large woman-run cultures. If it was true, there was no evidence in writing. Where could we look to? Mythology, religion, legends, archaeology, art history?

We would have to go back to the very beginnings of every story about history and examine it for remnants of a different past. Or else look for evidence of a great war or catastrophic event that changed the world from matriarchal to patriarchal.

And what if we don't find it? We are still dedicated to making changes to ensure women's equality. We don't need to prove ancient superiority to bolster a case for equality.

But what if the evidence was there and had been suppressed? Deliberately. Well, maybe not deliberately. Maybe men who were doing the writing just omitted us because they were ignorant of our accomplishments. Hmm. The status of women at the time of each writing was critical to the interpretation of the whole history of the world!

***"Anything you can do, or dream you can begin it,
Boldness has Genius, Power, and Magic in it!"***

***Goethe***

*THE POET JOYCE NOWER*

# 16
# SEEKER AND LIGHT: CONSCIOUSNESS RAISING

My first decision was to find another feminist. In order to organize women on campus, I would need to find someone who shared my new awareness and might want to work together. I started asking students, strangers or not, if they knew anyone who was a feminist. "A what? What's a feminist?" was the usual answer. After two weeks of asking students, I saw a man walking towards me in the Student Union whom I knew to be a radical professor. I stopped him and asked the same question. His answer, "Yes, I do, and she teaches in the English Department. She was a feminist before Simone de Beauvoir's book came out. If you want to talk to her, I suggest you call her up and ask her to coffee."

That threw me. I didn't drink coffee, and I didn't think I'd have the nerve to ask a professor to have coffee with a mere student. I thanked him for the information and took the phone number he wrote down for "Joyce." For several days I mulled it over. *I could call her up, but what if she said no? What if she said yes?* I had no plan for the conversation itself. I should have a thesis or a problem or a request. Next, I ran into Leon again, and he asked me if I had called her. "No, I, uh..."

"Just call her up, she will be happy to hear from you." Now, I had to do it.

Joyce answered the phone with a friendly voice, and I asked her to meet me for coffee to discuss feminism. Leon had told her about me. It turned out he was her husband! She was on a tight schedule, had two kids to get home to, and invited me to come to her home one evening instead!

Joyce and I hit it off right away. She was warm, casual, profound and willing. She was 16 years older than me, had firsthand experience in the Civil Rights Movement, was working on starting an alternative school, and had compiled the first "Bibliography of Black Writers" for one of her literature classes. We excitedly exchanged information on the Reno Conference and the Women's Movement on the East Coast, deciding to read everything we could get our hands on. Shulamith Firestone, Robin Morgan. In that first meeting, I realized that I, Carol Rowell Council, "the Seeker," had finally found Joyce Nower, "the Light."

Next we decided to start a consciousness-raising group by making a list of everyone we knew who might either have some feminist awareness or be open to learning about it. We identified about 20 students and three faculty wives, and assigned ourselves to approach each one. Soon we had our first meeting scheduled.

We started the meeting at Joyce's home by explaining how we came to meet and what some of the topics were that we were concerned with. Almost immediately the 12 or so women began talking about their perceptions that women didn't have much experience talking in groups. We were used to men doing most of the talking. Most leaders were men. How strange it was to be talking with only women! There was great excitement in the air. It was so outrageous and so right to be doing this.

We were becoming revolutionaries. You could feel it. Taste it. Smell it. We were excited and angry. The young male leaders in The Movement were mere radicals singing Beatles songs and talking revolution. They didn't know that the sexy backup singers were about to revolt and break out with a thunderous new melody of female freedom, which would later be heard around the world. Helen Reddy's hit song, "I Am Woman, Hear Me Roar" belted out our feelings.

Men didn't have a plan. They were busy "checking out what condition my condition was in." The men were in it for the Anti-War Movement, which would end with the end of the Vietnam War and the end of the draft. We, however, were in it, as the title of Juliet Mitchell's article said, for the "Longest Revolution."

The real revolution would be what *we* cooked up. Something personal and political. Something permanent. And, it would transcend their "revolution." The Longest Revolution would not be the transformation of capitalism to socialism under patriarchy. Nor of patriarchy to matriarchy. What would it be?

We would simply have to change *everything*. After our first Rap Group got too large, we helped start two more groups at the college. Toward the end of the summer, Joyce, Rhetta, and I were tired of talking and getting itchy for action. We attended protests and marches from People's Park in Berkeley to the Chicago Democratic Convention. I marched with thousands of anti-war protestors as we cried out, "The Whole World is Watching! The Whole World is Watching!" On TV countries all over the globe were showing the massive protests in the streets of America. I heard a sound like cracking a watermelon, but it was really the sound of a cop's billy club cracking the skull of a student. We didn't want more of that. Besides the men didn't really have a plan. We were angry. As Robin Morgan so aptly put it in her article about men in the *New Left*, "Goodbye To All That!"

One night, the members of the Rap Group filed in the front door of a small apartment and sat down in a circle on the floor as usual. Each face was lit up with the anticipation of sharing this intimate time of discovery and self-discovery together. Soon Maddie Farber entered with her baby on her back. Maddie was married to the famous professor Jerry Farber, author of *Student As Nigger*.

*What? A baby in our meeting?* The free-flowing conversation began stalling as people looked at Maddie and back at each other. Finally someone asked, "Why isn't Jerry taking care of the baby?" My friend Maddie, with her sweet Swedish looks, responded lightly, "Jerry doesn't do diapers." An unprecedented wave of silence swept across us.

Finally, someone spoke up, asking Maddie, "What, you're shitting me?"

Maddie smiled, and then grinned, "No, no shit."

The radical male professor's political position on diapers left me speechless. I thought it was so politically incorrect, reminiscent of Stokely Carmichael's pronouncement, "The only position for a woman in the movement is prone." The impending revolution seemed to confront us at every moment.

Panning the circle like a camera, my eyes took in expressions ranging from amazement to disapproval to empathy for our sister's plight. Maddie smiled at our shock, shrugged her shoulders and said, "That's the way it is, guys. When I can't get a sitter, I take the baby everywhere." My eyes glazed over as I remembered going to their house for dinner. Maddie had taken me into the room with the diaper-changing table to watch the procedure. She cooed at her baby, "I love you, and I'm going to have lots more babies just like you."

Flabbergasted again.

# 17
# "WHY DON'T WE START A WOMEN'S STUDIES PROGRAM?"

One summer evening, 16 women sat outside the lawn at Rhetta's house, talking about the future of our Women's Rap Group. The discussion centered on moving from study to action.

"If we want to change the world," I said, "we need to have a blueprint." Demands were not good enough. We were the architects of our future. We needed to envision structures and have blueprints for designing them. (The last section of my favorite book, Shulamith Firestone's groundbreaking 1970 book *The Dialectics of Sex*, has a diagram for the Women's Liberation Movement that I loved to look at. "For That Rare Diagram Freak, 3-D Revolution" is still a delight to my senses.)

*What do we want? What are we suited to do? We are connected to a campus. We are all interested in education. We have some important connections as students, faculty, staff, and wives of professors. What is possible? Let's not limit our thinking. Think big.*

"Why don't we start a Women's Studies Program at San Diego State?" asked Mary Lynn Clemente.

"Like the Chicano Studies Program my husband teaches in!" Anne Nuñez exclaimed.

We all looked at one another with wonderment. Gleeful smiles broke out on Joyce, Rhetta, and Chris's faces. I grinned back, "If they could do it, we can do it."

How had they done it? Anne said she'd ask Rene about it. Her husband Rene was the head of the newly created Chicano Studies Department. Joyce said she would talk to Gus Segade, a well-respected Chicano Studies professor and one of the architects of the Centro De Estudios Chicanos concept, of which the Chicano Studies Department was one component. I thought I'd call Leon and see what he thought.

All of them said, "Go for it. The time is right." All of these men were in their forties and I was only 20, but I knew they would treat me as an equal. We shared a bond based on the experience of discrimination. At our next meeting, we decided I should set up an appointment to go talk to the Chicano leaders. I put aside the thought that some feminists might think we were "talking to the enemy" by going to get advice from men. Besides, it would just be information gathering.

When I met the Chicano leaders at their offices, I was delighted to learn they had a blueprint! They showed me their organizational chart and design for a Center for Chicano Studies with seven components, including a storefront in the community, a recruitment and tutorial component, and the Chicano Studies Department in the College of Arts and Letters. If they could do it, we could too!

We had already been talking about needing a childcare center, an arts program, and services for women on welfare. From the beginning, it was clear to us that neither an academic program alone, nor an isolated service project would reflect the interlocking needs of women. We would propose an umbrella organization, The Center for Women, and make the Women's Studies Program part of it.

I looked upon this time as a battle. "Onward Christian Soldiers!" was a familiar battle hymn strain from my Baptist Church days. Just substitute some words: "Onward Women Soldiers!"

The coming days and months would be an uphill battle. It would take everything we had, and more, to fight the sexism in the college community and win over the male establishment of this ivory tower to allow a Women's Studies Program to even be started. It was like a civil war. We would be pitted sister against sister at times. It was like walking a tightrope. Don't alienate the unsympathetic women on campus. Keep the radical brothers thinking it's hip to support the radical women. Wear a dress when you go to see people in power, but proudly pin on that dress the red-and-white Women's Liberation button with the fist pushing out of a female symbol.

Be ready. Always be ready. For a challenge: "What do you women want?" For a catcall from the fraternity row. For rebuke: "You girls need to act more like ladies." For stupidity. "Yeah, I guess I think women should be equal." To clarify: "We don't want to be equal to men. We want to be free to be ourselves, whatever that might be."

For the battle, we would

need "weapons" and "ammunition." I began to think of all the possible tools and resources we could possibly conceive of or get our hands on. It became important to consider all strategies and tactics so that we would not look back later and see we had been blind to one opportunity or another.

Okay. We could have protests like marches and sit-ins but not disorganized and dangerous ones like the men did. After all, I had been in Chicago during the riots at the Democratic Convention. I did not choose to go there. On the last leg of our cross-country honeymoon trip, my radical leader husband told me the newspaper said masses of students were driving to Chicago and proclaimed, "We *have* to go. We can't be this close and miss it! This is where all the action is!"

I told him that would be crazy. I was afraid. I knew there would be violence. But when I saw the masses on TV chanting, "The Whole World is Watching," I caved in. This was the biggest development in United States contemporary history. It turned out to be a great learning experience and we luckily escaped the violence.

Our battleground at San Diego State was safe — so far. Diplomacy coupled with the power of a large constituency would characterize this battle. Ladies we could be. But underneath the "burqa" we were radical feminists. Leaflets, petitions, posters, skits, rallies, public speakers, demands, proposals, brochures, teach-ins, conferences, negotiations, lobbying, and presentations — whatever it took, we would do it.

It was also clear, however, that the male-dominated administration would not easily be persuaded by our analysis. We would need to build support for the idea throughout the campus so that, as with the Chicano experience, they would know that we had a power base. We needed to be viewed as representing a large movement, the Women's Liberation Movement.

The Rap Group was evolving. We called ourselves The Ad Hoc Committee for Women's Studies and wrote a "Proposal for a Center" with seven components to have ready to present to the campus authorities. The smudged mimeograph master we had typed it on is now in the Women's Studies Founders Archives.

Framing the idea in words that the university could relate to became essential. We said that our goals were "educational" and that a curriculum was needed because women had been omitted from the content of most courses. We were proposing the creation of a legitimate field of knowledge — Women. After all, we were the 51% of the population left out of intellectual endeavors, either as a subject for, or as an actor upon, society. In what other ways could we gain power?

The Committee began lobbying a dozen or so faculty women, speaking in classrooms, leafletting, and drawing up a petition for a Women's Studies Program. Newspapers began covering our work. Momentum was building. The fall semester was underway, and I had no time to attend classes. I considered dropping out of school so I could have more organizing time on campus.

Soon we were ready to select a spokeswoman and organize a rally. When this came up at a meeting, I squirmed. *Oh, no.* They were going to pick me. I wanted to do it, but I hoped someone else would. I could imagine speaking to the press and to the president of the college, but I didn't want to be a public figure. Could I ever speak at a rally? I didn't have charisma. What if they didn't like me or booed me?

"Carol, you should be the one to speak for the group. You are strong and articulate. You'll be the best spokeswoman." They all chimed in, "You should be the coordinator of the Ad Hoc Committee for Women's Studies."

I didn't know if I was ready for this and said, "Maybe Joyce would do it?" She was more experienced and articulate than I was, and, as a faculty member, would be automatically respected. Joyce made it clear that she did not want to be "It." She was a poet, not a politician, and she had her hands full as the director of Exploring Family School, which she had helped found the year before. Also, she was a faculty member and felt that, since all the women were students, a student should be the spokeswoman.

I stifled a gulp and said, "Okay." Then, looking at Joyce, I asked, "Will you still take some leadership?"

"I'll be there as much as I can — every step of the way!" she promised.

*I'm "It,"* I thought, with a mixture of pride and foreboding. Okay. *Jesus! My life is going to change now!* We would be trying to found the first Women's Studies Program in the world.

BUT was this really possible to do? Could a handful of feminists build a permanent feminist institution, here, in San Diego, in 1969? I heard the answer coming in Susan B.

Anthony's famous words of encouragement: "FAILURE IS IMPOSSIBLE."

# 18
# TACKLING THE ACADEMY

I needed another Joyce. Joyce was strong, mature, non-judgmental, wise, and light-hearted. She would make a good impression with the male administration. She was also busy. First, we needed to identify a "college" that would agree to housing us before we went to make our case to Vice President Walker.

We needed more women professors to support our core group. Respected professors, established professors whose names would cause men's ears to prick up with that thought of, "Oh, someone legitimate is behind what you are doing." That would make their eyes lock in with interest, and you could stick your foot in the door farther. Unfortunately, we had beaten the bushes and only found a handful. We already had the support of Dr. Ernie O'Byrne at the Foundation, and he did not know of any women professors who could be supportive. His advice about getting to know Dean Warren Carrier was good because not only was Carrier supportive of the Chicano Studies Department being put under the aegis of his college, the College of Arts and Letters, but when I met him, although an imposing man, he was supportive of Women's Studies and me!

Carrier thought I had what it took to get the job done, and I think he admired my doing it. I was fond of him, but didn't let on. I could use a father figure big time, but that wasn't in the Women's Liberation playbook. Carrier, who I suspected came from a more liberal bent than he could let on, had recently arrived from Rutgers, where he must have been quite distinguished for San Diego State to hire him as a dean of one of the largest colleges on campus. (The school was going through a transformation from a college to a university with several colleges and, although it was not yet totally official, he would be the Dean of the College of Arts and Letters once Walker became President of the University.)

Warren Carrier had a nice big frame, broad shoulders, and a ruddy complexion below bushy eyebrows. His round head with thinning hair barely concealed the thoughtful intelligence within. I liked to sit and talk in a relaxed manner with Dean Carrier. He was an astute politician, and I knew I could learn oodles from him if I had the opportunity. One day when exploring with him the possibility of getting "experimental" Women's

Studies classes going, he broached the subject of my working with him. I was stunned. Flabbergasted.

Did he mean like an office aide? Or just attending some meetings? Or what? I was waiting for him to explain.

"You're spending many hours of work organizing and getting this Ad Hoc Committee for Women's Studies going, right?"

I nodded.

"You have to think of your own studying, too. How are you going to get through school at the rate you are going?"

I let out a deep breath.

"Yeah, I know. I had to drop out of my French classes, and French was supposedly my major. I have barely any time to think about school."

"You are an organizer and leader. And a good one, too. If you don't think about school, you are liable to end up with a career and no education, and that won't take you very far."

His words profoundly touched me, because I could hear the echoes of truth. However, the irony of it and the reality of the decades is that I did achieve a great, wide education, but I never achieved a career.

I grew embarrassed at his praise, interest, and insight. We were talking about me? We were! Even Lonnie, and Leon, and Joyce didn't talk to me this way about my life. It was always about what we were doing for the Revolution.

"You may have the makings of a good administrator. Have you ever thought of getting a degree in Public Administration?"

"No, I don't know much about it."

"Well, why don't I give you the name of someone you can learn more about it from? Since you are doing what amounts to administration now, you may want to take some courses that are compatible with what you are doing. With some independent studies, you would not have to spend all of your time in the classroom. Why don't you make an appointment with Jim Kitchen? He is the head of Public Administration, which will be under the College of Professional Studies soon. He is a nice fellow, and I'm sure he will give you a good idea of what the program is. I am sure he will be interested in what you are doing with Women's Studies, and since Public Administration is his profession, he will particularly like hearing about the proposal for a seven-component Center for Women's Studies."

I was taking notes furiously now.

"My friend John Ash has been working to set up credited or paid internships," I ventured. "Do you know if they are doing anything with that?"

"I am sure that they are. Dr. Kitchen could put you in touch with the right person, tell you what the requirements are for the major and for internships."

Whew! My head was swimming, and we were running out of time.

"Well, I will certainly follow up on all these leads..."

"In the meantime you could think about writing a paper on your experiences working through this administration. I could give you three units of Independent Study, or you could see if they want to farm you out to me as an intern. Whatever works out best. Just keep going. You are doing well, the work needs to get done, and you should get credit for it."

*Wow!* I beamed.

He smiled and said, "Let me know what you think. I have another appointment." With that, he dashed into an adjoining conference room, late for a meeting.

If only there were Daddy Carriers all along your life's road.

I left jubilant, thinking something good was going to happen in my life. And, it would be more of what I was already doing! I was just going to get more mileage and credibility out of it. It was about *me* this time.

Lonnie would be thrilled, and John would be overjoyed to help cinch it. He probably knew Dr. Kitchen. Joyce and Leon would be excited and happy that my disrupted French major might be replaced by something better. Wow! I could have everything.

Oh, but I had forgotten that I was supposed to ask Dean Carrier if he knew any faculty women who might be supportive of Women's Studies. One woman wasn't going to be enough, and my search had not turned up anyone but Joyce.

*Thinking back on it now, it is almost like I had become a mother when I was too young. I had so many 'children' to look after every day, and I was still a child myself.*

*What had happened to me? My life had been happening so fast, I must have skipped some phases. I was expected to navigate this adult world of administrators and faculty who were all advancing higher education, and I was the only one who was not. What does it mean to lose that time in the summers to wonder? To wonder what you want to do, where you want to go? To have the freedom to try something and then, change course entirely. How precious a thing that is. Of course, I couldn't have that then. No, not until 20 more years as a Women's Movement leader, not until after my son was born, not until after my husband died... No matter. I have it now.*

*Later I would wonder what it would be like to take a year off from the Women's Movement. Was that a sin? I had promised to dedicate my life to the Women's Movement and I kept my vow as strictly as if I had made it before all of the deacons of the Baptist Church.*

*Sad, when you think of it, how we let those times rip us away from ourselves. Of course, not all of us did. But look at some other feminist memoir stories. They are full of lives that were put on hold. Arrested development. Trading in being a housewife for being an unsung heroine. That was our calling, our generation.*

*Had I only been a few years older, it might have been entirely different for me. The price not so high. So unrepayable. All the other feminist leaders I met were at least 10 to 15 years older than I was. They had already gone to graduate school, become writers, or gotten Ph.D.s. They had been in the workforce, whether as waitresses or as teachers, had taken lovers, been married, had children when I was still 10 years old.*

I remember in my late twenties when a long-time friend said, "Carol, you blossomed early as a feminist leader, and you've stayed inside the movement for ten years. That's who you are. Rather who you were. You need to get out beyond the Women's Movement world and adventure by yourself. Your interests — opera, dance, art history, and travel — are much bigger than this. You deserve the world!"

It was as if lightning had struck me again. I knew it was true. Why did it take so long for me to consider striking out for myself? The first words of survival advice you give others are sometimes the last you take for yourself.

Before the next Ad Hoc Committee meeting I sat on the lawn going through crumpled-up pieces of paper in my purse. The words "Nona Cannon" and "Home Economics" were scribbled on it. Who gave me that name? A Home Economics professor? Was there any point in calling her up? A pretty conservative department to go searching for feminists in.

Oh, yeah, didn't Rene Nunez say she had just guided some course changes through the Curriculum Committee, and we could benefit from talking to her while preparing for that step ourselves?

I strolled across the lawn, climbed the familiar steps of Aztec Center and headed to the new Student Lounge. Student organizing that Ron and Lonnie had participated in had resulted in the creation of this nice carpeted room with couches, designated as a "free space" where students could relax, study, or talk! Before that, the only place you could go to talk was the cafeteria. I looked through the glass doors and saw Rhetta, Karen, and Chris trying out the cushions on the new blue sofas.

"Carol, this is so cool," Chris said. She was grinning like it was Christmas morning. I sat down and found myself grinning, too. Lying on the carpet was a guy with long, matted hair and dirty bare feet! Comfort on campus. Luxurious. Soon I was grinning, and we were all giggling while we waited for Maddie, Mary Lynn, and Joyce. It was Friday afternoon, and we felt ready to party. When the others came in, we all got up and hugged one another.

"Okay, let's keep this one short. We are going out to dinner tonight and Maddie and Jerry have people coming over," said Mary Lynn.

"Oh, that's right, Leon and I have tickets to the opera tonight, and I've got to pick up the baby sitter and make dinner. What the hell am I going to wear?"

"Joyce!" Rhetta exclaimed, "Enough already!"

"Oh, yes, of course. Excuse me, but I was just realizing, oh..." Joyce mumbled.

"You're doing it again!" laughed Rhett uncontrollably.

Joyce grinned, "Okay I'll try to be good." She cleared her throat, took up a steno pad and her fountain pen, and looked at the blank page.

"So where are we here? No. I got it. We have to get five or six women faculty members who have nothing to do with us who will lend us legitimacy. At the moment, we don't look very credible with only one faculty member — me — behind the cause. The whole campus knows that we are trying to start a Women's Studies Program, and not one single female professor has contacted us. Of course, they have got their jobs to consider, and their marriages, if they align themselves with feminists. A handful of individuals must be out there that will support us if we can shake them out of the bushes. So we are bringing up the question once again. Does anyone have any names to consider?"

"Someone suggested Rose Sommerville," said Rhetta.

"Really? Do you think she'd want to be associated with us? Why?"

"I don't know, someone just said she would be worth trying. She's in Sociology, I think."

"I heard she gives speeches on women in the community. She's tenured, and older, so she might not have as much to lose as younger professors."

"Okay, who else?"

"Well, there is Lois Kessler in Health Science. I sat in on some of her classes. She's definitely progressive. She supports Planned Parenthood and talks openly about contraception. She is anti-war too."

"Maddie, can you ask her?"

"Who me? Okay, I guess so."

"Rose Sommerville's name keeps coming up. She's well known. She gives talks about people in other cultures and emphasizes the status of women."

"Joyce, you better ask her. She sounds like a heavy."

"Okay, but we still need..."

"What about Nona Cannon?" I suggested. "I've been carrying this note around with me forever. Someone said I should be sure to meet her, but I don't know...She doesn't seem likely to identify with feminism. She teaches in Home Economics."

"Home Economics!" Rhetta shrieked. "I'm not going near there — ever! I made an apron in junior high school and that was it! What a miserable looking thing!"

"I heard one of the campus ministers talking about her. She is a pacifist."

"Well, it would certainly help us look more legitimate in the public eye," Joyce pointed out.

Everyone was looking at me now. I looked back, hoping someone else would volunteer.

"Okay, put me down to call up Nona," I agreed.

"Great. We can go home now," Joyce said emphatically.

"No," I said. "We need to review what we are going to say when we meet with them. Remember that you are not calling to ask them to volunteer. You have to tell them they won't have to do any work. Say that you know they are very busy. Tell them we would just like them to come once so we can fill them in on the concept of the Center for Women and a Women's Studies Program. Say we'd like to get their input or advice, but they don't have to commit to anything. Right?"

"Carol's right. It's very important to cover all those bases. Now can I go home?"

"No! Let's set the next meeting time. Joyce! You're impossible today."

"But the opera is *Aida*! I don't want to miss the "Triumphal March" and at this rate Aida will be suffocating in the tomb with the tenor..."

"You like opera?"

"Well, of course. I like the Beatles, too, but opera isn't too highbrow for a good radical. Some of the most beautiful music in the world is arias from operas by Verdi and Puccini and Mozart. Opera is one of the best of the arts because it combines singing, music, acting, drama, beautiful sets, and paintings, not to mention the costumes and the history you learn from it. Leon and I used to go to operas at the Met as students. You guys really ought to take a music appreciation course."

"Okay, gang, same time, same place. Call me when you have an appointment set up!" I called after them.

It was a good meeting, but as soon as they left to meet their boyfriends and husbands, I wished I was going home with plans for tonight. I had not talked to Lonnie today, but I knew we did not have enough money to go to the movies. I pictured Joyce and Leon seated in red velvet seats as the lights dimmed in a gilded opera house. I had dreamt of going to any opera, but there were no operas in Corpus Christi, and I was way too poor to consider buying a ticket to the San Diego Opera. I tried to imagine the women in glittery gowns and furs there. Did it have a huge crystal chandelier?

I learned the music to *Aida* when I was a baby. Mother taught the "Triumphal March" to students on her piano at home, and my Aunt Helen had given us a record with excerpts from *Aida* on it. But that was long ago in Texas.

# 19
# GREEN-EYED WOMAN

I was vaguely aware that my relationship with Lonnie had been deteriorating. We didn't have any problems with each other. We just never saw each other. He had to graduate, so he always went to class, and he often used the classroom as a place to make anti-war announcements or get debates going about the kind of educational reform needed to make college more relevant to the students of the day. He was busy advocating that the college go to a Credit/No Credit system and was working with a few open-minded faculty in the Education Department, counselors at the counseling center, and campus ministers to make the academic environment more personal, and more political. Lonnie was everywhere at once. Every time he connected with someone, they got excited about what Lonnie was doing, and he would recruit them to teach a class in the Experimental College, help organize the Education Circus, or speak in the Free Speech area. Lonnie organized a huge rally that I spoke at, and helped form the committee to support professors Nower, Howard, and Emani.

He was a real rabble-rouser. Enthusiastic, angry, and funny at times, it seemed everyone was drawn to him. He called himself an organizer for Social Change, a term that magnetized people rather than repelled them. Of course, there were some students and faculty who dismissed him as a hippie or told him to go get a haircut, but for the most part, he was respected and effective. That is how he got doors opened to him with the administration. He and Don Walker were on a joking basis at the same time that Lonnie led a weeklong sit-in in the hallway right outside Walker's office!

Sex had not been a big thing in our relationship. He wanted it more than I did, especially on that trip around Canada, which was supposed to be our honeymoon. I did not like being close to him 24 hours a day, and at night in the tent we were often cold or uncomfortable.

I felt really bad about not feeling horny any more. I began to worry that I was, in fact, "frigid." We talked about it some, but when we got back to San Diego, we each got so busy that we rarely talked about anything except the problems in Amerika and the breaking news about Vietnam, the Nixon administration, or student issues across the country. Sex just wasn't a high priority for me.

I could see that girls were enamored with this good-looking radical student leader, just like I had been in Texas, but I was not jealous. We both thought jealousy was an unhealthy emotion, and that, by learning about personal growth in encounter groups, we were above such pettiness. He usually had a female friend who would help with the mimeographing or work into the wee hours typing and collating. Since I thought I should not be jealous, I did not feel jealous.

After the meeting about recruiting more support from women, I walked home humming the strains from "The Triumphal March" in *Aida*. I pictured what it would be like to attend an opera. The cost of a ticket made it out of the realm of possibility, but I loved the fantasy.

The sun broke through the clouds and gave us a gorgeous afternoon. I came home to our apartment next to the campus, looked in the bedroom door right near the front door, and there, sitting on the bed cross-legged, were Lonnie and Sharon, a sweet-looking freshman with long, fluffy, blonde hair. She had just pulled her see-through white peasant blouse over her head, and I saw her white cotton bra against glowing tanned skin as she lowered it. The strings that tied the opening to her neck were hanging loose. She didn't move to tie them back into a bow.

I didn't know what to say.

Lonnie said, "Sharon had a break before her night class and I told her she could hang out here. Look, she brought a copy of the new Associated Students Budget. They put in $500 for the Women's Center and the Cultural Arts Board is recommending money to bring Angela Davis."

"Oh. That's great."

Sharon said, "Here is an article in the *Daily Aztec* that quotes you."

"Oh. I'll look at it later."

I knew what I had seen. Their words were denying it. I couldn't compute the scene with the words and was getting pissed. I gave them a hard look and mumbled something about having come home to get my notebook. Lonnie followed me out to the kitchen, looking sheepish. I held my ground by saying nothing.

"Sharon's leaving now. You might say goodbye."

*Don't tell me what to do.*

I heard the screen door open and close. I was standing at the kitchen sink, frozen. Stalling for time, but ready to blow up. He reminded me that it was Wednesday, so there would be a 25-cent spaghetti dinner at the Wesley Center to go to and make announcements. "You should probably announce the next Women's Liberation meeting there, don't you think?"

*Oh, we are going to act like Mother. The less said the better. Don't be angry. Let's all try to get along and that shit.*

"Right."

"I think, uh, we should probably talk about our relationship," Lonnie said in an apologetic tone.

I quickly scanned his face, then turned back to examine the kitchen sink. He looked tired, worried.

Oh, he wanted to have a meeting, did he? I could play that game. God, though. A meeting about our relationship. That was a cold concept. Suddenly I wished I knew another young couple. How do you deal with your relationship? Instead, I said, "I don't want to talk about our relationship now. I need some space."

"Okay, but I really do think we need to talk."

I glared at him. "I've got to go meet Ron at the Student Center and then go to class." (*Get out, you bastard.*)

I didn't say goodbye. I was feeling pretty fried now. How had things deteriorated like this? We were a married couple. Weren't we? Everybody knew that. Or did they? Maybe sometimes he didn't tell girls! But I knew he had been faithful. We had made an explicit agreement to have a monogamous relationship and marriage. Otherwise things would fall apart. And now it felt like things were crumbling.

I always told people he was my husband, knowing it added to my credibility on campus. I was actually proud of the fact. He was proud of me, too, and often introduced people to me by glowingly telling them what things I was doing.

*Shit.* Here I was alone in "our apartment." It was no home. We didn't cook meals there. We never made any plans to be home together. We'd stopped leaving each other notes. Instead, we'd ask our friends on campus if they'd seen the other one and they usually knew what we were doing. The alternative community was our communications network in this time before answering machines or cell phones.

How did I feel about him now? We had argued a lot on our six-week trip to Canada and the Chicago Convention. He was petty and immature. I was irritated. For 24 hours a day, we were two feet from each other — either in the tiny VW Bug or in our cramped tent. I wanted to go to a historic house or an art museum. We didn't have any money. He wanted to go to the science exhibit at the World Expo in Toronto. He wanted to listen to football on the radio. I hated listening to football.

"She is a virgin."

That was a fine remark to make. Was I supposed to be happy for her? Or did he say that so I would feel relieved? He obviously wanted to fuck her. And I didn't want to have sex with him anymore — hadn't for some time. Maybe I was supposed to feel empathy for her. You know, as an older married woman, I knew what it was like to lose your virginity. She needed a girlfriend. I could be helpful. What the hell is going on here?

Was he asking my permission? Was she asking his permission? Were they asking my permission? Now it was "They." *Wait a minute. Just hold on. I live here. I am married to him. She has got to leave. Then it will be Us again. No. It can't be. It will* never *be Us again. Why am I sooo stupid? I should have seen it coming. There was very little of Us left. Was he in love with her?*

I gripped the edge of the kitchen sink with the realization that my personal world had just changed forever. My head felt strange, adrenaline rushed and fear rose up all around me. I was confused about everything. Should I go to class and act like nothing had happened? No one would know, would they? But I knew.

What if I ran into her on campus? Maybe I should stay home and feel my feelings. This was a crisis, and I was safe at home. Lonnie wouldn't be back for hours. There was no way I was going to meet him at the spaghetti dinner after this. People would ask him why I wasn't there. He'd be upset and try to cover up. It wouldn't work. He'd come home to find me and want to talk. Hell. I wasn't going to go on record saying anything yet. It was impossible to know how I wanted to deal with this.

I went to the spaghetti dinner with my heart pounding. As usual, I was greeted by every single person with a hug as I came in the door. I timed my arrival so everyone would have been served already and I could just grab a paper plate, pile it with spaghetti, snag a garlic roll, and join the group on the floor just as announcements were starting. I saw Lonnie at the front of the room planning the speaking order. He looked relieved that I had arrived, came over and asked if I wanted to be on the agenda. "Yes, I want to recruit women to hand out fliers tomorrow, and I have two announcements."

"Good."

*Good.* We had both pretended things were normal. Maybe they were. Maybe nothing had changed. I went home and pretended to be asleep when he came in.

Tomorrow would be another day. Like Scarlet O'Hara always said, "I'll think about that tomorrow."

# 20
# BROADENING THE BASE

Now that I had committed myself to recruiting Dr. Cannon, I couldn't put it off any longer. I called the secretary at the Department of Home Economics and explained why I was requesting an appointment. Without hesitation she scheduled a time a couple of days away. That was easy.

On the day of the appointment, I was looking forward to a sunny walk to the other side of campus and full of curiosity about the world of Home Economics in 1970. I passed the mission arches of the original main entrance to the campus built in the 1930s. What a tiny administration building they had back then! Past a little garden was the entrance to the "Little Theater," probably the original assembly hall. Some more formal gardens led to a vortex. The point of symmetry here was meant to feature a statue. It was the bronze bust of an Indian warrior chief. I stopped and took in his visage. Tough, wise, weathered-looking skin; the sculptor had arrested an ancient, a primitive, and the school had plopped him down in the center of an educational factory. I wondered how he felt about this.

Time to move on. I left Montezuma. Most people called him Monty, the mascot for the school and its football team, the Aztecs. He seemed lonely, out of place to me. What did radical Native American activists think about him?

Continuing down the old main quad, I heard the chimes of the clock and glanced up at the modest tower of yellow stucco, which matched the buildings and archways radiating from it. This part of the campus was nice. Beautiful in its symmetry, harmony, and welcoming proportions. There was a door that said "Department of Public Administration, Dr. James Kitchen" on it. Another doorway to explore soon. Ahhh. What would that doorway bring me to?

Passing under the windows of the three story Old Library building, I remembered the coworker who had lent me her wedding dress. She had brought it to me in a box at work one day, only two years ago. Three stories of green windowpanes looked lonely and dust-streaked, as it sat waiting for its occupants to move out into the almost finished Love Library building.

Rounding the backside of the Library, I saw the low one-story building on the cliff's edge overlooking the end of Mission

Valley and Interstate 8. It had a slant roof, angled walls, and a cement courtyard in the front. "The Home Economics Building" said the sign. Opening the double glass doors, I found myself in a corridor leading to another corridor and gazed through walls of half windows where students were walking around in cooking and sewing laboratories. A girl in a pretty dress and matching hair ribbon walked up to me.

"Are you looking for a classroom?" She asked — smiling?

*Oh! She thinks I'm one of them! Imagine that!*

No, I am looking for Dr. Cannon's office. Do you know where it is?

"Sure. I'll take you there."

My, this was a homey place!

As she chatted I noticed her Chi Omega sorority pin. If she saw my Women's Liberation button would she tell everyone there that a "women's libber" was in their place? I hated that derogatory label. She left me in the reception room. On the walls were posters that said "Family Studies" and on the table were a stack of brochures about a "Human Studies Symposium." There were also some flyers about a conference on childcare.

I didn't see any traditional pictures of a woman cooking in the kitchen.

"Carol, I am so glad you came," said Dr. Cannon in her naturally kind voice. "I've been looking forward to meeting you. Let's go in my office right in here. Can I get you anything?"

It was a standard issue office, but I felt like I had found the oasis on a desert campus.

"No, thank you. I appreciate your meeting with me."

"Oh, I just wish we had more time to talk. Let me tell you that I have been following your work on the Center for Women's Studies and Services and the Women's Studies Program; I believe it is to have seven components, and I think you are doing wonderful things. I hear good things about you and that is no small thing, since they are almost all men. Oh, some are well intentioned, but they have not had the difficulties we have of female socialization."

Her eyes twinkled and I laughed. This was going to be great! An instant ally!

"So, Nona, you are already aware of the concept and are supportive of the move to try to get a Women's Studies Program on campus!"

"Why, yes, of course I am. It is something that has to be done and the way it will get done is if someone like you and the group of women have the commitment to see it all the way through. I only wish I had more time to give it myself. You see, I am committed to a number of major efforts and heavily involved with the United Nations, as my husband is, so we travel a lot and have commitments to international projects. Then, of course, I am also head of this department, and...but I could go on and on and I want to hear about you. For example, what sparked your passion in women's rights? I like to call it human rights because personally I feel, when viewed in the proper perspective, human rights should include women's rights, but of course I understand your need to identify them as such," she said, then exclaimed, "Oh, but it's past lunchtime!"

Nona jumped up, went over to the refrigerator, and pulled out two homemade sandwiches. We sat on a bench outside the Home Economics building and chatted merrily away about changing the world. For the first time in the world, students would attend a Women's Studies class and get three units of credit. The College had not even sanctioned us revolutionaries, Yet many students can today look back on their transcripts and see official credit for completing one of the first experimental classes in Women's Studies in the spring of 1970.

When I reported back to the Committee that Nona had offered us her class I was hesitant.

All eyes were on me.

"Carol, that's wonderful. You gotta do it."

"Yes! Yes!" the chorus resounded.

"I'm only a student. I haven't even got a degree. I can't..."

"You can and you will," said a voice of authority.

"You already taught Women's Liberation in the Experimental College, didn't you?"

"Well, yes, it was terrific. If I could teach it like that..."

**Women's Studies Committee members sit alone in the courtyard of the San Diego State Student Union. They are instituting the first program of Women's Studies in the world. The Faculty Senate gave final approval to the program in May of 1970.**

What a thrill. Just think of it. To be the only teacher of the pilot program who was a student! I couldn't help but immerse myself totally, embracing the flames of my passion even if it meant I might get burned a little.

# 21
# THE DIVING BOARD STORY

One very hot and humid Saturday summer night I wandered into a late night swim party in the backyard of one of the campus ministry houses. To my surprise, guys were jumping in and out of the pool — nude! They were all shouting and giggling hysterically. Of course they weren't drunk, since alcohol wasn't allowed in the place, but it didn't take long for me to recognize that these guys were my stoned friends: Lenny, a long-haired free spirit; my good "brothers" John and Ron from everything radical; gorgeous blond–haired, blue-eyed Dave from Student Council, whom I had been flirting with madly lately; and handsome surfer Brian, who sported a trim, brown, sexy beard and flirted with me incessantly at Aztec Center. I guess they all kind of knew that Lonnie and I weren't much of a couple anymore, but we were married and still living together.

None of them hid when they saw me come inside the gate and continue walking down the sidewalk alongside the pool. I didn't want to look at their penises, so I scurried along.

"Carol!"

"Carol's here!"

"Hey, Carol, come on in. The water's fine!" I didn't know what to do or where to go. I thought I'd look for Lonnie. From the pool house I could hear that most exciting song "Light My Fire" starting up on the stereo. I decided to duck into the pool house but I smiled, said hello to my friends, and pretended to be calm.

Dave didn't acknowledge my presence. He looked my way, and then dived off the side of the pool. Was he playing hard to get? Or did he not care? Maybe he was embarrassed?

Once inside, I sat down in the safety of darkness. Three guys I knew slightly were pouring sodas. They were all wearing shorts and t-shirts. I sat down on a beanbag chair and someone handed me a coke. They were laughing, and I joined in.

"This is quite a party. How'd this happen? Where's the pastor?"

"Oh, he's gone for the weekend. Left me in charge. I've been staying in the pool house for the last three weeks. It's cool." He went to the record player, picked out another album, *In-A-Gadda-Da-Vida*, pulled out the record, set it on the turntable. The mesmerizing sounds of this masterpiece was wildly erotic now.

"Anybody seen Lonnie?"

"Yeah. He was here just a little while ago diving off the diving board. But he left. They were going to a midnight movie at the Strand."

So, I was on my own. Maybe this was a good thing. Something was supposed to happen tonight. I could feel the prickling on my skin. The thought of Dave and Brian out there nude gave me a warm, moist feeling between my legs.

A joint was passed around. When it came to me I eagerly inhaled deeply. I had never gotten stoned without Lonnie before.

*I'm going to get really high,* I thought gleefully. *I haven't had this much fun since I was a kid!*

From where I sat I had a narrow view of the diving board. I could look each one of them up and down and they wouldn't know it! In between puffs I would get one guy in my sights, zoom in on his genitals as he climbed onto the low diving board, and get a split second view before he ran forward.

Someone jumped on the board, sprung his butt in the air. Balls hanging way down, he bent at the waist and crashed into the dark blue waters. But there wasn't always time to put the penis with the face.

Years later, I read a grand article about Michelangelo's monumental statues atop the colonnade of St. Peter's Cathedral in the Vatican. The classic nudes were missing their genitalia since the Catholic hierarchy had cut off their penises hundreds of years ago and replaced them with fig leaves for modesty's sake. In the 1980s the church hired a young American female art historian to restore male integrity. Several cardinals ushered her through the labyrinth of storage rooms beneath the Vatican museums where she was shown roughly 15 crates containing carefully marked penises. Her job was to decipher the markings and match the dick to the saint.

Wouldn't you know such a job could only be accomplished by a new feminist, an American, part of our Movement?

"Carol, don't bogart the joint."

"Oh, sorry, I didn't know…"

"Yeah, we know."

"We know you didn't know, right."

"Know what?"

"I know what."

"What?"

"You're stoned."

"Are you stoned?"

"Nah! I'm ripped."

They all giggled when I nearly fell off the beanbag chair.

"Way to go, Carol!"

These guys never said anything about the guys outside being naked and me being the only girl around. So it was easy for me to act like nothing outrageous was happening. The room, though, was charged with electricity.

I was getting more and more stoned. I looked at somebody's pubic hair and was surprised that it didn't match the color of the hair on his head. Everybody's dick was really shriveled up. I had only made love with one man in my life, and his dick was hard every time I saw it. My, college could be educational!

I took another hit. Now I wanted feel the cool water surround me. It was so damn hot in the pool house. I was going to have to go outside sometime. I didn't have a bathing suit. I could walk back home and get one, but the two blocks to the apartment seemed miles away.

"Carol, you gotta come in the pool!" My mischievousness lion-headed friend John poked his head in the window. "We're playing a game and the guys said you can join."

"Oh, yeah? What's the game?"

"Marco Polo!"

"Ooooh, that's fun."

"There is one rule. The only way in is naked from the diving board."

"Oh, really?" I looked around at the two other guys who were smiling.

"Yup, that's the rule."

"Soooo..."

The step to the diving board was directly in front of me. If I could make it quickly with a towel to the edge of the pool...

I was feeling pretty loose. But, God, I could never do that!

I took another hit.

"Oh, come on Carol. It's only skin! Live in the moment! I'm going back in! Lenny's left, and Ron and I have to go soon."

That would leave me alone with Dave and Brian and night's magic. My heart was racing. I watched as John did a cannonball in the air. I untied by halter blouse, grabbed a towel and stripped off my panties and shorts in one quick motion. It was now or never.

I approached the diving board. No one was looking! I dropped my towel by the edge of the pool, walked carefully six feet down the plank, caught a glimpse of stars, and started to spring upward.

"Look at Carol!" someone bellowed.

All eyes were on me, on my perfectly proportioned body. For a split second, I felt free as a bird. But when I felt them looking over my naked body I jumped in feet first, so they couldn't get a long view.

When I came up for air, I saw a new world around me. I shed my marriage vows. I left my attachment to my parents, left my attachment to my husband, and I discovered a new realm. Female Independence.

I wonder what Freud would have thought.

When I rose dripping from the dark waters I was a Goddess. Sparkling eyes, waterbeds, bare shoulders, and beautiful nakedness turned the timid me into a seductress.

The advent of the birth control pill in the late sixties added fuel to the fire of the Second Wave of the Women's Revolution. The First Wave, for equality, focused on the long battle to obtain the Vote. During the Second Wave we were all struggling to gain control over our bodies and over the destiny of our lives. We would finally throw off the yoke of male domination. The Sexual Revolution often divided men into two camps, the ones who embraced us and the ones who feared that new freedom would mean their loss of control, ego, and power. Until now the men had been defined by these very attributes. I dove under and swam like a mermaid reveling in the fertile waters all-consuming…. Like a snake I rose again, searching out a mate. Brian on one side of the pool, Dave at the end. John and Ron were leaving. The music from the pool house stopped and a light went out.

Treading water now, I began my dance. A toss of the head towards Brian, an intense look cast at Dave. The water was dark. How much of my body was visible to them? I glanced down. My small but pert breasts floated just below the surface. Very white, like beacons.

Brian was the easy prey. He grinned widely at me, teasing me to come closer. Dave swam forward a little and began treading water in front of me, mirroring my moves. The night was silent now. Even the ripples in the water were soundless. Our eyes locked. Some time must have past because I thought I saw Brian going out the gate. When I turned around full circle in the pool, he had gone. Vanished.

Dave glided to the ladder. I watched his slim naked back, and he reached for a towel and tied it around his waist. Then he walked to the end of the pool, picked up my towel, brought it back, and set it down near the steps.

"I'm going to heat up some coffee in the kitchen." Was this an invitation or a retreat? I thought it best not to think. I got out, covered myself with the towel, and retrieved my clothes from the pool house. A light came on in the kitchen window, and I saw Dave at the sink watching me.

My bare feet took me into the kitchen. A charge of electricity went through my entire body as I felt his full presence.

He stared at me.

"Do you want coffee?"

I shook my head. "No."

He stepped forward, put a hand on my waist, bent down, and kissed my lips. I was in ecstasy. That blond mustache I loved was tickling me now. I felt a rush of heat come over me. Muscles around my vagina began pulsating. I leaned into him and pressed my breasts into his chest. His towel dropped to the floor, and he put his hand on my cheek, and then lowered it to take my hand, leading me to a room nearby.

Still in darkness, he led me to a couch. I felt another surge of lightning. Energy I had never felt before came from somewhere. I felt like I could do gymnastics. I was panting as I threw off my towel, and he pulled me down onto the couch.

His touch was so soft, but so definite. He was in no rush. It was exquisite. His fingers slid down one leg and up another so many times I gave up anticipating where he was going. I was letting go.

I brushed his neck with my lips, licked his chest, and played with his mustache, his sideburns. He was a golden god and mine for the taking.

I lost track of what was happening. Fingers were opening me, stroking parts I didn't know I had. How did he know how to make me feel so good?

*Oh, oh.* He was inside me and still fingering me. My back arched. My head swung from side to side. He was weightless and so was I. Then the part of me that went wild when I masturbated took off. He had come and was finishing me off. I had never had sex like this before. My first orgasm with a man. I wanted to tell him, but gave him little thank you kisses instead. We lay there out of breath, panting like two dogs. Then laughed at what we had done.

"Come on. I think we should leave. I'll walk with you to the gate."

I smiled a big smile of satisfaction.

"You know that song 'I can't get no satisfaction'? I just got some."

He opened the gate and, as I passed through to the other side, I was seized again with the feeling that the world was different now for me.

"See you at the Org Center, Dave," I tossed over my head.

That's what we affectionately called the Student Organization Center.

It would be fun to walk in there Monday with new knowledge between my legs.

# 22
# TEACHING THE LONGEST REVOLUTION

In the fall of 1969, Joyce and I threw around another earth-breaking idea: *Why wait for lengthy university sanctions? Let's just start some Women's Studies classes now, next semester.* It was a mad dream.

The vision was we would somehow put together several, say five, experimental classes in Women's Studies while we were also applying for formal status for the Women's Studies Program. *Yikes!* I was not only going to have to coordinate countless petitions, meetings, seven trials by fire (the Seven Steps), but also help organize five classes. At 21 years old, my adrenaline was off the charts. Good thing I didn't have medical insurance — they would have strapped me down.

When we pitched the idea at our next meeting, everyone loved it.

Maddie said, "We're going to knock Dr. Walker's socks off when he discovers we've already been doing what we're proposing!"

Rhetta chimed in, "I think we can get Joyce to turn her literature class into Women In Literature, right?"

"Righto. I've already got a syllabus in mind," beamed Joyce.

"So we've got to find four other professors who will revamp or lend their classes," said Chris. "I'll talk to my drama and health professors. I'm pretty sure they'll do it."

Soon we had four commitments and an artist working on a multicultural cover design for a brochure. The day I went to see Nona Cannon of the Home Economics Department about helping us get the official Women's Studies Program through the Curriculum Committee, I came home with one more class. Plus, she wanted me to teach it! It would be retitled, "Family Interaction: Male/Female Relations." Some dreams come true really fast.

The project would be unofficial, but students could get three units of credit from various departments. Faculty members who taught these classes were all paid. In my case, I was a student and a volunteer, so I was not paid. Suddenly we had five experimental courses for Spring Semester 1970 and were passing out brochures at Registration to advertise them.

My student heart danced as I headed across campus to teach my first class. On the north side, the college had purchased small houses. Some were offices, and others held counseling and police services. This was also where the campus ministries had multipurpose houses, welcoming students to address social change issues at forums, spaghetti dinners, and other activities. They respected the radical students and encouraged their organizing efforts. I reserved the living room of the Intersection House, where I attended many functions sponsored by the wonderful Quaker minister Dave Neptune. Dave was a quiet man who was very supportive of the Civil Rights, Women's, Anti War, and Student Rights Movements. He was a true friend to many people.

I walked up the steps, opened the door and sat down on the carpet near the doorway where I could greet students as they arrived. Chris joined me, saying she could help with some of the classes, but not be there all the time. As I looked at my watch, girls began to trickle in, asking if they were in the right place.

"You sure are. Have a seat. We're going to form a circle on the floor here."

That brought smiles and looks of surprise. This class surely was going to be different. Pillows came down from the couch, book bags piled up and the room filled with chatter. I'd never seen any of these girls at a feminist meeting, so I knew I would get to start out at the beginning. Sitting in a circle, I told them, was what women did in consciousness-raising groups to facilitate equality. I was the teacher, but this would not be a totalitarian classroom. We would explore male and female relations together and everyone who wanted would always have a chance to speak. There were nods of approval. We were bonding already.

The class was an enjoyable experience for all. We had guest lecturers from the other "Women's Studies classes" and occasionally Nona attended to ensure that things were going well. We read every feminist pamphlet or article I could get my hands on, and each student asked questions about her own role as a girl, woman, career woman, wife, mother, etc. The group was very supportive to its members. We were on a quest together. This is what Women's Studies would be like.

I would never again see that unanimous, lightning enthusiasm in a classroom setting. The five experimental classes in the spring of 1970 proved to be a piece of heaven.

Soon after the victory at the Faculty Senate, I was slated to become part of the faculty in the fall! I went from "student" to "faculty member" the day the Women's Studies Committee began the search to fill positions for the 10 courses. They wanted me to teach "Field Experience." There would be pay, but there would be dark changes.

A real teacher! Not that I hadn't already taught "Women's Liberation" in 1969 in the student-run Experimental College, and "Family Interaction: Male/Female Relations" in the spring. Now I was going to be PAID to teach. Only one other student without a Bachelor's Degree was a faculty member — Al Urista in Chicano Studies.

Organizing was my forte. The last two years I had honed skills I never knew I was capable of — all out of necessity. Now I could continue to organize <u>and</u> teach organizing, while degreed faculty took care of the more academic courses. My class, "Field Experience," would provide a link between the campus and community, combining Theory and Action. The Personal and the Political would be studied. We would identify problems, research who was beginning work on them in the community, look for resources and propose solutions. Of course, it could not all be done in one semester. The next semester, students could take the class again and continue or revise their work. As more issues emerged, new students would work to address them, identify other issues, and on and on each year. The new body of knowledge of Women's Studies itself would grow. I also knew that this field work might help lay the groundwork for building another one of the Center's other six components, the services component, the Community Storefront.

Working on the syllabus for the course was a delight. The reading list was: "Notes From the Second Year," "Women: A Journal of Liberation," *The Feminine Mystique* by Betty Friedan, "California Women: Report of the State's Advisory Commission on the Status of Women," and Evelyn Reed's article "Women, Caste, Class or Oppressed Sex." I was keenly aware of the different types of feminists who might enroll. Already I had seen various trends in the local Movement and studied them in articles written by East Coast feminists where the Movement started earlier and different factions had clearly developed.

I could expect students who were reformist feminists, those in N.O.W. who believed the political process was the correct focus for changing the status of women. There would be socialist feminists, who as Marxists ascribed to the belief that capitalism was the enemy and patriarchy an aspect of it that concerned women. There might even be Socialist Workers Party members whose aggressive and manipulative agenda was to recruit women for the overthrow of the organization of imperialism. Feminist separatists, those who were alienated from the male-dominated Left, and lesbian separatists fighting both against male domination and "male-identified women." Then there were women who were exclusively "cultural" or "spiritual" feminists, dedicated to creating a separate subculture of women like themselves.

My own beginnings in the Women's Movement stemmed from activism in 1968 in the Left — primarily the Anti-War and Student Rights Movements. All the leaders were men, most of whom saw women as secondary citizens, having been socialized with that understanding since birth. Moving amongst them was tricky, frustrating, and at times ("All she needs is a good lay.") completely maddening. It was easy for me, once I discovered the Women's Movement to decide that we needed an INDEPENDENT Women's Movement.

We had to do our own analysis of our oppression. The uniqueness of our type of oppression lay in the fact that we often lived with a member of the oppressor class, a man. The nuclear family was patriarchal and had been since little known times of ancient matriarchies. Our fathers, brothers, and husbands had dominated us, and personal issues of sex, birth control, sexual preference, and roles within the nuclear family were always suppressed. It was clear we needed our own movement. We had to get out from under, but particularly as heterosexuals or members of society in general, we could not separate entirely; after all, we were living within a patriarchy that wasn't going away soon.

My intent as a teacher of Women's Studies was to ensure freedom in the classroom for all viewpoints to be expressed. From the outset I planned to present some of the various positions, allow students to voice their theories, and emphasize that research projects and community work should be conducted with as much neutrality as possible.

When I read the enrollment sheet I saw the names of three students who I knew were there to dominate, disrupt, or take over the class. One was a rabble rousing Marxist, one was a leader of the Young Socialist Alliance, and another was a woman against having a women's center on campus. She was trying to start one at the YWCA which she felt was the vanguard because it had recently embraced fighting racism as a top priority. She believed that white privileged college women were inherently guilty of perpetuating racism if fighting it was not our focus. Each of them had their own style of long, preachy speeches, haranguing the audience. One had the habit of breaking into sobs as she wailed about our collective guilt as white women.

Another woman was a member of the new National Women's Political Caucus who was planning to run for public office. Then there were two men. I wondered what their perspectives would be.

Needless to say, when I faced the first class in a sterile room of metal chairs and desks I was on guard the whole time. I had to limit discussion more than I wanted to and listen to angry tirades, hoping non-dogmatic types would speak up too. It was not fun.

Some groundbreaking projects were accomplished, however. Students did community research, interviews and papers on discrimination in San Diego elementary school textbooks and teacher resources, sexism in high school counselors' methods, political prejudice against women in the local electoral and appointment process, employment discrimination in working class jobs, racism and sexism, and so on. One of the young men surprised me by choosing the topic on the role that the oppression of women plays in female suicides.

I enjoyed the real work that got done by regular students despite the disruptions of the ideologues, but I wished I had been back sitting on the floor with that enthusiastic group in the spring experimental class. The honeymoon was over.

# 23
# MORNING IN THE COMMUNE (1970)

At the beginning of the year, I slowly awoke to the realization that I was lying alone on the mattress on the cold floor of my new basement bedroom in a commune. I was 21, and my husband and I were now living in separate bedrooms in a houseful of student leaders. "Separate but equal." I liked that. I didn't have to think about anyone but myself.

Staring at the dull gray ceiling above, I wondered how much longer I could remain calm. An alarm clock and a big black telephone threatened to throw me into action again. In these days I was always reacting to one crisis or another. Christ! We were in the middle of a revolution. Or two or three or...? Who could keep track anymore? Every day leaders were being assassinated! Guys were burning their draft cards. Women were demanding equal rights in masses, organizing in one state after another. Gays and lesbians were coming out of the closet and organizing parades. Boys I went to high school with in Corpus Christi, Texas, would be coming home dead from Vietnam today. And I was supposed to go to classes?

The time was five minutes to 8:00 in the morning, which meant I had only five minutes to get myself together before the offices on campus would be open. Yesterday I had left a message with Vice President Walker's secretary that a group of women faculty, staff, and students wanted to meet with him about starting a Women's Studies Program at San Diego State College. It had never been dared before. This was the lead-up to a make-it-or-break-it situation. Damn, and I was their leader!

It just wouldn't sound professional to answer the phone with a sleepy voice, but if I went to the bathroom I might miss his call. So I ran to the bathroom, peed as fast as I could, ran back, sat back down on the mattress and hummed a few notes to have my good voice ready. Now I had a little time to contemplate what else was going on in the world today. I wished I had a TV or a newspaper. I grabbed my doctor's-office-size appointment book. *Oh! We have another rally in two days!* This meant another all-nighter mimeographing fliers tonight at the Peace and Freedom Party office with the guys. Hmmm. Maybe I would flirt with the older ones a little. The professors there were all married, but they did like to look me over, and they were sexy.

Then panic hit me. We hadn't scheduled the *next*

meeting of the Ad Hoc Committee for Women's Studies. Oh, no! Was I supposed to do this or was someone else? If *I* didn't do it, would it not even happen? Probably. And, what plans did I need to make to ensure it was a productive meeting? We couldn't afford to waste time, *any* time. I should be thinking of all the events of yesterday and who to inform about what since the last time I'd seen them. I didn't want to be called elitist again. I was killing myself to be democratic. Shit, nobody had taken minutes again! My eyes darted to the green portable Olympia typewriter across the floor by my boots. Thank God I had taken it with me when I ran away to California. Daddy had meant for me to use it in my UT dorm room, not here! I had finally shown him!

*Oh man!* I would be forced to make up some minutes from my head now. This could take a long time, but it would give me the context I needed to propose overall strategy and specific tactics for convincing the administration that they had to listen to us. Maybe I should work up an agenda by myself and then get the others to help call another meeting. But they were getting burned out. Were we in this for the long haul? Or was I alone? *Oh, hell, just get started!!!!!!*

*Shit, man!* What if the phone does ring, and Walker says yes? They'll want to set the time. Joyce has classes to teach, Rhetta was in so many organizations she was always hard to hunt down, and who else could I possibly scare up? Maybe the other woman ("sister," I should say) in the commune, Patti, could be coaxed into coming. Patti was an earth mother, smoking dope, baking cookies, knitting scarves, and cracking jokes. She was beautiful inside and beautiful outside. Half Cherokee Indian, she often wore her jet-black hair in thick braids, framing a large smile that broadcast her sunny nature to everyone. Even though she talked like a radical, Patti insisted that she wasn't political. This meant that she hated meetings.

So did I, but I couldn't afford the luxury of hating a meeting. Now my stomach began hurting again. In the beginning, in 1969, I used to love our meetings. Of course those were really consciousness group sessions or rap groups where we could laugh, scream, cry, and rage together. As the need for direction grew, we became more and more serious. No more days of spontaneity. The childhood of our revolution had faded all too soon.

I had to call the meetings AND run them. My good friend and student body president, Ron, could smoke a joint right before a student council meeting and proceed to run it with eloquence and finesse. He could kick back and debate or negotiate with any faculty member or President Love himself while he was stoned out of his mind. Afterwards in the Student Center, he would roll on the floor laughing about what he had pulled off and letting us in on his double entendres and their slips of the tongues. We had the best belly laughs then.

Anyway, Ron would convince Patti if I asked him. He understood how crucial every single meeting in this process was going to be. First, we had to win Walker's approval. Then he might help pave the way with the other power brokers of the college.

If I couldn't find Ron, John would convince Patti. *Why else are we all in this commune thing together?* John was a little older, had been in Vietnam, and was a now Business major with a long yellow mane that combined the hair from his head, sideburns, mustache, and beard. John was so light-hearted. He liked to loosen me up with a bear hug whenever he saw me. John could always make me smile — and that was not at all easy, especially in those days!

Maybe I could eat breakfast today. But that was not important. Besides I didn't have any food or money. *I'll think about that later*, I decided. Just like Scarlet O'Hara.

Time to go find out about the latest travesty of the Nixon gang that was fit to print. I held my breath. *Please don't let there be another riot.* What to wear? I had three pairs of bell-bottom pants, two sweaters from the thrift shop, two peasant blouses, a Women's Liberation t-shirt, and two madras short dresses Patti had sewn from bedspreads. Choosing from my wardrobe had become much easier since I had left Texas. There was no closet in this room, and everything I owned hung on hangers nailed in the wall. Just look up and say "Bingo!"

It was cold still, so I pulled on the corduroy brown pants, and a green sweater. I liked the way it brought out the green of my hazel eyes. Reaching for my watch — an absolute must — I reviewed my pin-on button collection: "Que Viva La Raza," "Make Love Not War," "Out of Viet Nam," "Free Angela Davis," "Eldridge Cleaver for President," and others, and chose my trusted standby. This button featured a red women's symbol on a black background. The stem of the biological symbol for women had a red bow tied about it — femininity. From the top of the stem rose a red clenched fist painted red — power. Yes! This was always the best! The one and only. My best piece of jewelry! By now there was a handful of women on campus wearing them, and it sure was a conversation starter.

Parting my long brown hair down the middle, I pulled the upper half back, clasping it together with the leather barrette I had bought from a hippie at a love-in. With my thrift-shop purse slung over my left shoulder I picked up my shield, the trusty brown briefcase, and looked in the mirror. I was ready. And I looked pretty.

No girls on campus carried briefcases. Bearing a briefcase, I became a woman, maybe even a professor. Without the briefcase, I was just a pretty girl.

Now I was ready to go forth, to take on the world.

# 24
# THE WOMEN'S CONTINGENT FACES OFF WITH VICE PRESIDENT WALKER

Four young students and one instructor, the radical feminist contingent representing a "large constituency of women," met in February of 1970 in front of the pale yellow SDSU Administration Building at five minutes to 1:00. Each face was tight, close to miserable looking. I was a very worried 21-year-old but wore my practiced calm and mature look, my stomach already gripped by the familiar daily aching that began with our first public presentation months prior. "Everybody ready? Okay let's go in."

Once I was inside, the putrid yellow green walls of the empty hallway repelled me. Nothing nice about this place. There was a counter window with bars across it, and it was shut tight. What was in there? A big red "EXIT" sign at the end of the hall, a glassed-in, red-handled axe, and gray fire hose were the only decorations here. Searching for the office directory, we found a black mounted felt board with little white plastic letters listing names and office numbers. There he was, second floor — Vice President Donald E. Walker. Joyce, newly pregnant, gripped her big black box of a briefcase and said "This way" when she spotted what looked like an abandoned staircase. The dirty greenish windows were double paned and reinforced with a crisscross of tiny wires. More protection from the unruly students outside.

As we sat in the waiting room outside, we already felt imprisoned. What could we safely say in front of the impeccably dressed older lady who was Donald Walker's private secretary? We stole looks at each other. Rhetta glanced at the secretary's beehive hairdo and sent an impish look, which threatened sarcasm around the group. Chris Spaulding,, a petite, shorthaired, no-make-up young woman with enormous wire-rimmed glasses looked bug-eyed, stiff. Maddie Farber, with her sweet Swedish face, had made it clear she was there only to be counted as a body. She scanned the stack of magazines and pointed with a giggle to *Ladies Home Journal* lying on the coffee table.

That magazine was infamous to us. Nearly two hundred women sat in at the office of the LHJ to protest a "women's magazine" whose advertisements routinely exploited women.

They demanded that the magazine include a special section on the Women's Movement. By August 1970, LHJ published a special eight-page insert titled "The Power of a Woman: The New Feminism" by the "Women's Liberation Movement." Our secret power was everywhere.

The silence was making me more nervous. "Pretty busy day today?" I asked the secretary politely. She looked up, glanced at our motley crew's couture, and answered, "Yes, the Vice President has had several meetings already this morning." She returned to her typing. Oh, well. *At least she knows I'm not scared of her.*

A man's voice boomed gaily, "Send them in!" We jumped in unison, and I led the procession into the inner sanctuary.

Vice President Donald E. Walker rose from his desk and stuck out his hand to me. "Hello Don," I said. Good God! I had done it. Not "Dr. Walker." I had planned this gutsy little tone setter. If he were going to call us by our first names, which I knew he would, I would call him by his. Besides, Lonnie, my husband and controversial student leader, had done this number on Don before and I loved the "teach *them* idea." Equality from the start.

My eyes scanned every inch of the room. I needed to know the turf. I imagined dignitaries from around the world — all men — having been in this room. He had never seen the likes of us.

I introduced Chris Spalding, Joyce Nower, Rhetta Alexander, and Maddie Farber, and there were warm, awkward handshakes all around. Vice President Walker, I mean Don, sat down at the head of the long conference table in front of his executive-sized desk while we took seats at the opposite end. The mahogany furniture was impressive but worn, the room small, the man informal. He gestured for us to begin. "This is your time."

Walker listened intently to every word of our joint presentation on the case for a Women's Studies Program. We had rehearsed and even set up the sequence his questions would come in, but we were on guard, nervous about what he could say that we weren't prepared for. Who could field the unexpected question? Would she blow it? Would I blow it? Who would get tough, but not too tough, with him?

"What kind of support is there on campus for this?" was Walker's opening question.

That was the cue to pull out the stack of crumpled papers from my briefcase. I had put the best looking petitions on top and hid the ones with missing addresses or duplicate names and coffee stains on the bottom, hoping he wouldn't ask to keep them. I had to prevent that precious pile getting reviewed to death, misplaced, or in any way out of my hands. This was cannon fodder we would need to carry to future meetings. If he did say he needed to have them, I was ready tell him these were the originals and that we would have to get copies made, hold my breath, and hope he wouldn't tell his secretary to copy them. He didn't.

Growing more at ease, I told how we had stood on the steps of the student center, Aztec Center, in front of the bookstore, and at other key locations, approaching strangers with the question "Would you support there being a Women's Studies Program on campus?" It was a chore we all hated since there was always a jock or a loud group of boys who'd laugh at us and call us "Women's Libbers."

Evidence began piling up on his conference table like documents in a courtroom. The stack of 600 signatures we had collected thus far; the Associated Student Council Resolution we had gotten passed without too much drama; the key professors, like Nona Cannon, we had consulted with; and the issue of *Time* magazine that carried a brief story about the experimental classes we were currently running. We were impressive, and we knew it.

"It looks like you have been doing your homework," he observed. "Is this being done anywhere else in the nation? Is there any precedent for this?" was his next challenge.

That was our cue to reference Florence Howe's research and Lucinda Cisler's Bibliography and to impress him with the fact that San Diego State would make the precedent for the first Women's Studies Program in the U.S.

*Hmmm.* That got his attention! He made some notes. "How do you know there will be enough students registering for the courses to justify allocating faculty positions to this?"

Now we cinched it with the story of five unofficial classes we were currently running — how they were sponsored by Professors Joyce Nower, Rose Sommerville, Nona Cannon, Lois Kessler, and Jacqueline Tunberg, how we had promoted them with leaflets at registration, and the long "waiting list" that developed to get in. I pulled out the wonderful green brochure we designed with faces of women of every ethnicity. The experimental courses offered in the Spring 1970 were:

- "Women's Roles in History and Literature"
- "Human Sexuality"
- "Women in World Drama"
- "Family Interaction: Male and Female Liberation"
- "Women in Contemporary British Literature"

We told Dr. Walker that students were already receiving college credit for completing these new courses. Yet, we had not attained official status from San Diego State. His eyes fixed on the brochure. Silence filled the room.

We seized the offensive. "Have you read the proposal we sent you?" I asked.

We had mailed Walker an advance copy of our Proposal for a Women's Studies Program and laid a copy of the full Proposal for a Center for Women's Studies on his table. We sat on the edges of our brown leather chairs waiting for his crucial opinion. Joyce gave me that look, *Had he read it?*

Don Walker matter-of-factly said for this proposal to be approved by the University it would need to pass seven decision-making bodies: The Curriculum Committee, the Academic Planning and Policy Committee, the Council of Deans, etc., and finally the Faculty Senate.

"Are you girls up to that?"

Joyce and I chimed in, "Of course."

*"You mean women"* we were all tempted to say.

Things began to heat up fast. He buzzed his secretary on the intercom, told her to consult the calendar and provide us with the dates for the meetings that were already scheduled as we left the outer office. It was over! My stomach relaxed a bit, but I was still holding my breath. I couldn't wait to lie down somewhere.

"What about the meetings that weren't scheduled?" one of our contingent asked him. "The dates will be scheduled so that items headed for a vote of the Faculty Senate can proceed along and be placed on the agenda for a meeting before the end of the academic year."

"When is the last meeting of the year?"

"Probably the last week in May. It will be a tight time schedule, but it is not impossible."

My heart was racing, my temples pounding. *NOT IMPOSSIBLE. This means close to POSSIBLE. He is not going to put up roadblocks! This is the closest thing to supporting it!!!*

"Do you mean that if the Proposal fails any committee, or if any committee meeting is *postponed*, the Proposal will not make it before the May Faculty Senate meeting?"

"Yes, that is likely to be what would happen. In that event you would need to start over again next year."

Silence. No one, including Walker, wanted to speculate on what our chances would be a whole year from now.

We thanked him for the information and ended the meeting with cordial goodbyes. Walking out of his office suite and moving down the hallway, no one spoke. Everyone let out audible sighs. "Let's wait till we get outside to talk," someone whispered.

We headed for the comfort of the green lawn and plopped down. "Well, he did seem to be supportive," Joyce ventured. "I think he wants to help us but can't be too committal."

"Good God, *seven* committees!" Rhetta exclaimed.

*That was too civilized*, I thought to myself.

"What is the Council of Deans?" asked Chris. "Well, we know Dean Warmer is on it 'cuz she is the Dean of Women Students."

"Oh, no. Not the Dragon Lady again," said Rhetta.

"More like The First Lady. She'll just agree with what the men say," Maddie observed. "I've got to go. I'm late for the baby sitter."

Chris chimed in, "Me too, I'm late for work."

Now there were only the three of us again. The same bedraggled threesome of Joyce, Rhetta, and myself, who had started the Rap Group what seemed like eons ago. "We have to go for broke," I stated. "It absolutely must come to a vote this year. Can you imagine what will happen if it doesn't? Next year we will have lost all the momentum, and the reactionaries will have more time to kill it."

Joyce agreed. "We've really got some work cut out for us. We're going to have to divide up the tasks and make sure people don't burn out before each committee meeting. And, by the way, I've got to make time to have a baby."

"When is your due date?"

"June 29," Joyce answered. My heart pounded harder. This was so heavy. What if she couldn't be there? I couldn't do it without her.

"Can you," I implored Joyce, "or the two of you," I looked at Rhetta's blank gaze and my eyes came to rest on the baby in Joyce's womb, "Can the two of you commit to being at the Faculty Senate the last week in May? *Please,"* I tried not to sound like I was begging.

"Hey, I know the Revolution can't wait, but I don't relish the thought of going into labor in the aisle of the auditorium, and I don't want Stokely Carmichael to get the last word."

Rhetta and I responded in a chorus of sarcasm, "THE ONLY POSITION FOR WOMEN IN THE MOVEMENT IS PRONE."

We all laughed heartily and hugged goodbyes. I walked away with my head spinning and my stomach too queasy to be hungry. It was 3:00 p.m., and I had had nothing to eat that day. I walked on alone across the campus, wondering how to orchestrate so many things at once. The spring of 1970 would surely be a time we would never, ever forget.

I remember thinking, "Seven committees and assemblies. Is it Seven Steps or Seven Pitfalls?"

**December 20, 1969 – Carol Council, then 21 years old, surveys questions she and others painted on plywood walls surrounding the construction site of the SDSU Malcolm A. Love Library to dramatize the need for a Women's Studies Program.**

# 25
# THE SEVEN STEPS

*In Mozart's opera* The Magic Flute *a prince awakens in a forest. He is young and lost. The sounds there are strange. Are they made by insects, birds, and wolves? Or, worse? Maybe there are monsters in this unknown world. He has no shelter, armor or weapons.*

*When a motherly like figure with a smooth voice appears to him, Tamino is first suspicious, but upon hearing her kind words and realizing his complete aloneness in this foreign place (and seduced by the beautiful soprano's aria), he decides to trust her. She paints the picture of a journey he must make, and foretells the signs and trials along the way.*

Donald Walker did this for me. Absent the aria and the beauty. I knew I could not trust any man in the University administration, but I decided I *needed* to trust him — at least for the beginning of the journey.

The path Walker drew for me seemed straightforward in my mind. Seven committees and assemblies. Very objective. Democratic. Linear. People would play fair, and at the end of the journey we would win or lose.

On the other hand, what if they didn't play fair? *They* had all the power, these administrators and professors; we were mere supplicants. If someone wanted to block our efforts they could start rumors, fail to show up at a meeting where they were needed to make a quorum, or give us a wrong meeting date. They could omit putting it on the agenda, or "table us" for a later meeting — too late for the next step.

We would just have to be vigilant, then. I would need to triple-check everything and everyone before, during, and after each of the seven steps.

There was an underworld, too, beneath these seven steps. The dark places of anxiety, confusion, fear, bewilderment could not be measured, tested, or seen. The Unknown was just that — unknown.

Furthermore, while we diligently followed the path Walker prescribed, he could, with one deft move, put the Women's Studies Program over the top by giving us his blessing, or destroy the entire project by saying there were no funds for it.

All we could do, then, was to follow the path while being ever watchful to anything on all sides or under the bushes. Too bad we didn't have spies in the administration!

The Seven Steps were:

1. The Sub Committee on Curriculum of the Faculty Senate
2. The Interim Advisory and Planning Committee of the Faculty Senate
3. The Council of Deans
4. The College of Arts and Letters Faculty Assembly
5. The Academic Policy and Planning Council
6. The University Curriculum Committee
7. The Faculty Senate

All of these groups were unfamiliar to us. As students we had never come into contact with this hierarchy. Joyce's only knowledge of the Steps was that the College of Arts and Letters Assembly was made up of about 300 people, some from her department, English, but none of whom were her best friends. She dreaded this step particularly. They were full professors; she was only a lecturer. Joyce guessed that they were all men, some of whom were old and crotchety. Then, that could be true of all of these groups. If there were any women at all, they would be a tiny minority trying to blend in with the majority. Not people to make waves.

So she preferred to start writing and focus on getting ready fast for the Curriculum Committee. Anticipating this, she had already gathered sample course descriptions from various departments, researched their origins and longevity, and begun to analyze the content and verbiage that were the most solid. Stuff we could plagiarize so the Committee would like its conformity. She started drafting samples. Comparative Literature would become Women In Comparative Literature, with notable women authors in the course description and a bibliography to serve as an arsenal if the going got rough.

We crossed our fingers that the date and time of the Curriculum Committee would fall at a time when Nona Cannon, our ally from the Home Economics Department, could make it. Nona knew exactly what we were planning, and understood the full importance of it. She trusted me enough to teach one of her classes as an experimental Women's Studies class. I titled it "Family Interaction: Male and Female Liberation." Twice when she came to visit, she was delighted with the enthusiasm of the students and the informal teaching and learning format I facilitated.

When I called her with the news of the Seven Steps Walker had outlined, she said, in her slow Oklahoma drawl, "Well, you know, you can count on me to be at the Curriculum Committee. You realize that I know everyone on it. I've been through it before. I worked very hard on getting that Committee to approve changes in Home Economics curricula to make it into Family Studies. They are not an easy bunch, but they are fair."

"We don't know the date and time of the meeting, Nona. We won't know until a few days before... I hope you can make it. If you can't, what should we do?" Dr. Cannon was an extremely busy woman as chair of her department and an activist with the United Nations; she was constantly in meetings all over San Diego and traveling all over the globe. She was already preparing to be out of the country while on a year's sabbatical starting at the end of the semester.

"Well, Carol," I remember her saying in her sweet but firm tone, "there is too much at stake for me not to be there, so I'll just make sure that I am!"

Bravo for Nona!

"Joyce is working up draft language for the classes now to have them ready for the next women's meeting. I'll get copies to you as soon as possible."

"Yes, please do. I'll not only want to review them, but I may run them by one or two of the Curriculum Committee members in advance of the meeting. If I can do any individual lobbying, I will let you know. Right now, though, I'm afraid I'm about to be late for a speaking event downtown."

Hurray! Dialing Joyce, I knew we had just scored big time.

"Joyce, Nona said she not only will be at the Curriculum Committee, but she will make the presentation for us!"

"Really? That's wonderful. I don't have to be the token faculty member for once! No, you know I would have done it, but Nona has got her Ph.D., and credentials up the kazoo. Plus, she's not officially identified with us. The perfect advocate. Yes, I think she's just the ticket. If anyone can persuade them it's Nona!"

"Okay, so we got that lined up."

"I've got a class to teach in fifteen minutes."

"Okay, but we need to strategize about the Interim Advisory and Planning Committee. It could be coming up soon too."

"I talked to Leon. He said it's like the Federal Ways and Means Committee. They decide where proposals go next. Many ideas die right there."

"Great. I'll call Walker's office and try to get a list of the members. Meanwhile we've got to start working on printing the Center for Women's Studies Proposal, and then a document describing each of the seven components."

"Seven steps for seven components. Sounds like a mantra."

"Or a musical, 'Seven Brides for Seven Brothers.'"

"See you tonight. I hope more than three or four of us show up. Maddie said she can't get a sitter, Karen is not coming, and Mary Lynn is a maybe."

"Yeah, the group is getting smaller just when we are going to need a presence at seven committees. Let's discuss how to recruit more feminists tonight, okay?"

"Righto."

That night five women showed up. We reviewed the Seven Steps and asked for people to sign up to attend at least one of them. Although everyone was willing, only three promised to be there. Not everyone was as committed as me. And others had scheduling conflicts. Joyce had classes and committee meetings, and childcare considerations, that wouldn't make it possible for her to keep such a promise. So, in the end only one woman promised to be at all seven presentations. Yup, that was little old me — the youngest of the lot. For a moment I wondered what a wig and makeup would do for me.

Everyone was a little overwhelmed by the sheer number of committees we had to win over in such a tight timeline. It was the end of January. We had five months to progress through seven bodies. The Faculty Senate's last meeting was in May.

And, that was just for the academic component. Anticipating a lot of questions throughout the process, we decided to host an invitational event to formally present the Proposal for the Center for Women and get the head honchos briefed well before we might be making presentations before their groups. We booked the President's Lounge in Aztec Center and invited President Love; Vice President for Academic Affairs Donald Walker; Vice President for External Affairs Ernie O'Byrne from the Foundation; Dean Warmer, the Dean of Women Students; Dr. Ned Joy, head of the Council of Deans; Dean

Carrier, Dean of the College of Arts and Letters; Ron Breen, President of the Associated Student Council; and Judy Haller, a friendly young administrator who was the new head of Student Affairs.

Our plan was a one-hour presentation, complete with lemonade and cookies, followed by a press conference in the courtyard of the student center. The Ad Hoc Committee started cranking out mimeographed copies of the Proposal Karen had typed on the IBM electric typewriters. The faded purple ink on white paper looked dismal and cheap.

Joyce came in, stared at them, and left. Later she called me up. "Carol, is there any way we can make it look more professional?"

"We could never afford colored paper."

"Even on colored paper, anything mimeographed looks cheap."

"Maybe we could have the Proposal for a Center for Women printed on an offset printer and the rest mimeographed."

"Wow. What if we could have each of the seven components printed up on different colors of paper?"

"Seven different colors spread out on the table when they come in the conference room!"

"That would be impressive."

"Wouldn't it?"

"It would cost a mint."

"We are going to need all of these documents for many different occasions, and to send to foundations."

"Foundations. Hmmmm. I have to be at O'Byrne's office this afternoon. Maybe if I just called him up now and told him about the situation..."

"He could slip it into the foundation's printing budget!"

"Yes!"

"I'll give it a try."

Three hours later I handed O'Byrne our ditto masters. He had his secretary ready to retype them to make them print-ready. Then he picked up the phone and called the printing office, making an appointment to have them run off by the next day. I was practically in awe of his power.

"He looked back at me. How many copies?"

I shrugged, "Four hundred?"

"Make it a thousand of each. What colors, Carol?" He smiled at me. I was elated.

"Golden Rod, Green, Blue, Beige, Yellow, Purple.... and what?" *Orange? Yuck. Pink? No, never pink. Pink was the color that labeled baby girls inferior in the hospital bassinet. But, then, we could give it new meaning. Yes, why not?* "Pink!"

The day of their debut, on February 10, the pretty colored paper documents made a great rainbow spread out over a table covered in white linen. All the dignitaries attended. Joyce, Rhetta, Chris, and I made presentations. Everyone politely shook hands, ate cookies, and never raised an eyebrow at the language they heard that day: "feminist," "chauvinism," "oppression," and "male domination." We could just as well have said "sorority," "fraternity," "brotherhood" and "sisterhood." It was easy. There was no voting today.

It was like a dress rehearsal. On February 17 we made the same presentation before the full Council of Deans, that is, the Dean of every school in San Diego State. Two very hard-nosed Deans said the idea was all fine and good, but that it was not a priority given other needs on campus. I had heard rumors of worse things they said about us. A third said, "I wonder where you think the faculty positions are going to come from?" We made the surprise announcement that Vice President Walker had committed one faculty position already in a memo I brought with me, and that Dean Carrier had promised one half-time position. Carrier nodded his affirmation.

"Well, if they have already gotten approval from the Subcommittee on Curriculum and have 1.5 positions allocated, I say we give our approval so it can go on to the next step."

"All in favor?"

"Aye."

"Opposed?"

Silence.

"Abstentions?"

Two hands went up.

"The motion passes."

I said, "Thank you."

Joyce shook hands.

We left, relieved to leave the roomful of wise old men.

The Committee had organized a "Response Rally" in front of the library to report on the meeting publicly and try to force a commitment from the administration. The flyer for the rally read, "We are an unforeseen need," using their favorite language for why they couldn't allocate money or positions yet;

the argument was always "We have to have money left for 'unforeseen needs.'"

Since we had news to give them of the 1.5 faculty positions, it wasn't very much of a rally; I mean, we couldn't get very angry. We knew, though, that regardless of good news, we had to keep the momentum up, and, of course, there were always powerful speeches to give on the oppression of women in general and individual cases that fired up the small but enthusiastic crowd.

With 1.5 faculty positions so far (we got one more later) we felt rich, but in reality we had nothing. The gifts were the votes of confidence that the Program would exist. We had planned for 10 to 15 courses minimum and a "Department Chair" position. Our original proposal demanded 4.5 faculty positions. The gifts were welcome, but nowhere big enough. On May 1, we had to be at the Academic Policy and Planning Council that would no doubt challenge how we could operate with only 1.5 positions. They were likely to conclude that our plans should wait another year.

We were at a crossroads. How to keep our good relations but make larger demands? Requests wouldn't be effective. We needed to show power, and make demands. I called a special meeting of the Ad Hoc Committee to reassess our status and strategize for the rest of the fight.

The turnout at this meeting was bigger, because we sent out the message that the Women's Studies Program was in jeopardy. The press, however, touted the 1.5 positions as a major victory, and some women we counted on never showed because they read the good news.

The joint meeting of the Ad Hoc Committee for Women's Studies and Women's Liberation had new blood in it. Some were from the Young Socialist Alliance — we knew their faces and outrageous behavior — while others came from who knows where. It was impossible to bring them all up to speed about the work that had gone on in the last year, but we did our best. We needed consensus that 1.5 positions was only token support, and we got it. We needed bodies we could call on to make a show of support, and we got names, phone numbers, and commitments. What did not come out of the meeting was a strategy. Joyce, Rhetta, and I sat limp on the conference table after everyone else left pumped up.

**Student protestor holds sign, "UP AGAINST THE WALL WALKER !" during rally and sit in.**

# 26
# THE HAND THAT ROCKS THE CRADLE

I remember vividly the day we had to present the Women's Studies Proposal to the entire faculty of the College of Arts and Letters at San Diego State. We were at the midpoint in the Seven Steps, or seven committees, path to the Faculty Senate and the Proposed Program (quasi department) was to be housed in the College of Arts and Letters. If they didn't want it there, it was the end of the road.

We were seated on a stage before a sea of male professors. Joyce Nower says she remembers feeling like we were beer cans lined up on a fence for target practice. There were four or five of us and over 300 of them.

We finished presenting the justification for an academic program, the need for a separate program like a department, and the support on campus for the cause. We recited our successes at the various committees and dropped the appropriate names to lend it legitimacy. Then it was their turn.

A sympathetic male professor stood up and gave his wholehearted support. An unknown man stood up and fired the first question. It was neutral! So far, so good. I scanned the audience looking for women professors. There were only two, and they did not move. I spied Rene and Gus, the two Chicano professors who had been my secret advisors. They would not speak unless things went very badly. They had made enough enemies and did not want to give us more. Next, an elderly man began to rise. He had to be assisted by the man sitting next to him. Dr. Claude Shouse's voice crackled as he stated emphatically that there was no need for a program about women. "One only has to look at history to know that *the hand that rocks the cradle rules the world*."

I felt that seething feeling in my chest. My eyes darted around the auditorium and back at our group as I tried to assess if we should respond to that, or if someone in the audience would counter it. Suddenly I realized this was a godsend. Male professors would have to debate each other and take a stand. Three men stood up at once to object to Dr. Shouse. As they took him on, others rose to make middle-of-the-road statements. Nobody wanted to be aligned with Shouse's overt sexism. No women stood up. There were very few in that room.

I was confused by the quote. Mother rocked my cradle,

but she didn't rule the roost. What did he mean? I didn't get it literally — but I knew it was insulting. For years afterwards, I quoted him as saying "The hand that rocks the cradle, shouldn't rock the boat." When Joyce and I spoke together, she would always correct me, but since we were in a public setting I couldn't ask her about it, and then I would forget until it happened the next time. I still wasn't sure until I looked it up on the Internet. It is a quote from the 19th Century English poet, William Ross Wallace.

All I remember after Dr. Shouse's outpouring is that the audience nodded agreement with those who were outraged by his proclamation. Soon somebody called from the question. A motion was made and seconded. "I call the question!" a man shouted.

Dean Carrier said, "All in favor signify by raising your right hand." A large number of arms shot up. "All opposed?" Dr. Shouse shoved his hand up high while a sprinkle of hands were barely raised. *The cowards.*

"The motion passes," Dean Carrier announced with a broad smile and shook hands with each one of us. We filed off the stage and out the door stunned, but grinning. I think we all felt we had just made it over the worst hurdle. Onwards!

Our unheralded Goddess, the Centaur for Women's Studies, had won the day. The Centaur swiftly marched through the vineyards of the College of Arts and Letters and trampled where the grapes of men's wrath were stored. Our truth was marching on. Now, if only we could climb the rest of the Seven Steps.

THE CENTAUR FOR WOMEN'S STUDIES

# 27
# THE RALLY AND THE SIT-IN

One day in March Lonnie came home with Ron and John, talking excitedly about the news that they were planning a big rally with lots of speakers.

"This is going to be the biggest rally San Diego State has ever seen," Ron, the Student Body President, was saying. "We are going to have representatives for every major group: Chicano Studies, African-American Studies, Mecha, Maya. The Black Panthers are going to be there and so will Young Social Alliance, and the campus ministries. We'll cover all the issues. We may even get one of the radical professors besides Jerry Farber to speak, like Leon Nower or Norm Howard. You can have two speakers, one from Women's Liberation and one from the Ad Hoc Committee on Women's Studies."

Lonnie said, "Let's do some guerrilla theater or something to make sure the TV stations really show up this time. That's crucial."

"Oh, yeah," John added. "I've got to contact Vietnam Vets Against the War. I could speak as a vet, but I think it's better that we get their president to be there."

"What's the date?" I asked.

Lonnie replied, "March 12th at noon. Carol, we swore we wouldn't tell anyone, but I know you can keep a secret. Is it okay if we tell her, guys?"

Ron said, "Yes, but you have to keep it a secret, and remember that I was never a part of this." He always had to cover his butt to keep his position as Student Council President credible.

"You know I can. Come on and tell me! Are guys going to burn their draft cards?"

"No, not there. Some of us are talking about having a sit-in after the rally if our demands on the administration aren't met."

"A sit-in where?"

"In the Administration Building, either on the first floor or on the second floor outside Vice President Walker's office!"

"Oh, no. You can't do that. Lonnie! That's the day when we are going back to Don Walker's office to push for the five faculty positions!!!!"

"Oh, my God!" He looked really worried and then grinned. "That's perfect, don't you see?"

"No it's not. Are you crazy? We have got to go in there and have a serious negotiation and not while there is a disruption outside. Besides, I might want to be at the sit-in if it were on a different day. This could be terrible timing."

"Well, we can't change the date of the rally," John said. "I've just gotten the permit approved to use the lawn, and that was no easy thing to accomplish. Plus we've already got major speakers committed. Change your meeting with Walker."

"I can't! It's one of the Seven Steps. We can't go to the next committee unless we have already worked out something with Walker. We have absolutely no choice. Shit! I wish you would have told me about this sooner, Lonnie."

Lonnie shrugged, "It just happened after the meeting last night."

I felt like two trains were headed towards each other and were going to collide.

The day of the rally, March 12, 1970, was a heady one. Lonnie and the guys were out at 6:00 a.m. passing out flyers all across the campus, lugging speakers and microphones from one place to another, doing radio and TV interviews, and revising the growing list of speakers. And the San Francisco Mime Troupe had arrived!

I reviewed my notes, and rehearsed the speech I had read out loud to Joyce and Leon the night before. I knew I wouldn't be a very good speaker. The other speakers were charismatic and could ad lib passionately. They had done it many times before. Leaders from the Peace Movement, the Chicano Movement, Vietnam Vets Against the War, the Farmworkers, the campus ministers, MECHA, Black Studies, Free Huey, and the radical professors — they were all orators. I was not. So, I would have to get over the fear of the crowd, and rely on good enunciation and the power of the microphone. Oh, yes. "SPEAK SLOWLY" I wrote in the middle of the first page. I knew I had a tendency to talk fast when I was nervous. "MAKE EYE CONTACT HERE: SCAN THE CROWD," and "PAUSE FOR AUDIENCE REACTION" were the other cues I gave myself.

Then I had the pleasurable thought that by now there could be a lot more women on campus who would like hearing a feminist speaker! Our ranks had not grown in terms of meeting attendees, but the campus, and the world, had been saturated with feminist news and slogans since we began organizing in the summer of 1969. Now we'd get to see the fruit of the Movement!

I glanced around me and realized all of the other speakers were men. It was a revolution and yet, the men almost completely dominated the event. Nevertheless, my voice, the only feminine voice, would be heard.

Consequently, when I delivered the speech to the largest crowd ever assembled on campus, 2,000 people, I was proud, angry, and happy. The moment Lonnie, the MC, introduced me as a feminist student who would speak about the need for a Center for Women's Studies, I heard women's joyful screams, applause, and "Right On Sister!" When I paused, they applauded and whistled loudly. People jumped up and down and waved handmade banners. Cameramen from two TV stations scurried to get their heavy equipment closer in on me. I was nervous, but was able to slow down, control my breathing, and end the speech with a rousing cry: **"POWER TO THE WOMEN!"**

The reaction of the crowd thundered and shook the earth. The podium shook as I nervously removed my notes. The men cheered and applauded. The women, o' contraire, leapt to their feet in a frenzy of ecstasy. Among the vast male majority, the female jubilant dances and hugs sprouted up like morning glory lightning bolts throughout the mass assembly. As I looked out over the sprawling crowd, I realized I had never seen such a thrilling division between the encouraging, yet subdued, men and the unbridled celebration of women grasping their freedom.

If only I could have savored that moment. I wanted so badly to stay and talk to the feminists in the crowd. I could almost taste their jubilance, feel their sweaty t-shirts hugging me, and dance around with the euphoria. But, it was not in our strategy. Instead I hurried over to a corner of the quad to meet up with our contingent of eight women who were going to Don Walker's office to demand five faculty positions.

We stood and waited while the last speaker, Leon Nower, gave a rousing speech about student power, black power, Chicano power, womanpower, and people power. He called for people to stand up and take action. "Do It!" he ended his speech, and the crowd went wild.

John got up and asked everyone to follow him in a march to the Administration Building. "If all our demands aren't met we are going to have a sit-in!" With that Lenny, John, Patty,

Gordon and other friends picked up kazoos, drums, pots and pans, wooden spoons and led a chanting group of 300 or 400 students to the windows of the Administration Building. As planned, we stayed behind. Our meeting with Walker was in 45 minutes.

The happy crowd swelled around two sides of the building, singing songs and shouting slogans. There were no campus police visible. John got up on the steps and asked for everyone's attention. He read a list of student demands, pausing to look up at the second floor, and asked, "Can you hear me, President Love? Are you listening, Don Walker?" Then to the audience, "We mustn't forget Ned Joy; he is part of the triumvirate too."

"Love and Joy" someone shouted. All the students laughed and began chanting, "Love and Joy, Love and Joy, We want Love and Joy!" Someone opened the doorway, and the marchers snaked inside the building and up the wide stairway. Outside we came closer, watching people as they started jumping and dancing. A news reporter wanted to talk to me, "Not now," I answered. "You'll have to set up an appointment."

Lonnie had planned ahead and picked up his bullhorn.

"We can't all fit into the Administration Building hallway, and it is not our goal to stop business, just to get heard. When the hallway is filled everyone inside must sit down, and the rest of us must stay outside, all right? This is the way to keep it peaceful, brothers and sisters. Are you with me?"

"Right on!"

"Peace, Brother."

"And Peace to the Sisters."

"Right on!"

Lonnie disappeared into the building. Patty took the microphone. "Okay, why don't we sing some Beatles songs together? Tammy, bring your guitar up here!"

A peace monitor wearing a yellow armband ran up and whispered to her. "Good. They are beginning to sit down in the hall," Patty announced. "The hallway is filled up, and we are closing the door. Let's all sit down, so the rest of us can show support for the brothers and sisters in the Sit-In."

"All we are saying, is give peace a chance," sang a soprano, and everyone joined in. The group of hopeful, happy students locked arms and swayed from side to side.

I looked at my watch. Eight minutes until our appointment with Walker.

"Let's go in," I said.

It wasn't easy making it through the crowd of 600 people and staying together. Some people told us to sit down. When we got to the doorway, I opened it and saw bodies crowded next to each other, crammed in like sardines, with yellow balloons floating above. I tried to step through some people and they jeered at me. "We have a meeting with Walker," I pleaded. "We're not cop outs. We support the Sit-In."

"Then sit down."

I spied Lonnie at the end of the hall stepping over someone. He saw me, and waved me to come on. I couldn't move. He reached for the bullhorn.

"Brother and Sisters," he bellowed. "Make room for the Women's Liberation. The sisters are here to make their demands personally to Don Walker. Let's show our support by making an aisle down the middle."

People turned and looked at us, then tried to squeeze up against the walls. There wasn't enough room. Hands extended out to us to help us crawl over the bodies and backpacks. I grabbed my briefcase in one hand, and reached out for the hand of a big strong guy who guided me on to the next outstretched hand. Joyce, Rhetta, Karen and the rest followed. It took almost five minutes to make it down the hallway.

"Women's Studies! We want Women's Studies! We want Women's Studies!" they chanted. We smiled and laughed back at everyone along the way. What a reception! Leaning out of their doorways, secretaries smiled and waved to us too!

We safely made it into Walker's secretary's office and reception room. I was trying to control my smiles and so were the others. I tried to find that familiar worried place within myself by reminding myself that we were here on a critical mission. "Demands," right. I am to tell him that we must demand five faculty positions.

At that moment Walker came out his door and said, "Let me see what's going on out there. My, that's quite a support group you brought with you! Carol, that sure looks like your husband outside Love's door. I've never seen the two of you together!" He laughed, and waved to Lonnie. Lonnie smiled and waved back.

I don't remember much about the meeting itself. Somehow we got serious, I made our "demands." Walker told us the budget was really tight, but he might be able to come up with one more position. He'd get back to us.

He opened the door for us to rejoin the protesters at the Sit-In. Later, he issued a statement that "The student actions were perfectly all right," and, "As far as I have observed this is a peaceful, lawful assembly, protected under the Constitution." At a previous rally, white haired President Love had stood on the sidelines and told the press "I am proud to be the President of San Diego State."

The Sit-In lasted for seven peaceful days. Leon and the other professors did not get their tenure or promotions. Students did win the right to have more classes on a Credit or No Credit basis and the demand to make student evaluations a significant, but not major factor for consideration in faculty retention and promotion.

Although there were few concrete victories as a direct result of the Sit-In, the process, as we often said then, was more important than the product. Numerous reforms in the following years stemmed from that day of student protest and pride.

CAROL AND LONNIE ROWELL

# 28
# VICTORY DAY

May 22nd was a warm spring afternoon. The campus was strangely calm. The place looked virtually abandoned. A few students were having finals; many others had no finals because their professors had cancelled them. Many campuses had shut down for the year to avoid any more bloodshed like that at Kent State. I had to go on to the end, regardless of the situation.

I had just turned 22, but there had been no party, no celebrating at a bar. The mood was deathly serious now, and I had important work to finish.

By now I had grown used to being alone when I went to a crucial meeting. This one was the penultimate, the final one of the Seven Steps. Today was the meeting of the Faculty Senate. I walked by the old Campanile, glanced at the bronze bust of Montezuma in the quad, passed by the Library where I had worked before my wedding day, strode passed the Public Administration Building where Drs. James Kitchen and Marco Walshok had given me their approval for independent study credits to establish the Women's Studies Program, and headed west to the Old Social Sciences, or SS, Building where the Faculty Senate assembled in an auditorium for its final meeting of 1970–1971.

I could relax, be passive. I didn't have to give a presentation to this body. I was there to observe the proceedings and answer questions if need be. I was weary. I did not know our fate. What the outcome would be. They would vote whether or not to approve a Women's Studies Program and curricula under the College of Arts and Letters. We had done everything we possibly could. Our fate was in their hands.

I went in and sat down somberly. They were finishing other business, but soon turned to the recommendation for a Women's Studies Program. I was introduced, and I nodded back. The Chair read a paragraph of background and asked for discussion. I was too tired to care whether or not there was to be a debate. I scanned the room for women faculty and saw none.

A man's voice said, "I move that the Faculty Senate approve the establishment of a Women's Studies Program to begin in the fall of 1970."

There was a second to the motion. The Chair asked for discussion. A professor stood up and said these women had done a remarkable job presenting their case, that they should be commended, and that he was 100% in favor of the motion. Someone else stood up and asked a question that showed he had missed a few meetings. He was told to refer to the minutes. "Call for the question!" came a booming voice.

I waited. The Chair called for a show of hands in favor. I saw a lot of hands. Those against? I saw two or three. Things went into slow motion for me. My breathing slowed. The Chair announced, "Motion passes."

I stood up in a bit of a daze to leave so they could go on with the next item of business. There was applause. As I walked down the aisle, a number of professors reached out to shake my hand. I barely heard the word, "Congratulations."

At the end of the aisle I pushed opened the doors, walked out into the sunshine, crossed the pavement, and saw that the familiar grassy lawn seemed to greet me. I knew that the world had changed. The creation of the first Women's Studies Program in the United States meant that "Women" was now a new intellectual field, which would transform history.

At that moment It would have been fitting for trumpets to sound the opening notes of the "Triumphal March" from Verdi's opera *Aida* as an endless number of women and men poured forth singing the victory news in a gigantic chorus.

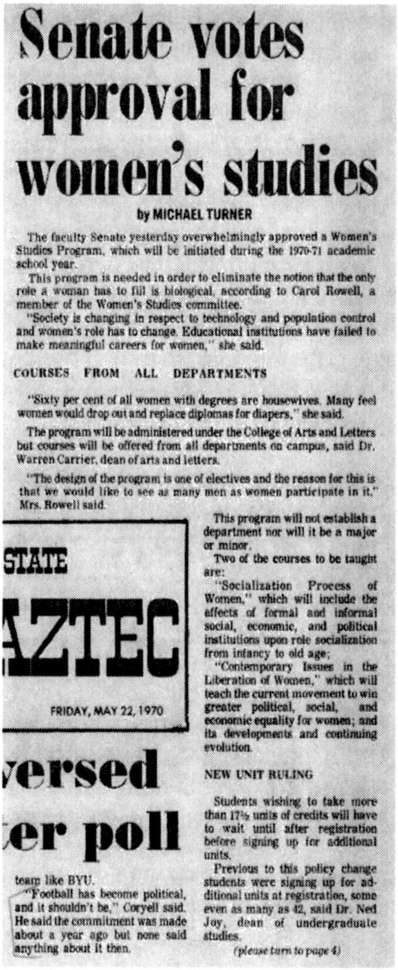

**Senate votes approval for women's studies**

by MICHAEL TURNER

The faculty Senate yesterday overwhelmingly approved a Women's Studies Program, which will be initiated during the 1970-71 academic school year.

This program is needed in order to eliminate the notion that the only role a woman has to fill is biological, according to Carol Rowell, a member of the Women's Studies committee.

"Society is changing in respect to technology and population control and women's role has to change. Educational institutions have failed to make meaningful careers for women," she said.

COURSES FROM ALL DEPARTMENTS

"Sixty per cent of all women with degrees are housewives. Many feel women would drop out and replace diplomas for diapers," she said.

The program will be administered under the College of Arts and Letters but courses will be offered from all departments on campus, said Dr. Warren Carrier, dean of arts and letters.

"The design of the program is one of electives and the reason for this is that we would like to see as many men as women participate in it," Mrs. Rowell said.

This program will not establish a department nor will it be a major or minor.

Two of the courses to be taught are:

"Socialization Process of Women," which will include the effects of formal and informal social, economic, and political institutions upon role socialization from infancy to old age;

"Contemporary Issues in the Liberation of Women," which will teach the current movement to win greater political, social, and economic equality for women; and its developments and continuing evolution.

NEW UNIT RULING

Students wishing to take more than 17½ units of credits will have to wait until after registration before signing up for additional units.

Previous to this policy change students were signing up for additional units at registration, some even as many as 42, said Dr. Ned Joy, dean of undergraduate studies.

(please turn to page 4)

STATE AZTEC

FRIDAY, MAY 22, 1970

versed

er poll

team like BYU.

"Football has become political, and it shouldn't be," Coryell said. He said the commitment was made about a year ago but none said anything about it then.

Colorful banners and balloons rose high as the procession snaked its way past the point of the scene of our massive rally on the green lawn. As the swelling crowd advanced, the Centaur for Women's Studies galloped along the ranks waving the purple and gold flag of our suffragist ancestors. The California sky blazed crimson as the light of the setting sun struck the golden brass of flutes and horns.

The Centaur waved the flag at the auditorium where we won the vote of the College of Arts and Letters and crossed the quad where we were hailed by friends during the Sit-In the day we hand-carried the demands into Vice President Walker's office.

Joyce with her enormously pregnant belly rushed forward. "I shortened the students' final exam! I wouldn't miss this for anything!"

As our Lady Centaur arrived at the feminist-slogan-covered fence of the Love Library construction site, a winged 1959 red Thunderbird convertible rocketed in and screeched to a halt. The dirt-spattered wheels looked like they had traveled five thousand miles. Out spilled Gloria Steinem, Kate Millet, Robin Morgan, Juliet Mitchell and Simone de Beauvoir, in blue jeans and cowboy hats, running to catch up. Their red banner billowing in the wind proclaimed: "WOMEN UNITED CAN NEVER BE DEFEATED."

My vision lingered as we all danced up the steps of Aztec Center. Cymbals clanged and elephants roared, calling everyone to a halt for the victory celebration — the lighting of the Women's Eternal Flame.

Reality check. The campus was quiet. Students dreading their last final exam day trudged along. Tired faculty members headed for their cars. I was alone. Oh, well. That's politics. Besides, I could hear that magnificent orchestral march in my mind.

# 29
# SUMMER BEFORE THE STORM

Summertime began peacefully. It was the aftermath of the shootings at Kent State, and many kids had gone home for the summer. Professors took long vacations to Europe, Mexico, or other destinations for relief and research.

Quickly, though, I realized how little time we had to recruit faculty and do mounds of administrative work to be ready to run classes at the end of August.

When I met her, she passed for normal. Jackie Wertz, who taught full-time in the Psychology Department, was in her late thirties, wore loose–fitting, attractive, '70s-style hippie clothing, and had a very curly and full head of brown hair. One of the men in her department told her she should meet me, and Leon had told me I should meet her, so we had a nice lunch on campus. She told me of her previous experience assisting a Chair of a department (how she basically did everything for him), and I was eager to get the big picture and the details on what had to be done. She told me of the minutiae involving a continuous stream of memos, correspondence, her phenomenal speed at typing, record keeping, enrollment reporting, grade posting, and, of course, committee meetings, department meetings, and meetings required by the Chair of a department.

Already afraid of getting overwhelmed with Women's Studies administrative work, I listened intently. I had to focus on being the Development Coordinator for the Center for Women's Studies or I wouldn't get the fundraising done to start up the other six components.

I shared my worries. She told me she had an "in" with someone in her department who owed her something. "I might be able to get them to loan me to Women's Studies for one quarter of my time. You wouldn't have to pay for anything, and you would get a Chair for your department."

*You're kidding.* This was too good to be true. Wasn't it? I didn't know what to say. I was leery of getting expectations up, so I smiled gleefully, told her I would talk it over with others. "Okay, but let me know this week. It is getting late for putting things into place in the fall."

Right. More pressure. But what an opportunity. In hindsight it was a case of beggars couldn't be choosers. I went over to Joyce's house and told her.

"This could be a godsend." She was at home with her newborn baby girl, Rhetta, named after our good friend. But we knew nothing about Jackie Wertz, and had little time to find out. Leon came home, and we told him the news. He brightened up.

"Really? I've heard some good things about her. I think you should go for it."

To this day he regrets his advice.

That's how Jackie became the first Chair of the first Women's Studies Program in the nation — for one year. She pretty much stayed in her office on the other side of the campus, and I had little idea of what she did. I was her supervisor, even though I was a student, and she was 10 or 12 years older. I forced myself to ask her to write weekly reports. That didn't go over very well. The reports I got were perfunctory listings of correspondence that had come in, meetings attended, and reports that had gone out. Oh, well. At least we had a figurehead and someone was doing the bare minimum to hold down the fort.

I was still the one pouring through documents, budgets, resumes, and conferring with Joyce and Rhetta, when they were available, on whom to hire for the faculty and how to staff an understaffed office. If only we could get a big name from the East Coast, a heavyweight, someone charismatic, capable, and knowledgeable who could take the load off of me. Someone like Florence Howe? She was known for having experimented with her freshman English classes at Goucher College by adding fiction by women writers and, in 1969, her course had been very popular. Of course famous speakers Robin Morgan, Gloria Steinem, and Kate Millet would be fabulous, but they were over-committed writers and non-academics.

There still weren't very many feminists with strong academic backgrounds at this point. And, since there had never been a Women's Studies Program before, it was difficult to find anyone who had taught more than one or two classes directly related to women. And then, it was usually only in their field, often literature, which Joyce was already slated to teach and had developed a rich syllabus for.

We had only two full-time positions to fill. One would teach three courses, the other four. Joyce was planning a rich syllabus for her "Women in Literature" class, and I was preparing research and community projects for the "Field Experience" class I was hired to teach. I was terrifically excited about teaching. After all, I was still a student! And teaching "Field Experience" translated into keeping the organizing part of the Women's Liberation Movement alive within and without the academy.

The 10 courses were: "Women in Contemporary Cultures," "Socialization Process of Women," "Self-Actualization of Women," "Contemporary Issues in the Liberation of Women," "Women in History," "Women in Literature," "Human Sexuality," "Status of Women Under Various Economic Systems," "Women and Education," and "Field Experience." By the end of the summer we had interviewed a handful of teachers. The one we were most impressed with was Marlene Dixon, a real "heavy" (brilliant and eloquent) and a counterculture lesbian. The administration would be freaked out, but let them be; we had the right to hire anyone we wanted.

# 30
# FIVE MONTHS LATER: THAT TERRIBLE NIGHT

My jaw was set, breathing was very difficult, and my heart pounded out of my chest as I methodically made the last preparations for the evening's events. Packing up papers from the office, I tried to calm myself by reviewing my outline and neatly stacking papers in my briefcase. No good. I knew they would have their own agenda and none of my well-crafted documents or brochures would impress anyone tonight.

My shield, my trusty briefcase, would just weigh me down, and I felt better having both hands free. Besides, if I brought it and had to leave abruptly, I might never see it again. Better to travel light just this once. Just myself and handwritten notes. *Stand straight. Forget you are only 22 years old. When it gets really bad, don't make eye contact with anyone but Joyce. No matter what anyone says, stick to "the principle of the thing." Stay near an exit.*

I really had no clue what to say to them except to reiterate our position. And this would only infuriate them. They were hunting for bear. They wanted to see me down on my knees, or better still, crying. With a sinking feeling, I set the briefcase back down on the ironing board desk, clutched 20 copies of the Position Paper, turned the key in the lock of the kitchen door, and walked out into the pitch-dark night. I wondered how I would feel the next time I unlocked that door. Would the kitchen be a sanctuary, a refuge, or a graveyard? I was expecting a nasty confrontation tonight at the so-called Women's Studies Board meeting. Since I was only teaching one Women's Studies class, "Field Experience," I didn't have to attend the weekly Faculty Meetings Joyce dreaded. I was the paid Coordinator for the Center for Women's Studies under a college foundation grant. They might try to ignore me, claiming I had no vote. I knew they had stacked the meeting. Dread spread down my head and over my whole body. I felt weak all over.

There were no lights in the backyard of the little house on Linda Paseo Street. It wasn't safe out here. Women should walk in pairs on campus at night, part of our rape prevention teachings. I knew this well, had told it to my sisters, but tonight I had no choice but to walk alone.

My narrow feet began to wobble in my shoes, and I was alarmed. These high-top brown boots had always kept me steady. I pushed on, crossing the moist grass, and coming out of the shadows onto the main promenade leading to the bell tower. Joyce would be coming from another meeting and Rhetta from work, so there was no one to walk with me to the showdown. As my feet carried me forward, I wanted to turn back. This was not a legitimately constituted meeting. This "board" was not in any of our plans; we had planned for a broader-based board to be implemented later in the year. To us this was just an interim board of the first component in the Proposal. Dean Carrier and the Ad Hoc Committee for Women's Studies had created a Faculty Advisory Committee as the only group with any authority above the Women's Studies Program and that was clearly spelled out to be primarily advisory in nature. They were there to be helpful, friendly advisors, not to wield power, and we all knew it. So there would be no officials from the University in the room, just fractious "sisters" and the four full- and part-time Women's Studies faculty members.

Why should I allow *them* to pass judgment over me? I resented their audacity. I would not allow them to destroy the Program or me. They could say whatever they wanted to, and I would take it in, then I would leave it. And, of course, there was that small chance that someone else would stand up to them, defend me, or, at least, agree with my position.

Maybe it wouldn't be too bad, but how could standing in a minefield not be terrible? Of course, this fear was unfounded compared to the legitimate fear of our boys in real mine fields in Vietnam. Yet, these women were vicious. Like pit bulls. I had felt their hatred coming to a crescendo in the past several days. It was as if an arsonist was setting a lot of small fires all week and tonight would be a bonfire. Would these feminists really turn on their sister? Did ancient Christians turn on Christians?

Peering over my shoulder, I realized that if I were a Chicano leader, or Black Studies leader, bodyguards would surround me right now. We women were not organized like that. How naïve.

I trudged on. Now it occurred to me that I guessed that Joyce and Leon had tried to spare me some details of things they had heard people saying about me, but I sensed I had no clue as to the full extent of it yet. I remembered one day, a time I wanted very much to block out, when I was climbing up the steps of the student center. A girl who used to come to our planning meetings walked up to me and said, "Have you seen this?" I remember thinking she was the bearer of bad tidings. She looked upset, embarrassed, worried for me. "I think you should know about this."

Just then, another member of Women's Liberation meetings stopped, listened in, touched my arm lightly, and then walked away. What was that? Could it be that she was now afraid to be seen with me?

Didn't they know that if you try to change the world you have to be ready for adversity? Yes, they knew that, but it was supposed to come from the enemy. From men. Not from our sisters! "Out of adversity comes strength," Leon reminded me when he gave me a copy of *How the Steel Was Tempered*. This was different, though. The storm I was walking into was not one of a clear disagreement of position. I learned later that a hideous form of character assassination, which amounted to psychological rape, was what they had in mind for me.

The girl held up one sheet on mimeograph paper. Someone was distributing a flyer proclaiming that "Carol Rowell is an elitist. She does not represent the students. She is paid by the patriarchy. She has sold out to men, and should resign as Coordinator of the Center for Women's Studies." It was signed by six women, two of whom I had done battle with numerous times and knew hated my guts — hated me so viciously they were inarticulate. They were not full-time college students, but feminists from the community who had registered for a class so they could be where the action was. I had never met such hostile people in my life. Who had fired them up? To me they were incoherent, but their angry outbursts got a lot of attention from students who were very new to the Women's Movement. I knew I wasn't ready for this. It had all happened too fast. At 22 years old, I was too young and fragile. They made me out to be a demagogue. And for what?

At the time, I could not understand the depth and breadth of their hatred. It took me many years to understand Trashing. In fact, I still cannot fully explain it today. A phenomenon seemingly unique to the Women's Movement, Trashing, as Jo Freeman (Joreen) named it in an article written for *Ms. Magazine* and published four years later in April of 1976, is "manipulative, dishonest, and excessive. It is occasionally disguised by the rhetoric of honest conflict, or covered up by denying that any disapproval exists at all. But, it is not done to expose disagreements or resolve differences. It is done to disparage and destroy. Whatever methods are used, trashing involves a violation of one's integrity, a declaration of one's worthlessness, and an impugning of one's motives. In effect, what is attacked is not one's actions, not one's ideas, but one's self."

I walked on towards the fire. Joyce and Leon knew how vulnerable I was. They coached me day and night to stand my ground. No matter how they goaded me, I must resist replying. Don't dignify their behavior with an answer. It would just lead to more arguments, more issues, and add more fuel to the flames. My job was to get in there, be stoic, make my position clear, and not seem afraid. I knew I could be stoic, and by reading my Position Paper aloud, passing it around, and remembering not to speak freely, it would be clear what my decision was. I was sticking to the original concept of the Women's Studies Program and the Center for Women's Studies, and I would not be bullied into leaving my job. But, to not show fear! How do you do that when you fear for your very safety? These women were tough-looking, mean-talking, and deliberately intimidating.

Where were my friends and supporters now? Why had they abandoned me? Most just said they did not have time for meetings anymore, but others said they were fed up with shouting matches and could not take it anymore. I did not beg them to stay with me. Maybe I should have, but I saw the look of defeat in their faces. I could have asked Nona to be there that night to support me, but they would not have listened to her, a peaceful-talking Home Economics professor. They would have laughed at her. I think she would have wanted me to ask her to come had she known then how badly I needed any sense of comfort or support in that room. I was staying on to the last to stick to our original principles and save the Women's Studies Program from a takeover or even total collapse. A righteous fight. An unnecessary war, but one that could no longer be avoided. Even the media had caught onto it. A newspaper in Riverside, California, printed a huge article titled "Lib Gals Split on Philosophy." The oversized photo was of me consulting with Rhetta at a table in the courtyard of Aztec Center.

All of a sudden the crazies had come out and taken over Women's Studies. It had been less than six months since the Faculty Senate had approved the Program. We had rushed to hire expert faculty from out of state and not checked them out thoroughly. Even if we'd had more time that summer for interviewing, I doubt we would have learned the truth about these two feminist socialist friends who were trained by and accountable to the New University Conference. That, of course, was something they were not keen on revealing. They passed as feminist professors. In reality, they were socialist women professors who wanted to bring socialism to the hinterlands by gaining positions of authority teaching classes on women. Barbara Kessel and Roberta Salper were recommended to us by Marlene Dixon, who had made headlines in the feminist press by being fired by a university in Chicago. In those days, being fired by the establishment was a credential for being hired by feminists. Later we learned that Dixon was a leader of this NUC group to which she held primary allegiance. At this point, though, we were still ignorant of their agenda, just caught in the web of dirty tricks.

Suddenly I was in front of the room. There was nothing for me to do but go inside. I still wasn't ready. I guess this is the way a prisoner feels when he has to keep walking towards the executioner.

Opening the door, I stepped into a dimly lit chamber with a long rectangular conference table that left little standing room. It seemed so dark. Was it my fear, my distress?

I spotted Joyce right away, at the head of the table with the other faculty — Roberta Salper, Barbara Kessel, and Jackie Wertz. Roberta and Barbara looked stiff, focused, and uncomfortable. Their eyes avoided mine when I entered, so I avoided theirs. Did they have any sympathy for me? Jackie with her big frizzy head of curls, long skirt, and heavy boots, was buzzing around, dumping odd items out of her huge soft leather pouch of a purse, putting them back in and muttering with no particular purpose. Jackie was Chair of the Program, but she had very little to say. She looked more like a stoner than a psych professor.

I searched Joyce's eyes to give me strength. Joyce wasn't looking my way, and when she did, she looked down. I understood. She was nervous too and trying hard to appear neutral. I took the only free chair at a table on the left side. It was not close to a door. I sat down, adjusted myself in the chair, swallowed hard, and looked right and left for someone to say hello to.

I saw only strangers and enemies, or friends of enemies. Behind the table across from mine four large, tough-looking women stood against the wall, almost blocking the exit. My heart pumped faster as I felt the wild instinct to run. The brain and the body. Two parts of me battled fiercely. I felt like I was whirling in karate moves against my shadow. Slowly my brain began winning. I tried to breathe, looked down at my feet for meditative relief. When I looked up again, the panic attack grew. *Look back at your feet.*

"Hi."

Startled, I turned and saw the girl sitting next to me.

"Hi." I croaked.

"It's getting hot in here, isn't it? I didn't know there would be so many people."

I tried to smile. She looked like an angel to me. I desperately wanted her to be my best friend at that moment.

I turned and faced her directly, to shut out the rest of the room and get my bearings.

"I hope this meeting doesn't go too long," she said smiling. My boyfriend walked me here and is coming back in an hour." She added that she had thought of asking him to come to the meeting with her, but...

I laughed and said, "I don't think he would have felt welcome, do you?" There were no men in the room.

"No way," she agreed. "Men are supposed to be allowed to enroll in Women's Studies classes, but I haven't seen any."

"Which class are you in?" she asked me.

"Well, actually, I'm not in a class. I'm the Coordinator for the Center for Women's Studies."

"Really? How wonderful! You must love your job. I think it is such a great thing, this being the first Women's Studies Program in the United States."

"Yes, it is... isn't it?" I nodded.

"And you must be really proud to have been a part of this."

"Uh, well..."

"No *really,* you should be proud of yourself. You are a leader, a model for other women. Congratulations!"

I let go of a big sigh, looked into her eyes and accepted the compliment with a soft "Thank you."

I was still trapped here, but I knew there was one other kind person in the room.

Roberta Salper, the faculty member we had hired from Chicago using the Visiting Distinguished Professor position from

Dr. Walker, stood up and tried to tell everyone the meeting was about to get started. She had a soft voice, and no one heard her. I wondered why she really was here. She seemed, strangely enough, like her mind was elsewhere, like she didn't want to be here, not just in this room tonight, but also in San Diego. Strange. It couldn't be true.

I hoped no one would hear her. A delay could mean Rhetta would be here from the start. Maybe Maddie or Patty would come after all. Oh, there was Yolanda! I saw Pam glaring into my face. She hated my guts. She was a sidekick of that pit bull drama student Paula, the outspoken member of the Young Socialist Alliance. I looked for Sherry Smith, the charismatic YSA leader, but she had moved to try to take over the group organizing a childcare center. They weren't really feminists. They were confrontationists. Later I learned why they glued onto Barbara and Roberta. These two young professors were members of the New University Conference, an aggressive socialist alliance that trained faculty to go into communities for the purpose of "organizing the masses."

Barbara Kessel, the other full-time faculty member (also from Chicago) was taller than Roberta and had a louder voice. She stood up, gave a little smile, and asked everyone to settle down so the meeting could start. She nodded hellos to several young women who must have been her own students.

I counted those present: about 20 women were there now. There were over 300 students in the 10 Women's Studies classes. I had heard that my enemies were recruiting in the classrooms that week. Someone said Carla was doing a guerrilla theater skit about the Women's Studies split and was making announcements in different classrooms about tonight's meeting. Joyce mouthed "Hi" to two of her students. I breathed a little easier. I remember thinking, "I can take it from this size of a crowd." Fewer witnesses, fewer curiosity seekers, fewer reporters, ***fewer people to remember me being burned at the stake.***

Roberta was a young, attractive brunette who looked like she'd be more at home flirting with men in New York City. Why had she accepted our offer? On the other hand, maybe they were lovers. Looking back on it, I think I understand now. It is this simple. My conversion to feminism (in the back seat of the car returning from my first feminist conference) was so complete, that I only saw the world through revolutionary rose-colored glasses. How naïve I was. And Joyce, my older, wiser friend, was too. In the beginning she and I both had trusted most other feminists — especially the radical ones. Since Roberta and Barbara talked the talk about revolution, I thought that was their pure motivation. Now I see, as they admitted to a researcher later, that it was their careers and their commitment to socialism that primarily motivated them. Feminism was interesting and came at an opportune time for them.

Looking over at them, I realized that neither of them alone or together intimidated me. They were kind of lightweights by themselves, but when bolstered by their newfound loyal following of young feminist pit bulls, anything might happen, and that did scare me. Which were their leaders, which were their followers? It wasn't clear, and that served their purpose. No accountability. It didn't matter anymore. I was outnumbered. I was now facing a mob.

Barbara yelled out, "Quiet! Everybody, quiet!" That got their attention.

Roberta said, "We are all here tonight because of a crisis facing the Women's Studies Program, because women from the Center of Women's Studies were acting like they were not accountable to the Women's Studies Program. The purpose of tonight's meeting is to clarify that relationship and the position and role of Carol Rowell."

*Oh, great, here it comes.*

Joyce interrupted and cleared her throat. "Before we begin, I would like to provide some historical context for those who have never been to a Women's Studies board meeting before tonight. It is unusual to have so many visitors," she said flatly.

Roberta patiently waited through Joyce's recounting of the last two years of organizing the Women's Studies Program as part of a larger concept of a Center for Women's Studies. Speaking about the early days, the Consciousness Raising groups, the Action group, the progression to forming the Ad Hoc Committee for Women's Studies, the organizing of five "experimental courses," and of the year-long seven-step process to win University approval, she eloquently taught the history. She told of our grass roots organizing with leaflets, petitions, rallies, Women's Liberation meetings, coalitions with minority groups, drawing up demands, principles and position papers, and ultimately the proposal for a seven-component Center for

Women's Studies, of which the Women's Studies Program would be the first to be implemented.

I listened to her account of our history and thought sorrowfully that her presentation was necessary, impressive, but futile. I knew once they attacked me, I would look guilty. Either I would bow to them and be "tolerated," or I would refuse to obey them. To obey a new self-appointed, self-serving, hateful group of dictators would be impossible.

Roberta said, "This board has been organized as a democratic organization, one where all the women are represented. This is an open meeting."

Barbara added, "Everyone here is equal. Every woman has one vote."

*Every woman!* Not "each faculty member, staff member, and student representative from a classroom" but everyone who showed up! Who did they think they were? Lenin? Stalin? What a blatant tactic to seize power. Not only had they stacked the meeting. They had imposed a rule that promised to outvote us. My cheeks burned red hot.

"Now is the time to hear from the students. Faculty members will not be speaking so that we can be sure that the student voice is fully presented. The faculty will be listening." Joyce's eyebrows went up in surprise.

*Oh, I get it, that move silences Joyce.* She could not defend herself or me! Just then, I saw Rhetta standing near the doorway. She jumped right in, "These are not democratic rules. No democratic organization has a rule that anyone who shows up can vote, and that they represent the larger group! Only the Socialist Worker's Party does this, and everyone knows how underhanded they are. This meeting is a sham and an embarrassment to the Women's Studies Program. I challenge this rule, and I call on others to challenge it as well! Speak up now or this whole meeting is a hoax!"

*Hurray for Rhetta!* Where did she get her guts, her wisdom? God, I admired her courage. Only two years older than me, she was incredible at 24! What made her so strong, so daring?

"This is the first time I have attended a Women's Studies meeting," said a young woman with a nice face. "When I came here from Barstow, I needed an elective, so I took a Women's Studies course because it wasn't filled up. I don't know anything about the Women's Studies Program or Department, but I think that only members should be allowed to vote, just like we do in the sororities. Maybe this is a stupid question. Who are the members?"

Silence followed. Everyone seemed stunned. *A sorority girl was here!*

"Who is the membership?" asked another newcomer as the girl next to me got up to leave to meet her boyfriend peering in the doorway. An hour had passed already. Two or three more students trickled out past the "toughies" in black leather jackets standing by the open doorway.

Contradictions were being exposed. Things were unraveling.

I looked over at Joyce. She was taller, stronger, and more dignified than me or anyone else in the room. Joyce had always held her own, but tonight she looked miserable. She was, at her core, a poet. Joyce wanted to teach literature, educate about feminism, craft powerful poetry, and have a private life. But here she was tonight. Fighting against crazies whom she had helped to bring to San Diego and given jobs.

Joyce called them the "lunatic fringe," but often said that even that did not explain away the viciousness of those "feminists." They were much-damaged people. As Ruth Rosen said in her book *The World Split Open*, published in 2000, "Many of us were damaged people. How could we have not created a damaged movement?"

Like me, Joyce must have felt increasingly that we were losing the war. Or, worse, that her teaching career was at stake. At 38 years old, with three children, she valued her role, her independence, and her salary dearly. The old guard of the college had demonized her dear husband Leon for his radical teaching, and she was resigned to that. This, however, was very different. She, a woman, a feminist, a sacrificer for her sex, was being demonized by her own kind!

Maybe they weren't our own kind. Years later, reporters, interviewers and researchers would ask us if these women were on drugs or were government infiltrators. We always honestly said, "No, not to our knowledge." Although we had proof later that one was on drugs, the rage seemed genuine at the time, not drug-induced.

Joyce also wondered if some FBI agents had infiltrated us; it all felt so contrived, unnatural. They had done it in Chicago, San Francisco, Los Angeles, and many other places under the

Nixon administration and J. Edgar Hoover. Why not in provincial San Diego? If so, it did not change anything. We could never expose those powers. What would be would be.

"So, who is the membership? And why did you faculty members ask us to be here tonight?"

It was getting late and people were leaving.

Paula's shrill stage voice yelled from the front of the room to silence the last speaker. "Any woman who is a student is a member, and any from the community is a member. This is a grass roots movement of real women." Then she turned and pointed at me. "Carol Rowell does not represent real women."

I turned away from her and waited for the next volley. It came from her sidekick, a woman some speculated was her lover.

"You, you don't represent women, real women. Feminists don't believe in having leaders, that is why the Women's Movement is a leaderless movement. You are not from the grass roots. You are like one of the men; you're male-identified, sleeping with the enemy, co-opted."

Rhetta sneered, "And you, you ARE the grass roots?"

Joyce jumped in, "I don't think that whom you sleep with has anything to do with the work that needs to get done. Besides, if we eliminated women from the Women's Liberation Movement for being married, having a boyfriend, or just talking to men, we'd hardly have a Women's Movement left, wouldn't we? Women join the Women's Movement freely," she asserted, "and should be able to address the inequities and work to change the world TOGETHER."

The room went quiet.

Veins pulsing in my temples told my body to halt the flight instinct. My head was spinning. *Fight!* said the shooting adrenalin. *No, Carol! Don't move, look calm, stay still*, commanded my inner voice.

## *CHORUS OF THE SEVEN SISTERS*

*All the courage of the wounded women leaders was drawing together in an unseen force. In the winds from the East came voices of my heroines. The Seven Sisters — Shulamith Firestone, Kate Millet, Robin Morgan, Simone de Beauvoir, Betty Friedan, Roxanne Dunbar and Jo Freeman — called to me in unison:*

Hear us, O Sister!
Young Leader in the West.

Would that we could come to your side.
We are seven sisters who have been vilified.
To your aide we cannot come
So, instead we have each taken one.

Seven components build the center.
Seven sisters represent a pillar.
Each of us has taken one
Consecrated it as our own.

You strong women of San Diego shall build our temple
With columns of white marble and open ceilings of glass
Dedicated to Education, Diversity, Community
You will preserve Herstory forever.

The vision is strong and will withstand the test of time
It will not rise today
It may not rise in a decade.
This is what is important:
The foundation is made.

Others will come after to right the wrongs
They will bring music, dance, and song
The muses, too, will guide them along.
Think not of the small crowd today,
But of women becoming a million strong.

*Oh hear the anthem of the early suffragists:*

~

## *BREAD AND ROSES*

*As we come marching, marching in the beauty of the day,*
*A million darkened kitchens, a thousand mill lofts gray,*
*Are touched with all the radiance that a sudden sun discloses,*
*For the people hear us singing: "Bread and roses! Bread and roses!"*

*As we come marching, marching, we battle too for men,*
*For they are women's children and we mother them again.*
*Our lives shall not be sweated from birth until life closes;*
*Hearts starve as well as bodies; give us bread, but give us roses!*

*As we come marching, marching, unnumbered women dead*
*Go crying through our singing their ancient cry for bread.*
*Small art and love and beauty, their drudging spirits knew.*
*Yes, it is bread we fight for — but we fight for roses, too!*

*As we come marching, marching, we bring the greater days.*
*The rising of the women means the rising of the race.*
*No more the drudge and idler — ten that toil where one reposes,*
*But a sharing of life's glories: Bread and roses! Bread and roses!*

~

Still we are scorned by arrogant men everywhere.
We have each led many women into battle.
We who understood we could not wait any longer,
Our fate was to retaliate.

But who attacks us now?

Must we face yet another enemy?
Now come the Pretender Feminists
They attack us from within
Vilifying and demonizing sister leaders
Scorning their own.

For what cause do they scream?
To destroy the builders of self-esteem
It is the builder they revile
Out of envy and rage they are beguiled.

We too have borne the False Sisters' treacherous acts.
Betraying precious principles of sisterhood
We bear witness. They victimize the innocent.
Seeking glory while damning us, unwilling "stars," as glory seekers.

Be steady then and beware!
The worst is yet to come.
Be ready. Allow no surprises.
From here you must go it alone.

Draw now upon that well of courage
From which you were born
The forces grew within you
At an early age
Fed your youthful rage.
Must now be harnessed to command the stage.

Yes, younger sister, there will be one Sister true,
Older and wiser than you
She will guide you through dangerous paths,
But she cannot accompany you.
Destiny demands you go on alone.

Hear us, oh sister. We feel your pain
We cried for ourselves; we cry for you
We rush to you side
Tend your wounded flesh.
The battle rages on in both
The East and in the West.

Soon we will have learned great lessons
Put all trials to the test.
For tonight though, be still
This act, though you do not know it yet,
Will be your best.

A slow stream of young women squeezed through the doorway, lining the walls. They kept on coming. Each time someone entered, she looked surprised, and someone equally surprised had to move down the wall to make room for her. Still they kept coming. Marching in one by one. Who knows where they came from. Were they Paula's gang?

Someone moved a whole classroom over here. Since Barbara let Carla team-teach with her, it was probably their doing. The line turned the corner and slowly filled the back wall, pushing more women behind my back and up towards the faculty table. I scanned their faces and recognized no one. Funny, thinking of it now, I am reminded of a scene from *Dr. Zhivago* in which the people are in the street and, one by one, soldiers on horseback line up in front of them, blocking their way.

A handful of women were trying to revolt in the name of the masses. Then they could seize control. Tonight they would purge the old leadership by vilifying me until I surrendered.

As a Women's Studies Ph.D. candidate who researched the archives, Catherine Orr, later wrote:

"What is truly ironic here is that faction that was so dead-set against Rowell-Council because of her attempts to fund the program through foundation money ending up... appealing to the President of the San Diego State Foundation to affirm their authority as the leaders of the Women's Studies Program."

But their two leaders (Salper and Kessel) weren't planning on staying very long! Salper's position was only funded for one year, although had she wanted to stay on, she might have been rehired from other budgetary sources. Kessel stayed for two and half years.

"When I first came to the Women's Liberation Movement I was a housewife with two kids and in an abusive relationship," said Judy Fry. "I learned that the personal is political, and I am very angry now. I am now divorced and no longer male-identified. I am a woman-identified woman and proud of it. This is what the Women's Studies Program can do for other women too.

No one will ever have power over me again, and Carol Rowell should not have power over the Women's Studies Program. That's power hungry, elitist and patriarchal. The Women's Studies Program should be run by real women!"

*Wow. Hmmm.* Joyce used to like Judy. So did I. She had turned from a housewife to a witch hunter overnight, all in the name of feminism.

I heard a voice behind me saying, "Which one is Carol Rowell?"

"I don't know," came the reply.

*If only I could remain invisible.*

Ellen, short, heavy-set, and freckled, said, "Carol Rowell and Joyce Nower want to set up a monolithic women's center with seven components and keep the Women's Studies Program under it so they can control it. We didn't ask them to do this. We don't need another hierarchy that is accountable to the male administration. There is a grass roots movement to have a women's center at the downtown YWCA. It will represent the real women, not white, privileged college students." (Ellen was white and taking a Women's Studies class. She ranted on and on for several minutes while students began leaving one by one.) "These women sold out to the Establishment, and they are trying to get more grants from the foundation! We should disassociate from them entirely, and Carol Rowell should resign."

"We are going to stay here until we take a vote. This has to be resolved tonight however long it takes," said Paula as another woman crept out the door.

Roberta and Barbara looked at each other and said nothing. They seemed completely wrung out. After having relinquished control of the meeting hours earlier and watching the process descend into anarchy, they didn't have a clue what to do. I still sat there stoically.

Paula stood up and said, "There were no leaders of the Women's Studies cause at SDSC. There was a spontaneous grass roots movement of real women. It was a true mass movement. No woman was more important that the rest. You're elitist!" screamed Paula. "It never happened like that. We were all equal and didn't have leaders." (Paula hadn't even been involved the year before and she was acting as historian.) "It was a grass roots fire. A wildfire, sweeping from the East Coast to the West Coast in just a few months."

So, in her gang's version (which she stuck to for 20 years) the same ideas sprang up naturally in this conflagration. There were never any founders — unless it was a large group of founders. As if a flag were raised, SISTERS UNITED, and the oppressed masses of women came forth. The fires were fueled by millions of bras thrown off the breasts of screaming women in the streets. They spilled out onto sidewalks, across campuses, along corridors, where sparks from the unstoppable revolution ignited each other, connecting, forming paths, moving westwards, northwards, to the Canadian border and south to the impermeable stone walls which stretched like the Great Wall of China across an entire continent. Walls guarded by men, countrymen, media broadcasters, and working class people everywhere. In her dogma the major enemy was capitalism and its twin brother imperialism. The Women's Movement for her was an opportunity to swell the ranks of the Socialist Movement. When Paula, well-liked by Barbara and Roberta for her ardor for socialism, got too far afield from our cause of defeating patriarchy, she lost her audience. Roberta and Barbara remembered this was Women's Studies.

Roberta said, "Let's hear from Carol. I think it is her turn now."

I'll say it was. This, finally, was going to be the real climax. I picked up my Position Paper and read it out loud. My throat tightened. I spoke in a strained monotone. That paper made it crystal clear that the Women's Studies Program was part of the Center for Women's Studies — not the other way around — and that an Interim Board would be established to work on the development of all of the components. It would lead to a board with representatives from all of the components and people from the broader community.

I sat back down.

"You elitist sell out!" yelled Paula.

The yells of "elitist" hurt to this day. I was frozen. I had been sleeping in a basement, on a mattress. I worked over a year, countless hours, for no money, for an ideal. Now there were more and more yells. I had no idea what a powerful weapon slander could be when used by a clever, calculating mind.

"You're a hypocrite!" screamed Judy.

"Let's try to be civil," said Roberta.

"Well," said Barbara. "It has finally been made clear tonight that Carol refuses to be held accountable. She is not going to change and she is not going to resign."

Joyce and I had reached one of our goals, the start of Women's Studies. They had suddenly achieved their first goal: Eliminating me. That is their legacy for Women's Studies. They eliminated Joyce from the faculty at the end of the first semester.

There was mumbling, whispering, stirring. The room had emptied.

Only 17 people were in the room now, and three of them were headed for the doorway. It was after 11:00 p.m.

Someone at the front table said, "I make a motion that the Women's Studies Program publicly disassociates from the Center for Women's Studies."

"That's all we can do."

"Who can vote?"

"I think whoever is still here can vote."

"I call the question."

"All in favor raise your hands."

Thirteen hands went up.

"All opposed?"

Joyce's hand went up along with two others.

"Abstentions?"

One hand.

A pall fell over the room. Something died in that moment.

I thought that now would be the best moment to make my escape. Back into the night, alone, I trudged to the desolate parking lot. My little car was my goal. It would be my temporary sanctuary. I walked on in a daze.

My career as the catalyst of Women's Studies ended that terrible night. It would be 27 years before I would muster the strength to enter a dark room and confront the unleashed hatred of a sister.

# 31
# AFTERMATH

Oh, Sister! Oh wounded heroine.
We hear your silent agony.
We are tortured by your pain.
Singed by the terrible flames
From funeral pyres
Salem women burned as witches
Joan of Arc, a virtuous leader
Sacrificed as a heretic

Our hearts and spirits go out to you
Though you do not know.
You cannot hear us.
Now you will suffer alone.

I stumbled through the darkened campus toward the deserted parking lot where I spotted my refuge — my little faded red Toyota. I jumped inside as fast as I could, locked the doors, saw no one in the rearview mirror and tried to breathe. No good.

I remembered that the two tough-looking women at the door hadn't voted. Was that because they were engaged as security or because they felt the whole thing was a farce? I had summoned all my dignity, stood up, stared them down, and passed them by out into the cold night air. I remember that I could barely breathe and would have dropped to the grass and curled up into the fetal position, except that someone would have seen me. I felt as if I had been tied to the stake and the little flames were following, trying to catch me and burn me alive. Freedom for me now could only be in a dream. My body was beginning to shake as chills ran down my spine.

I would have to wait until I got inside my apartment before normal breathing could slowly return. I visualized the homey duplex that was the one concrete benefit of my paid position. It was in the old neighborhood of Kensington where regular lives were lived. A big oval hooked hug, a mahogany dining table and an old overstuffed sofa would embrace me. Once there, I went straight for the bottle of Jim Beam I'd bought earlier in the day in anticipation of the need for medicine. I found the Valium stored away for emergencies, swallowed it, and wanted another.

Here I was again — alone. It was 11:30 p.m. Joyce had gone home to the baby. Lonnie and I were no longer pals. I wanted to collapse, but I was more keyed up than I had ever been. Everything had changed. I felt I was in danger. I could no longer keep my cool. I wanted to run fast and long. Or hide under the covers. But I knew I could never sleep.

The phone rang. *Thank God. Was somebody going to save me?* It was Joyce, my one true Sister, my fellow warrior.

"Carol, I feel so bad. It was a Kangaroo Court. I wish I could have done more to help you. I should have said...."

"No, no. You did all you could do. Really. They made that rule up to silence you. Besides they wouldn't listen to you anymore."

"It was terrible, just terrible." Joyce sounded defeated, but as the older, wiser one, she wanted to cheer me up. I knew her job was on the line, too, tonight.

"I really wish I could be there with you now. You shouldn't be alone. They ran out of breast milk because the meeting went so long. The baby is chomping on my tittie and, when she is finished, I'll have to pump more milk. I thought I was going to squirt it right into Paula's ugly mug. Would have served her right."

There was little to say. We enjoyed a few jabs at the inquisitors and then she had to get back to the baby.

Leon got on the phone. He was forceful, "Carol, don't let them get to you!"

I started to cry.

"Listen to me. They will hang themselves eventually. Trust me, they will hang themselves."

I broke down sobbing. "I don't want to go on."

"I'm coming over there," he said.

Joyce's voice said. "Yes, go."

I hung up, unlocked the front door and fell on the couch, crying hysterically.

When Leon came to the front door, I couldn't get up. The room was dark. He knocked, then let himself in, came over to the couch and leaned over me. I turned toward the back of the couch and hid my head in a pillow. I was embarrassed, ashamed, out of control. He turned on a lamp, brought me some Kleenex, and told me to blow my nose. I felt like the doctor had arrived, but I didn't know if he could save me from myself. I have always wondered what a nervous breakdown feels like.

Leon mixed me a drink, sat down and asked me to tell him the entire story of that evening, not leaving anything out. I pulled myself together, found some analytical brain cells still working and reported on the events. It was somewhat cathartic to repeat the facts, but the pain did not subside. It was creeping all over my body.

It was very late. Leon had to leave. I was afraid to try to sleep. He turned on my bathroom and bedroom lights, guiding me in the right direction and told me to first go into the bathroom and brush my teeth and then go to bed. I nodded. "I'll lock the front door behind me and make sure the kitchen door is locked. We'll call you in the morning," he said. Then he was gone. I waited to see how I felt now. I followed the orders, and managed to brush my teeth and crawl into bed. In Leon I had a father and a friend, but it was not enough to ease the pain. This pain was all consuming. Nothing could erase what my "sisters" had done to me, forever.

I tossed and turned. I couldn't stand the pain of not being able to relax my muscles. My neck muscles had never been tighter. Back muscles, face muscles, hurt. Sleep was impossible. My leg muscles began to cramp. I couldn't stand the memories of hateful faces. The mattress became stiff like a board. The sheets itched. My skin crawled. I tried to keep my eyes closed, so I could fall asleep and forget.

Voices rang in my ears repeating over and over: "Elitist," "Co-opted," "Male-identified."

I felt deep shame. Was I guilty?

Remorse.

Grief.

Unbearable pain.

Throat choked. Exhausted. Weren't you supposed to feel better after crying? What was wrong with me?

*Help me, somebody, help me!*

If only I could wake up in the morning back in Texas in my comfortable bed under the blue canopy again. Pale blue is so calming. I thought of the blue morning glories at home. Nothing in that thought could chase away the agony of that terrible night. Not even now, years and years later.

# 32
# RAINBOW SNAKE

In the days that followed, things began to move in slow motion. I had absolutely no motivation to go to campus, much less into the office. There were no more battles to fight and I had lost hope about raising money for the Center for Women's Studies. Since the Women's Studies Program had officially separated the two entities, the foundation that was funding it was not optimistic about grant opportunities. Most phone calls I got had to do with the fallout from that terrible night. They made me cringe. Everyone wanted to know if there had been a "split," including the local media. I didn't what to call "it" or if "it" was permanent. Was that meeting "official?" Did the vote count? Could we coexist peacefully? Where was the base of support for them? Where was our base of support? I felt isolated and almost paralyzed.

So I tried to reach out with a diplomatic phone call to Roberta. She was rude, saying there was nothing to talk about. Dean Carrier met with "us" and tried to meet with "them" to assess the damage and maybe patch things up. They were intransigent. They were so infuriated by his contacting them that they put out a memo stating the Women's Studies Program was not accountable to the College of Arts and Letters or to the University. They were now totally autonomous and refused to talk to administrators. Both Walker and Carrier warned them not go down that road or they would lose the "semi autonomy" WSP had enjoyed before largely out of respect.

Towards the spring, I began to see that it would be impossible to continue. We were besieged from all directions. I had been vilified. Our support base had dwindled to next to nothing. Money was not forthcoming.

We would never be able to finish building the seven-component Center for Women. An impossible dream. What had been a fertile environment at San Diego State College had now become toxic, a hostile, barren land.

None of the grant proposals I wrote to outside sources for funding for the next year were funded. I only had two more long shots pending. The angel we hoped would someday appear as major donor didn't materialize, though it was not for want. It was too soon anyway. We needed more time for the many letters of inquiry I had mailed out to result in follow-ups that could yield relationships. If those relationships developed, they would have to be nurtured for months before they could bear fruit. What's worse, our modest college foundation funding was contingent on getting outside funding.

While I sat in my office at the ironing board worrying about the "big picture," Joyce popped in bringing me the name and phone number of a new volunteer to cheer me up. Her cheeks were pink, and she had bounce in her step that I couldn't remember seeing before.

In our relationship, I had always been the strategist, public speaker, and meeting Chair. She was the writer, sage, critic, and editor. Now her own organizing of fellow women poets buoyed her. The results of the first All San Diego Women's Poetry Reading, which she pulled off before a small but packed audience at the Wesley Center adjacent to the campus, had yielded a core group of campus and community poets that bolstered her spirits and gave us some unexpected publicity.

"Carol," she stated confidently, "I am going to put together an anthology of women poets!"

I remember feeling embarrassed. *Do I even know what an anthology is*? By now I was 22, but had some gaps in my education since I had dropped out my sophomore year to do Women's Studies work full time.

Mostly I just felt tired. Her enthusiasm for something I had no interest in was weighing me down more.

"The publisher can be The Publications Component of the Center for Women's Studies!"

Us! Publish a book? Had she gone nuts? That was a huge idea, and not necessary and not politically important. "It will be mainly local poets," said Joyce, "but I think I can get some nationally known guest poets like Denise Levertov or Collette Inez! Alta from the Bay Area could be in it."

I indulged her by listening. I had nothing else to do anyway.

Watching her as she spoke, I was in awe and disbelief. She amazed me. She had incredible energy and enthusiasm. A 38-year-old mother of three, one just a baby, she was still devoting hours of training and tutoring time to Exploring Family School (along with Leon and Lonnie), was teaching, and was serving on several committees. The defeat at the Women's Studies "board meeting," though terrible, had not set her back like it had me. Besides she had "other interests." I had nothing except the Women's Movement.

"Publish a book, huh? We can't afford it."

"I'll look into it. The underground press has been using a printing house called Grandma's Press. We could print it on inexpensive, recyclable paper that wouldn't be ugly. Something like oatmeal looks and feels. I'm not talking about thousands of copies or the mainstream press. Maybe just a thousand copies. We can pass the hat and do some fundraisers until we've got the money."

"Hmmm," I said, not able to take it all in or make a commitment.

"Well, I gotta go relieve the babysitter, before I go to tonight's meeting. Think about it, Carol. You wouldn't have to do a lot of the work. I'll be the editor. You could do the proofreading and write an introduction. Oh, shit, I'm really late. See you later. Don't forget to call up that volunteer. Bye!"

*Me, write the introduction to a book? That was a huge compliment. A very prestigious thing. Especially since I was not a writer. All I had ever written were school papers and grant proposals. Something literary? Impossible! Not without a lot of help. How the hell would I do that? I didn't know anything about poetry and wasn't really interested in learning. Didn't Joyce know that too? My God, she was a literature teacher! Or was she going to try to teach me?*

I knew this was really important to Joyce. After she shut the door to the ironing board room, I had an idea of how we could fund this poetry book. The arts. This would come to be the first time the arts bailed me out of a nervous breakdown.

I had the power to make line-item changes under 10% of the foundation grant without requesting approval of anyone. We had some money we wouldn't need for supplies, and the printing allocation had barely been touched since we mostly did everything on the mimeograph machine. Women's Studies now had its own budget it used for printing the course brochure. The line item called "Research and Educational Materials" hadn't been touched, because we weren't sure what to do with it. That was $500 right there! If it cost under $1,000, we had the majority of the money already! This was one of the few joys of being an administrator — finding money. I'd sleep on it, then probably tell Joyce tomorrow!

The next day I called Leon about the idea. "I'll donate $50.00 towards the book,'" he said. "But you have to say it is from an anonymous donor. Promise?"

"Okay, I'll tell the others we've started fundraising. Thanks." I hung up. *Wow. Something is happening here. Something good, something creative. Again.*

I remembered the phrase "Hope springs eternal." Then I thought that this stuff was all fluff. We were still facing the probability that CWS would be in the toilet by summer. But you know what? I did feel much better. Out of our own battle, burning, chaos, suffering, something new and interesting was coming. Out of the ashes rises the phoenix.

*Wow.*

I looked back at all the papers stacked on the ironing board and the piles on the kitchen counter. There sat today's mail, a thick bundle tied in a rubber band. Low rays from the setting sun began to come in the window of the back kitchen door, beckoning me outside. "When the deep purple falls, over sleepy garden walls…" *Leave the mail until tomorrow. Hell, why not leave my whole briefcase there till tomorrow?*

I locked up and drove back to my Kensington apartment feeling lighter. Maybe things could get better.

*I'll stop at the liquor store for a half pint of Jim Beam, swing around to Kentucky Fried Chicken for takeout, and put the Carole King album on my record player when I get home.*

*"Lay down, lay down, and lay it all down. Let the white bird lay down."*

*For the morning I'll set out the album for "Morning has broken like the first dawning."*

I spent a couple of hours listening to popular music, and then switched to excerpts from operas. Verdi's "Triumphal March" from *Aida* rallied me always; who could resist that rousing chorus? I was reminded of my early music lessons with Mother and the Sunday morning performance with horns and trumpets of Handel and Hayden. I turned out the lights, put on a long flannel nightgown and strolled about in the moonlight thinking of … the lullaby from Barcarolle. I had left all that behind — Mother's sheet music library and Daddy's record collection when I ran away from Texas.

*Maybe I'll water the morning glories on the back fence before I leave for work.* Their deep, blue-and-purple hues were a celebration of life itself.

Usually there was no time or money for classical music in my revolutionary lifestyle. Tonight was rejuvenating. A departure from the routine.

Yet, didn't Leon say that the Arts are as important as politics? And hadn't Daddy volunteered hours and money to start an FM classical music station in Corpus Christi when I was still a kid? He knew...

I couldn't have known then I would be living in Florence studying art history 12 years later.

The next day I went to the office to sort through the mail. There were precious handwritten letters from women in Iowa, New Jersey, Illinois, Wyoming, France, Germany, and Holland. Typewritten envelopes from universities, a copy of the magazine *Women: A Journal of Liberation*, a feminist newspaper put out by the Chicago Women's Liberation Union, a flyer from the Comision Femenil Mexicana and a poster about a women's music festival with Chris Williams and Holly Near. I loved receiving these rare treasures in the mail. They used to be so hard to find, so underground. Now the college paid for the subscriptions to be sent to our office! Oh, boy I was going to have fun looking through these tasty morsels. It was going to be a good day.

I almost didn't see the expensive white envelope from the San Diego State College Foundation. The phone rang. It was Rhetta. She was calling from her job downtown at the Crisis Center, a new suicide hotline, and said she didn't think she could come in today. I told her it wasn't a problem since there wasn't anything to do. Rhetta was excited about a meeting she attended at the Neighborhood House, where she'd had an important talk with Merkle Harris. Merkle was organizing women on welfare and wanted Rhetta to help out. This was her calling. Rhetta was really good one-on-one helping someone. She was excited to be learning so much and said it would be useful if we got the Storefront Component going someday. She said there was a slight chance we could get a desk and a phone at the Alpha Project, a grass roots drug prevention and services non-profit in North Park. I didn't say anything but I thought it was interesting.

*Joyce was trying to start the Publications Component and Rhetta was trying to start the Storefront Component. Good for them, I guess, but we barely have the money to stay on campus and pay our bills here.* Back to the mail.

A terse letter from a committee at the foundation commended us on what we had accomplished, but said we had failed to attract alternative funding. The foundation could not continue its grant after May 30th. Our office would need to be vacated on the same date.

There it was. The bombshell. Although I'd feared exactly this, I was shocked. I felt hurt. I had really tried my best to get the funds raised, hadn't I? Had I missed something? Been lazy? Could I have done more? Was I a failure?

It was all over now. The long exciting struggle to organize a Women's Movement on campus, to build a Women's Studies Program, to found more programs, to establish seven components…that was all to end soon.

I dropped the letter back down on the ironing board, walked out the door and put the key in the lock.

"I haven't been fired," I told myself. "Don't feel too bad. Walk to your car before you start crying."

I drove home with tears blinding my eyes. But by the time I was driving down the familiar calm of Kensington Drive I couldn't let out a single tear. Instead, a sense of relief was coming over me. Once inside the duplex, I plopped on the comfy old couch and let it all out. Then it was gone again. I looked around the room and felt a breath of fresh air. The terrible times were over. I was free.

No more fear. No more dread! No need to worry about all those details. I could let go. I imagined going to Balboa Park to bask in the sun by the lily pond, to gaze at babies learning to walk, to savor a hot dog with mustard, and to stroll aimlessly past the Art Museum. I would be consoled by the Moorish architecture of the lovely, embracing Organ Pavilion. Its welcoming arms of arcades spreading like those in front of Saint Paul's Cathedral in the Vatican never failed to be awe inspiring.

I wasn't going to tell anyone about the bombshell. This was my moment. My shackles were unlocked and there was springtime in the air. I could live worry free, in the present.

*OUR DREAM*

## *THE CENTER FOR WOMEN*

*became a GHOST that day. She still roams in the hearts of SDSU dreamers. Some of the Lucky young ones have claimed to have seen the white ghost of the Centaur gallop out from the hidden frescoes of the campanile.*

# 33
# WOMEN'S ARTS FESTIVAL

The next time Joyce popped by my office she brought a young artist friend to introduce to me. Chris MacDonald was bright-eyed and excited to be in the Women's Center Office. She carried some sketches rolled up under her arm. Joyce asked her to spread them out on the ironing board and the kitchen counter tops.

The first one was a pencil drawing of a woman's face made in the shape of a strong oval and looking directly at the viewer. Near the right side of her face she held upright a long, thick artist's brush and below was the faint outline of an artist's palette. The smiling face stays in my memory as one as happy as that of a bride's. She was rejoicing in her work. Chris was clearly pleased with her work and thrilled that we wanted to see it. Her husband did not like her paintings, and she kept them hidden behind a door. We were the first to see them.

The next drawing was of a female centaur. Her breasts were small and muscular; her face had a pointed chin and high cheekbones like mine. Dark wavy hair flowed from the crown of her head below to her waist, where her torso joined with the graceful body of a trotting horse. In one hand she held a round shield. In the other a long spear. She looked like an athlete in her prime. I stared at each sketch in amazement. They were symbols of our work and dreams! Feminist art. Art made for the Center for Women's Studies. What a precious gift!

"What inspired you to do this kind of subject matter?" I asked.

"You did. You and Joyce and what the Center for Women's Studies stands for. I haven't met you before, but I have been hearing about everything you are doing. When I met Joyce, I was so excited. These things just kept pouring out of me. She said you need a logo for your new letterhead, a cover for the poetry book, graphics for the newsletter, and I just started working.

"These are just some ideas, of course, some samples. If you want to use any of them I will volunteer my time."

When Chris left, Joyce and I jumped up and hugged each other for joy.

"I've been thinking we should mount a women artists art exhibition."

I sat back down to earth with a thud. She was on a roll.

"There is still time to do it this spring if we can find a space."

"Space?"

"A large space on campus with lots of wall space for paintings and some floor space for sculpture and three-dimensional art."

"It won't cost much. Every artist who shows her work will be expected to volunteer. Besides, artists want to be involved in hanging their own work. It will be hard to keep them out of our hair!"

This was too much for me. *First she wants us to publish a poetry book, and now she's proposing a major art show!!!*

I didn't know anything about artwork or artists. My one art class, in 7th grade, was a trying exercise in drawing vases and a still life, and building an abstract three-dimensional object out of Popsicle sticks. Of course, we had designed one of the seven components to be a cultural component to encourage women artists, present their work, and serve as a vehicle of expression of our feelings and aesthetics, but that was something way off in the future.

Joyce wanted to start the future now. And we had no plans or money for this.

Nevertheless, somehow, an angel had arrived on our doorstep with inspiration. Chris entered our world of ashes and delivered the revolutionary image of the galloping Centaur. We ended up using all of her work and more for decades. Holding that wondrous piece of imagination, I felt the redemption of Art inspired by our years of struggles. The dark forces of chaos had destroyed our dream of a Center for Women's Studies on campus, yet in my hands for the first time I held the Centaur for Women's Studies. Her spirit showed us the pathway through our darkest hours and her victories directly led to the emergence of the first Women's Studies Program on a university campus in the world. She adorns the cover of this book. The Centaur charmed all who came to the Women's Arts Festival.

# 34
# CWSS: MOVING ON

We proceeded to implement the original design of the Center for Women's Studies and Services off campus, securing funding from private and public sources. The Storefront evolved into a crisis center, helping women on welfare, women needing jobs, victims of rape and domestic violence. Volunteers working there saw a need for an Underground Railroad (as Harriet Tubman had organized for runaway slaves, by housing battered women in other volunteers' homes and sometimes ferrying them out of San Diego to a shelter in another city. When calls for help became overwhelming, Laurie MacKenzie and Sue Kirk, members of the CWSS collective, organized a 24-hour-a-day telephone hotline staffed by volunteers they recruited, trained, and supervised. It was another impossible undertaking, but somehow they managed to always keep it running, by always implementing a backup plan for every situation. Often, they had to save the day, taking calls in the middle of the night and working other people's shifts. This was before cell phones. Consequently, the calls were patched through to a staff person's home and they literally had to sit by their phone ready to answer it regardless of personal situations. They lived the Revolution and saved many lives.

Sue and Laurie also created an innovative Feminist Counseling Component, reflecting the adage, "The personal is political." Joyce organized a consciousness raising group at the Viejas Women's Detention Facility and we traveled to women's prison's, putting on poetry readings, women's rock concerts, and presentations on the facts that the majority of the women were there because of boyfriends' actions, the women most often being left literally "holding the bag" of drugs the men were dealing.

Another innovation was the publishing of a national newspaper, lovingly titled *The Longest Revolution*, edited by Lisa Cobbs (now Dr. Lisa Cobbs Hoffman), recently the chair of the SDSU History Department. CWSS also initiated a Feminist Free University, the Seneca Falls Art Gallery, and Project Safehouse. Our Student Chapter still on campus mounted 13 consecutive years of magnificent regional Women's Arts Festivals. The opening festival, in the spring of 1970, featured a spectacular soft sculpture cascading down the four-story stairwell consisting of hundreds of white sanitary napkins and blood-red balloons!

The Center itself has gone through many transformations as the times have changed. Now that most of the original organizers and activists have gone on to other jobs and endeavors, it operates as a very successful service center, with 120 employees and a seven-figure budget. It is now the Center for Community Solutions, in Pacific Beach, with satellite branches in La Mesa and Escondido. There is talk of reclaiming the feminist focus, which would help awaken the dormant remnants of the Second Wave.

In 1971, CWSS came out with the publication of the anthology *Rainbow Snake*. I love the Introduction, which reads as follows:

*Introduction:*

*In a society dedicated to hardware and merchandising, a work of art is intrinsically political. In a society dominated by men and male values, a work of art by a woman is doubly political. And in a society torn by competition and dehumanized by the lure of profit, a cooperative effort by women artists is revolutionary.*

*The volume you are holding in your hands is all of these things and more. From writing to graphics to production and distribution it was done cooperatively by women, under the aegis of the CWSS Publications Component. It grew out of an all-woman poetry reading held on Nov. 20, 1970 at San Diego State College. The reading was organized by Joyce Nower, one of the poets represented in this volume, who is also the current coordinator of the Publications Component. Kris McDonald, whose paintings formed the visual background for the reading, did the art work for this anthology. The editor of this volume, Barbara Miles, had also participated in the reading and is represented in this anthology. Each is an active member of the Board of CWSS, and is deeply involved along with other participants in the struggles of women and oppressed people in general.*

*This first large-scale endeavor of our Publications Component illustrates the CWSS guidelines under which all of our components operate: to be at all times women-oriented, community-oriented, and participant-controlled; and to provide the opportunity for women to receive first-hand knowledge and training in realizing their potential for management, control, and creativity. The Center for Women's Studies and Services is a comprehensive program of services by and for women that includes Recruitment, Tutorial, Research, Cultural, and Publications Components. The comprehensiveness of our program, and the way the several components cooperate, is exemplified by the fact that while the Recruitment Component is working with women prisoners, and ex-convicts, the CWSS-sponsored Women's Festival of the Arts is presenting a panel on and by women prisoners, and the Publications Component is planning a monograph on the subject.*

*The obvious economic, social, and political inequities, the disastrous psychological damage, all conspire to keep Womankind from ever transcending the here-and-now, to keep her chained to the material, to keep her imagination from roaming freely in the lands of her history, and from developing visions of a more beautiful, self-determined future. For those of us in the women's movement, our daily struggles for social change, for dignity, for equal rights, for full liberation, involve tearing down the many decadent, exploitative structures that surround us; and it is easy to lose sight of the many tasks of building and creation before us.*

*The rainbow snake occupies a prominent place in the nearly lost female mythology. The efforts of a few pioneering women are now directed towards reconstructing this mythology with the hope that a popular awareness of its existence will contribute to Woman's growing sense of personal and historical wholeness. In addition to its obvious merit as poetry, the rainbow snake will hopefully advance this process, thus fulfilling one of the aims and aspirations of CWSS.*

Close to home . . .

# PROFILE

Carol Council came to California from south Texas in 1969 to join the political activism of the Vietnam War-era that was flowering in the Golden State, but she stumbled instead upon the budding feminist movement.

At a Bay area lecture on sex-role stereotyping, Council, then 20, experienced what she describes as "an awakening," and found what would become her life's work and abiding passion. She was reborn a feminist who would become one of the pioneers of the women's movement in San Diego.

She and others of like mind became the instigators of the women's studies curriculum at San Diego State University and then moved their efforts into the community to create the independent Center for Women's Studies and Services.

The recently widowed mother of a 5-year-old son, Council is now executive director of the center, which provides educational and support services, including aid for battered women and victims of sexual assault.

The feminist movement's greatest achievement over the past 20 years, Council says, has been to spur "a change of attitude in convincing society that women, indeed, have been in an inferior position and discriminated against . . ."

The movement, less strident than in its 1970s heyday, is ready for the 1990s, Council says.

— Darla Welles

*Tribune photo by Jerry McClard*

**Carol Council came from Texas to the Golden State and found what she calls "an awakening" leading to her life's work. That was when she became a feminist and one of the pioneers of the women's movement in San Diego.**

# 35

# FIFTEEN YEARS LATER: THE MAN IN THE WOMEN'S CENTER GALLERY

One fine spring Friday evening at our new, bigger location for the Women's Center, next to the Library in downtown San Diego, we were preparing an opening reception for a well-known group of local women artists. As I greeted visitors and met each of the artists, I noticed a man on the other side of the exhibit hall. I watched his strong, sexy body move lithely from painting to painting. Tall, well built, with reddish brown hair and a trim beard, he had a wonderfully casual air about him. I watched as he took time with each painting, absorbing the details. Pointing to certain aspects of a work, he conversed comfortably with his two companions, and strangers joined in. Over his shoulder was an Italian leather borsa. A man wearing a purse! I liked that.

As Director of the Center for Women's Studies and Services, and a member of the managing collective, my job was to greet each guest. Somehow this man had slipped by me. He must have arrived early. That evening I looked both simple and sophisticated in snug-fitting blue jeans, a short-sleeve turtleneck, and a brown tweed tailored jacket. So did this man with the reddish brown hair, round face and rosy cheeks. As usual, I knew that I surprised strangers with my intelligence and savvy.

If I were going to make an impression, I would have to be brazen. I could manage to meet him after the program. *Please stay for the wine and hors d'oeuvres.* After my brief marriage in college, several years living in a feminist commune, only four or five dates with a radical attorney friend who was on the rebound, and a hopeless love affair, I was the equivalent of a feminist nun. Time to break on through to the Other Side.

I went over to Chris Kehoe, our Gallery Director. "Chris, do you know who that man over there is?"

"Oh, I had a great conversation with him. He's very nice. He came with two artists. Don't know who he is, though."

Chris, whose standard outfit was a white T-shirt and faded jeans, had dressed up for this occasion by donning a long-sleeve, button-up cotton shirt. She usually cracked jokes and laughed easily, but as it grew closer to the time for her to welcome the crowd, her face grew tight, her manner a bit nervous. (Later she became a California State Senator.) Her lover came closer and said something encouraging to her. They were both "out of the closet" and comfortable in groups of women and gays, but this exhibit had drawn strangers from Del Mar, La Jolla and Rancho Santa Fe. These affluent guests probably didn't even know they were among feminists, having only read about the reception in the art gallery listing in the Union Tribune.

I called out "Welcome everyone" to get their attention. People gathered toward the middle and took their seats. I gave my usual speech about the mission of the Center for Women's Studies and Services, its vast array of social services, educational and cultural events, mentioned an upcoming local performer Whoopie Goldberg, and introduced Chris. When Chris took over, she began to warm to the audience, explaining her concept for this particular show and some of its highlights. She read a short bio of each artist, and said something complimentary about their unique artwork. I loved listening to her vivid descriptions and watching as the artists swelled with pride. As Chris grew more comfortable with the crowd her Irish wit became entertaining. She had the group in stitches several times. It was going to be a great night.

I was already in art euphoria land. Two weeks earlier I learned I had won a scholarship to study art history at the Villa Schifanoia in Florence. Mother had sent me a news clipping from her Corpus Christi chapter of the American Association of University Women (AAUW).The tiny article announced a scholarship competition to the Master's Program of Rosary College of Chicago in the hilltop town of Fiesole. Since I had starting taking art history classes at night and fallen in love with Florence on a bus trip of Europe, Mother remembered that I said my dream was to spend a year studying in Florence.

I submitted a paper into the competition. Incredibly I won! The Collective of the Women's Center then met to make a difficult decision. If I was to be gone for a year, who could do my job? Lisa, the youngest member of the group, was the obvious choice. After protesting that she didn't know how to do everything I did, she reluctantly agreed to do her best. I knew she would do very well, and I promised to write detailed instructions, review her progress reports and do anything I could from thousands of miles away to help her. The CWSS Collective let me accept on one condition — that I would return to my job as Director of CWSS. I have Lisa to thank for freeing me up for the most stimulating year of my life!

So it was that when I sauntered over to the couch where the handsome man with a ruddy complexion and jolly manner sat talking, I confidently perched myself on the arm of the couch, and listened to their conversation. When the man looked up at me, I felt a warmness envelope me. I turned towards him and saw a spark of some kind of wonder mixed with recognition. His eyes said *I know you,* or, *We need to know each other.* Mine must have said exactly the same thing.

When Patrick looked into my eyes, I thought, *This could be the man who will be the father of my child.* It was love at first sight. Not only did he call himself a feminist, but he had also lived in Italy, and loved classical music, opera and dancing! What a find, and right under my own nose. We strolled into the far side of the gallery, and toured the offices, and talked excitedly about many interests we shared.

A week later I got up the courage to call and asked him out. Ordinary women didn't do that. Patrick was stunned and delighted. "How 'bout today?" was his reaction. "It's Sunday so there should be some good events going on. I'll check the newspaper and call you back, okay?"

"Great!"

Ten minutes later the phone rang. "There is an oboe concert at the San Diego Museum of Art in Balboa Park. How does that sound?"

"Wonderful," I drawled. Waiting for him by the old marble fireplace in the Victorian house where I lived with seven other members of the 24$^{th}$ Street Collective, I felt my world expanding into infinite possibilities. The doorbell rang, someone answered it, and brought him into the old parlor. I felt like I was 16 again. The bunch of sweet peas he carried effused the room with an intoxicating aroma. He was gorgeous, smelled delicious, and I was drooling.

On the way to the concert, he said he had made fried chicken and biscuits if we got hungry. It was impossible for either of us to focus on the musicians, and when I spied a side door by our chairs, he nodded. Soon we were unpacking the picnic basket and pouring champagne on a grassy knoll in the sculpture garden. "Carol," he said, "tell me all about yourself." I leapt at the chance to tell my coming of age story. He shared his, and from then on we were inseparable.

We avoided counting the days before I had to leave in

August, and when he put me on the plane he promised to come see me at Christmas. His visit at Christmas became a five-month stay, and we moved to Impruneta into an idyllic cottage on the grounds of a lovely Tuscan villa with acres of vineyards and olive trees. Patrick taught "English as a Second Language" to Italian medical officers. When he told his students that his wife worked with battered women in San Diego, they asked him to invite me as a guest speaker. Since there was nothing in their curriculum on the topic, I was happy to address future doctors (all men) on my work at CWSS.

Patrick did odd jobs around the villa and spent many an afternoon cooking gourmet dinners with Anna, our landlady, who had attended the Cordon Bleu Cooking School. Francesco, her husband, had written musical scores for movies when he was younger, spent his afternoons painting, was a great conversationalist and hopeless flirt. One day when Patrick was out and Anna had gone to market in Greve, Francesco came over to our cottage and tried to persuade me to sit for him. I had the uncomfortable feeling he meant to paint me nude. When I asked Patrick, he said, "Of course that's what he meant."

I avoided being alone with Francesco as long as I could. When he knocked on my door to bring our weekly demijohn of wine made in the cellar, I was prepared for him. I took the offensive.

"About you painting me, I'm flattered, but I've decided I really don't have the time. And if you wanted to paint me nude, that's out of the question."

"Oh, no, una bella donna come tu must be painted by a maestro."

"No thanks, Francesco," I grinned and pushed him back out the door. "See you at dinner." The white-haired gentleman bowed, lifted my hand, and kissed it softly.

Needless to say, more of my time was now spent on dinner parties and hangovers than studying. It was a miracle that I did get my Master's Degree that year. When I was on deadline, though, Patrick walked four miles to convince the ancient contessa (whom the locals called a witch because she let her vicious dogs go wild when she chose to) to loan me a typewriter, and he typed my entire Master's thesis on it for me.

For the summer we had planned a three-month trip of Italy in the old Fiat we bought for $300. Three days before my graduation ceremony, I came out of a lecture at the Villa

Schifanoia. Sister Mary, the Director, said Patrick was on the phone and I could take it in her office. Hmm. Maybe a graduation surprise. I was delighted to cross the loggia, past a preening peacock, to the private corridor leading to her enormous office overlooking the three tiers of formal gardens. Long heavy drapes were pulled back to let the light in and double doors to a balcony were pushed open for the spring Tuscan air. Plush Renaissance style furnishings surrounded an oak carved desk and red velvet director's chair. I felt giddy as I sank into her chair and picked up the receiver of the heavy black phone.

"Hi, honey" he said. He sounded strangely different.

"Hi, darling. What's up?"

"Your mother called." I knew something was wrong. Phone calls to Italy were extremely expensive.

"Your father is in the hospital."

"Okay*." I damn sure wasn't going to let this news ruin my time in Italy. Why are they bothering me?*

"They think he might not make it*."* I was stopped in my tracks.

"I think we should go to there," Patrick stated.

I was silent. *I don't want to go home.*

*I'll miss my last exam and graduation. And how would we get back for our summer road trip? We can't afford the tickets.* "Can't we talk about this later? I'll meet you for coffee at the place by the Duomo after my last class. I gotta go now."

"If I start walking right now I can catch the one o'clock bus from Impruneta. I have some things I need to do in Firenze, anyway. I'll meet you around five o'clock."

I got off the phone determined to guard my summer in Italy with my life. Why was Patrick, of all people, willing to risk that?

Passing the green, pink and white marble stones of the great cathedral I adored, the thought of leaving this Renaissance paradise now was horrible. It had awakened all of my senses. The smells, sights, tastes were intoxicating. This is where I wanted to live. With my Master's Degree and friends on the faculty I actually could get a teaching job after our summer vacation in the south of Italy.

I spied Patrick in his herringbone jacket, sipping cappuccino outside the bar. My happy-go-lucky guy who was always ready for adventures looked somber. I slid into a chair at the little table, kissed him, and sipped my cappuccino.

"What precisely did she say? Why is he in the hospital this time? Did he fall or anything?" My barrage was like a prosecutor's.

"She sounded very upset. He has pneumonia and he may have leukemia."

I saw my mother's worried face and froze inside. *She needs me.*

"Couldn't this be something that would linger on?"

"Carol, I think he is dying. Your mother didn't want to upset your graduation and she said if you do come she doesn't know if he'll be alive by the time you get to Corpus Christi."

"But..."

"You're saying my mother needs me."

"Yes."

"Then, how...can I arrange..."

"I talked to Sister Mary. She'll move your French translation exam to tomorrow and grade it immediately. Meanwhile I've been to the post office and gotten all the right specifications for the boxes we'll need, the weight, and the payment process. Francesco and Anna could mail the rest."

My head was spinning.

"I guess I should talk to Mother tonight." *Then I would decide*, I thought, but already I knew I should do the right thing..

"Honey? I called your Mother back and told her we are coming. I'm working on a flight for right after the graduation ceremony."

I sighed deeply with relief. He had made the decision for me, and, of course, it was the right one.

At the funeral Mother, Kay and I sat in the same pew. I cried profusely. Mother managed to keep it together and Kay sat there stony faced. It felt like she didn't like him getting all that attention. I would only comprehend later that she was making plans.

Later that day I sat on my mother's bed looking at a framed photograph of Daddy when he was about my age. I began to ponder what my father's life was really like — I mean from the standpoint of an outsider.

This was a wholly new concept to me. Of course he had a life story of his own, and I had heard pieces of it, but I mainly knew him as a bad father and a sick man.

The framed photograph of him striding along a sidewalk in downtown San Antonio in 1938, arm in arm with a striking beauty, came to mind. They were both tall and thin, wearing stylish suits and slanted, sexy hats; the moment captured was divine. Each of them stared into the others eyes, clearly in love. It was the only picture I had of him when he was young. Where had I buried it years back? Probably with some of Mother's things. I started digging through boxes from the hall closet. Or maybe she still had it with her. The last I remembered seeing it was on her bedside table in the rehabilitation hospital she stayed in after her first hip injury. Reaching further into the box I found the familiar family photograph of his mother's family.

It was a vintage piece, this faded 1890s portrait of a west Texas family in front of their modest home. The formal scene was set on the low front porch and single step to a worn wooden house. No columns adorned this southern façade. An oriental rug, obviously provided by the photographer, cascaded from the porch into the dirt. The German couple sat in formal wood armchairs, surrounded by their eight children between the ages of 10 and 21. The photo was evidence that the mother had borne about one child a year. And I knew there had been more, that at least two had died young or been stillborn. It didn't take a feminist to realize that Margaret Sanger had not visited this couple. Birth control was a topic not discussed by most Americans then, and it was probably against their Lutheran upbringing.

No one smiled. People had to freeze for the time delay of cameras in those days. All the young women wore frilly, hour-glass-shaped long, white, linen and lace dresses, their thick, dark hair piled atop their heads in charming hairdos. The youngest, about age 10, were twin girls decked out in pinafores and high white stockings, their long brown hair pulled back from the bangs and tied back above the forehead with big floppy white bows. There was my chatty Aunt Isabelle with her crossed eyes, blind Aunt Marie with her eyelids lowered, pretty Louise, my father's mother, with very pronounced eyebrows and her hair in a pompadour. Uncle Charlie, Uncle Bill who was a twin to Aunt Nora, were awkward teenagers in their black suits and ties topped off by slick black hair that was far from flattering.

Daddy's mother married Montrose Calhoun Council not long after that photo was taken. They were both schoolteachers at nearby towns when they met. Montrose went on to law school and by the time Daddy was a young boy, his father was a popular judge in the county in which Clyde, Texas lay. He was known as “The Orator.” People would come to his courtroom just to hear him speak. Daddy loved to go to the courthouse with him and spend the day watching his hero balancing the scales of justice.

All this came to a sudden end when Montrose drove his buggy out into a cold winter night to help someone in need. He was stranded in a wild west Texas “norther,” a fast-moving storm with high winds, driving rain, and dangerous white bolts of lightning striking and splitting trees in half.

Although my grandfather made it home safely, he was ravaged by pneumonia, and died not long after. Or, so the story went. Unfortunately I never got to meet my Grandpa, nor did my son.

Daddy, who was only 12 years old, was devastated by his death. He mourned him all his life. Worse than that, he became angrier and angrier about his father’s fate as time wore on.

The way Daddy told it, he had to drop out of high school to support his mother and his sister Lois. Times were getting harder and the Stock Market crash made survival next to impossible. Daddy sold newspapers, walked door-to-door selling insurance, took odd jobs, but couldn’t make ends meet. One of the family values of his parents and aunties was that it was more important for girls to get an education than boys because there were more jobs for men, and a woman could only support herself, if she had to, if she had a college degree. Then she could teach. Lois, then, was destined to become a teacher, and my father, Frank, along with other relatives, had to provide the money. Perhaps, he agreed with this. Most likely not. Though he never complained about it, or said it was unfair, he was always bitter that he didn’t get to go to college.

Suddenly Patrick and I were back in San Diego prematurely with no jobs and no place to stay. We found a tiny love nest on Fir Street and CWSS scraped together money in the budget to take me back part-time. Patrick couldn’t find steady work, was grumpy, and slept a lot. When he did take a decent job, we decided to get pregnant. He worked extra hours and volunteered at the San Diego Repertory Theater on the weekends. His behavior became erratic and I didn’t know what to make of it, so I did what my mother had done. I coped.

When Mother called and told me her trust officers advised her to help her children buy two affordable houses, one for Kay and one for me, I was ecstatic. Mother came up with a small down payment. We would be responsible for the loan payments and taxes. Within three weeks I found a fixer upper that reminded me of Grandma's house and was only $89,000. Patrick had carpentry, plumbing, and electrician skills, so he would do the work. We moved into Blue Haven with our six-month-old son and Patrick went to work tearing out windows, re-plumbing, roofing, etc. I went back to work full-time, putting Timmy in day care nearby the Women's Center. We lived there for five years.

## 36
## A GHOST FROM THE PAST — SEVEN YEARS LATER

I had been alone for less than a year when the realtor came. At the advice of a therapist, I determined not to make any major changes for one year. Anyone, especially the mother of a five-year-old child, was too vulnerable and disoriented to be objective in personal decision making abilities at this stage in the grieving process. I might function all right at the Women's Center, although that was also in doubt, compounded by the fact that no one on else in the core staff, the CWSS Collective, was a mother. Dear sisters they were, but they didn't share my experience of motherhood, widowhood, and single parenthood. There was a gaping hole in my life. I knew I had to protect it carefully before the wound could even begin to heal.

The realtor knocked on the wide Craftsman-style front door with its inset squares of beveled glass and stood waiting by the porch swing. Constructed in the Pennsylvania Dutch style in 1907, the cheery blue house at 3365 B Street sat on the hill in the ghetto part of the neighborhood called Golden Hill, a historic residential section above downtown San Diego, destined someday to be gentrified.

I watched the short woman with dark, graying hair get out of her car, put on her sunglasses and survey my unkempt lawn surrounded by a hurricane fence. One side was completely covered by a 10-foot high overgrown hedge of pyracantha bushes, hiding completely the tiny frame house next door. On the other side was a garish yellow stucco house built in the fifties. My blue morning glories couldn't climb high enough to hide that site. Across the street two rows of shabby rental houses lined up opposite each other. Parked on the street were three beat-up old cars covered with dead leaves and other debris. The flat tires were rotting away. Opening the door, I noticed the realtor was somber as she stepped from the blinding San Diego sunshine into the darkness of the doorway and said "Hello."

I had phoned her because someone at the Women's Center had spoken highly of this woman as particularly knowledgeable about our unique neighborhood. I was keenly aware that the housing market in San Diego had been rising for years and was close to its peak. But, I reminded myself, I was not going to put it up for sale yet. I only wanted to get information on sales trends in the neighborhood and, perhaps, an opinion about the current value of the house which Mother had helped us buy five years ago. I loved my home because it bore a striking resemblance to that wonderful old house far away in Premont, Texas, where Grandma and Grandpa had given me so many happy days. There I ran carefree with my cousins Clyde David and Ruth Marie. All who came there were loving, happy, modest people. I wanted the same happiness here for years to come.

I let the woman inside, and hesitated. Her black eyes stared deeply into mine.

"We've met before," she said.

"Yes... we have," I stumbled. *Where? When? I know.* The memory returned, sweeping down, covering all my flesh and digging into my gut. It was on the battlefields long ago. What flashed before me were scenes from the months of torture when I was treated as a traitor in the first months of the Women's Studies Program. I felt the fear of that Terrible Night creeping at me. The troops were many then. Now I was face-to-face and alone with one of them.

"I used my married name then."

"Yes, and I was Carol Rowell then."

*No need to offer refreshments.*

We both sat down and looked at each other. Older, yes, but, we were the same people. I took the seat of power, my high-back lounger chair I had upholstered in blue and purple hydrangeas. Judy perched on the edge of the couch across the room.

"Carol," she said slowly, "I know I have owed you an apology for many years."

She paused and cleared her throat.

I tried to play back her words in my eardrums. I strained to remember how she looked in 1970, 19 years back.

Then the sound of those words penetrated my brain, falling over me like a warm blanket.

I looked straight into her eyes and nodded my agreement. *Yes, you owe me an apology. And I am waiting.*

"I meant to look you up," Judy began. "I've heard good things over the years about what you have done at CWSS; two of my friends went there for counseling, and I've thought of volunteering on the Rape Crisis Center hotline. Anyhow, I meant to look you up over the years."

I felt stunned. A compliment. *Okay that's good.* Who were her friends? *Oh, my God.* Suddenly I remembered that Joyce had told me a few years ago that Judy's long-time partner had committed suicide. We were both widows.

"When you phoned I wondered if it would be the same person. I knew you had changed your name..."

"I went back to my birth name," I clarified.

I stared back into her eyes.

"What we did to you that night was unforgivable. No one could have withstood that. No one."

So she knew they were going to treat me like scum. Labeling me "elitist" just for being a leader — one who wanted to go on past Women's Studies and finish building the seven components. The Women's Center, CWSS, which had gone on and on, successfully serving thousands of women throughout San Diego County.

"I got swept up into Carla Kirkwood's tirades, and I ended up being part of a mob. I am sorry," she said genuinely.

"I forgive you. No one has ever said that to me in all these years," I blurted out.

She stifled a sob.

I got up and went towards her, sitting on the couch. We embraced and sobbed together.

There was nothing more that needed to be said.

Judy stood up. "I didn't come here to look at the house."

We both laughed.

I said, "I didn't want to sell it anyway."

We laughed again. I thanked her for the apology, walked her out onto the front porch and said "Goodbye."

Closing the heavy wood door behind me, I felt the first sensation that some closure had come to my wounds.

# 37
# THE INTERVIEW

In the early winter of 1998 I sat waiting for a Ph.D. candidate named Catherine Orr to arrive at my home. I was living in a pretty new condominium with arched windows, white stucco curving balustrades, quatrefoil windows and Ionic columns, tucked neatly into the foothills neighborhood called Belsera. I pictured her drive from La Jolla, where she was visiting her mother. It would be a pretty ride, one that undulated eastward along the wide 52 freeway. Sparse traffic on the new freeway and the scenes of uninterrupted low-lying hills were deceptively rural for the metropolis of San Diego. A canyon of eucalyptus trees gave way to nothing but small bushes of chaparral like in Texas as far as the eye could see. Miles of vacant land owned by the military merged with the open space of Mission Trails State Park at her exit, Santo Road, where the tree-lined community of Tierrasanta lay. "Tierrasanta" is the Spanish name for "sacred land," though its mostly Republican residents fondly call it "The Island in The Hills."

When she arrived she would enter a walled garden draped with fuchsia-colored blossoms of bougainvillea, and be greeted by a small, white West Highland terrier, barking and hopping up to get a view out the slender window adjacent to the front door. Catherine had just phoned to say she was running a little late, and I knew her cramming this interview into a busy holiday schedule was a last minute feat, one she hoped she could do justice to when writing Chapter Two of her Ph.D. thesis. Her draft, "On Becoming Subjects of Knowledge: The Emergence of Women's Studies at San Diego State College," was due too soon. It was part of the larger manuscript, *Representing Women/ Disciplining Feminism: Activism, Professionalism, and Women's Studies.*

I knew that lunch two days before with Joyce Nower had given her a wealth of information already, and she probably would want to get right to the hard questions. Joyce, as usual, had set the stage with fascinating details of the socio-political times surrounding the birth of Women's Studies at SDSU, and she wanted to make sure Catherine got the details of the Seven-Step process clear from me.

I sat waiting for her on the long sofa I had custom-made for our last house, of blue and pink hydrangeas on polished cotton, gazing at the beauty of the cornflower blue carpet as it climbed like a vine up the spiral staircase up to Timmy's bedroom. It was a lovely home. I didn't know how much longer I could afford to keep it, though. The realtor said if I put it on the market, I absolutely had to change the carpet to an off-white Berber. Cornflower blue would never sell. What nerve! Was he the god of realtors? Yes, in fact, Saied Mojabi, with multiple awards had been the No. 1 realtor in the area for many years running. Damn. I was revolted by the idea of eliminating colorismo out of financial necessity. What the fuck was the Renaissance for anyway? My training in Florence for my Master's Degree was insulted. I had used up all of Patrick's life insurance money to move out of a "bad neighborhood," and get Timmy into a good school, and currently I had no job. Social Security Survivor's Benefits and occasional oil royalties wouldn't meet the mortgage payments. I had begun living on credit cards. Ironic that so many women had made money off of good careers in Women's Studies for decades now, complete with health benefits and retirement. Here I was, a founder of Women's Studies, but besides being paid as coordinator for a year, and teaching one class, I never made any money off of it — not even for all the subsequent public speaking events!

What would today's interviewer be like? Another person coming to extract more livelihood from me. I sighed. It was noon and I had to pick Timmy up from the Recreation Center at 2:30. That would give us two solid hours, and a good excuse to cut it off at 2:15.

Every few years someone, usually a student writing a paper on the Women's Movement, or a reporter doing an article on the anniversary of Women's Studies at SDSU, came to meet me, hoping for some good quotes, a glimpse into this glorious (or giddy) past, or insight and inspiration. On the coffee table before me were spread out some of their news clippings and photos.

They always had a deadline that was two days away. I obliged somewhat reluctantly. Sometimes I felt like I needed graying hair and a rocking chair in order to not disappoint them. I was still not "an older woman." Most feminist leaders were about 15 years older than I. People often said to me "You certainly were an early bloomer" when they learned I was a leader and founder at age 22. I felt this meant I had to go out to pasture earlier than most, since I hadn't found anything else stellar to do since then. Often they left saying, "You really should write a book about this!"

Dredging up horrible memories made me tense. Skirting them with an interviewer was hard work. I knew it was very tough on Joyce too. There was still too much unresolved.

Would I ever feel okay about my story? I mean the whole story.

I doubted it. But, I reminded myself that it came a little easier each time. I had to admit I loved telling the stories about the exciting times and the battles — to a point — to that point where it got so very raw and personal. But I owed it to history to do it. More importantly, the truth had still not been recorded anywhere — not even in the San Diego State Archives — something we had better get done soon.

I was 47 years old now. As a widow and a single parent of a 13-year-old son, I had other things on my mind. Then that phone call from Geri, Mother's trust fund officer back in Texas, had me worried. What exactly had she said?

I remembered Geri's tense voice when she called unexpectedly from Texas earlier in the morning.

"Carol, I'm going to say this very directly. Your sister is not normal."

"What exactly do you mean?"

"Kay came into our office with your mother. She rattled on and on about how tough her life is, that no one understands what it is like to be diagnosed with Adult Attention Deficit Disorder late in life, to be a single parent and the mother of a girl with ADD. She blamed her family for claiming 'they are so loving' and not giving her any help at all. Said she is 'handicapped' and should get special assistance."

"Why was Kay even coming with Mother to see her Trust Officer?"

"That's a good question. Perhaps she is not happy about the will. She may be trying to get her to change it to eliminate you. Your mother seemed very intimidated and embarrassed by Kay. I can only guess what went on when they went home together. I don't like the idea of her being alone in the house with Kay."

Now my heart was pounding. Kay had become belligerent with Mother just like Daddy and she was going home with Mother where she could badger her endlessly! I should be there. What a horrible thought. My sister could have turned into my father and history was repeating itself.

The iron gate creaked, Sport barked, and the doorbell rang.

I welcomed Catherine by offering her refreshments and motioning to seat herself in a chair across the coffee table from me. I was eyeing her and she was eyeing me. Trevor came in from the garage where he had been working on a project that would balance the stand of Timmy's basketball hoop on my sloping driveway. Always one to put people at ease, he cracked some jokes and told her that her research into the story of the Women's Studies Program was very important. He was glad she had chosen it for her Doctoral thesis and certain that I would be of great help to her. Then he excused himself and left on his bicycle. I was right. Before she turned on the tape recorder, she referenced her interview with Joyce Nower and "others." That got my attention. Had she interviewed my enemies? Did she know about all that? Then she listed documents she had studied at the SDSU archives, citing memos I had written and other key documents I didn't know were there or wasn't sure I even remembered. It had been a long time.

Catherine preceded each question with a statement of what she had learned. This was unlike any of the other interviewers who mainly asked open-ended questions with no clue as to their knowledge of time, place, or significance of the questions. Her format kept me focused and succinct. I was used to less-experienced interviewers who enjoyed letting me tell stories, ramble, and have spontaneous exchanges. Catherine, though, was an academic, and I was only part of a broader investigation. Soon I found myself not so eloquent. Her insightful questions about the dynamics at work revealed not only that, for the first time, I found myself in the company of someone who understood the complexity of it all better that I did, but that I found myself growing eager to read her thesis!

What a strange feeling. I had been the expert on the SDSU story — from my experience — until a young woman who reminded me a little of myself turned out to be a "knower" of all facets of the history of the development of the first Women's Studies Program in the U.S.

The interview sped by. We chatted a bit, exchanged email addresses and she was off, promising to mail me a draft as soon as it was ready. It hadn't been hard. I wondered how she would quote me and the women on the "other side." But as soon as I closed the door behind her, my thoughts turned to what Mother's Trust Officer had said.

# 38
# MOTHER

I tried to remember the rest of the phone conversation with Geri. *Something terrible was about to happen to my Mother!*

"If you ask me, and I know it may not be within my formal role as a trust officer, but Kay has been given too much help already. More than her fair share."

"What did you say to her?"

"I said, 'I have an adult child with ADD and, believe me, I know exactly what's going on.' I don't think she liked me saying that, but I am not afraid to say it, it's the truth. Grownup kids have to take responsibility for their own lives, not leech off their family. My son has been homeless several times. I had to learn to practice tough love. Your Mother is a wonderful woman, too nice a person to have to become a co-dependent after her husband passed away."

The message hit home double time. Geri didn't know what I did. Mother was a co-dependent all the years of her marriage. I thought she was finally free.

I was speechless; trying to be analytical.

"Does Kay have a job now?"

"She said she was writing for that little newspaper on the way to Padre Island, but they only publish once a month. She can't be making enough to support herself and a child on that."

"Where is she living?"

"Your mom says she has an apartment over a garage, but they mostly stay at your home so Grandma can help by taking Laurie to school. Kay has to get her precious sleep, you know, because it is so debilitating being an insomniac."

I was stunned. Kay and her daughter are living in my mother's house. Mother is raising her granddaughter! She is 80 years old. Buying the groceries, the school clothes, the gasoline. Supporting two more people. Mother was either in denial or keeping this secret from me.

I could feel my mind shifting from one reality to another like I had learned to do after having been conned for years by a boyfriend. I recognized the tone and words of someone who had tried to stay out of other people's business, but could no longer be silent, or she would be complicit.

She said Mother seemed embarrassed and intimidated by Kay.

How bad was it? I had learned the hard way, shortly after Patrick and I had returned from our year in Italy, and I was pregnant with Timmy, that a con artist tells half-truths in order to never be caught in a lie. So, to figure out the truth, you take the bad information and double it, the good information and slice it in half. That's a lesson in logic they should teach everyone in school. "How to get an objective perspective on someone you love." How bad does it have to be before a woman can admit the truth about someone she loves, or your mother loves, without facing the terrifying fact that you have to go to war?

Was it bad enough that I shouldn't have been here giving an interview to Catherine Orr, but, instead, be boarding a plane to go to my mother's side? And if so, what could I do there? And what would I do with Timmy?

When I embraced the Women's Movement, I felt I took a vow to protect every woman against domestic abuse. Was this what I was looking at now? Was my mother the victim of a perpetrator who was her very own daughter?

I remembered that Geri said Mother would be back on Monday to sign some unrelated paperwork. Late Monday morning I got another call from her.

"Carol," she said, "Your Mother arrived for her appointment this morning with bruises on her face and arms."

"Oh, my God."

I brought in a colleague and together we asked her if Kay had hurt her. She was surprised and said, "How did you know?"

"Look in the mirror at your bruises."

"Your mom said as she was going out the door to come here Kay grabbed her arms and later squeezed her check saying "When are you going to change the will? You keep putting it off. Get it done today!"

"Oh, Geri, thank God you knew the right thing to do." I remembered all my training in the cycle of domestic violence, the denial by the victim, the certain escalation, the need to confront reality, and the need for the perpetrator to be confronted and stopped.

"I told your mom that we were going to take some photographs, and that I was going to call you about this. Kay has gone back to Austin for a few days, so your mom is alone now."

"I think I should call Mother's attorney about getting a Temporary Restraining Order and fly out there immediately."

"I already spoke with her. She said she'll be in her office for the next hour, after that she'll be in court."

"Okay, I'll call her right now. Then I'll call Mother. Do you think she will be willing to go to court to get a TRO against Kay?"

"I think if anyone can persuade her, it's you."

When I arrived at the airport in Corpus on Tuesday, Mother was obviously glad to see me. She was a little relieved that everyone now knew the truth and that help had arrived, but she was embarrassed, ashamed, and afraid that Kay would be back, angrier the next time. On top of that she was worried for her granddaughter and afraid she might never be allowed to see her again.

She grew quiet as we drove closer to her attorney's office. She was struggling with her fear that taking Kay to court would make matters worse and, at the same time buoyed by the caring she was receiving from three competent women — her Trust Officer, her attorney, and myself — all very knowledgeable about elder abuse, a term Mother was just learning applied to herself.

Sitting across from her lawyer, Jeanne, Mother tried to explore any other options. There were none. So, she woefully signed the statement that would go to the court that afternoon requesting a Temporary Restraining Order. The TRO would, if granted, make it illegal for Kay to come within a certain number of yards of Mother until the court had a hearing from both parties and made a final determination that week regarding a long term Protective Order. If Kay didn't show up, it would be automatically granted.

That morning Mother had gotten a call from Kay saying she was driving back today. Mother said she started to tell her that I had called and Kay hung up in a huff. Meanwhile the attorney had arranged for a courier to serve Kay the papers that evening.

When Mother and I got home to the house where I had lived from kindergarten through high school, she could tell that Kay had been there. She'd left a trail where she had tossed things aside while gathering up clothes and other belongings from my father's bedroom at the far end of the hall.

The place felt ominous, like an intruder had been there or, worse, still could be. I told Mother to close the blinds on all the windows in rooms facing our street corner so Kay couldn't see that I was there, and then to call a locksmith and tell him it was urgent. The next priority was to make sure she was gone, so I got up my courage and opened the door to the room with blackout curtains where insomniacs had slept. It was stone quiet and I couldn't see anything clearly until I found the light switch. It confirmed no one was there, but there were clumps of clothing, girls' toys, linens and who knows what piled so high that I didn't know what *else* might be lurking there. I checked the bathroom and the closets, then went back to assure Mother that Kay was gone and make sure she told the locksmith to come right away. She was on the phone and told me he was saying he could come tomorrow morning and it would be cheaper. I got on the phone and said there had been a break-in and we needed all the locks changed now.

Then I went back to the dark, foreboding room — the sight of my father's writhing body when he overdosed many years ago still vivid in my mind. Instinct told me to search the room for *anything* that could be dangerous. I checked the outside door to the backyard, concluding it was locked. As I did so, I remembered the sound of a shotgun going off in the middle of the night and my mother screaming, "Frank! Frank!" My father had shot a stray cat whose mating cries kept him awake one night.

I started sorting through piles of clothing, junk, and trash. Suddenly I realized I was exhausted. After the two plane flights, the meeting with the attorney, no food, and a huge adrenaline rush, I needed to lie down. I was about to leave the room, but told myself that if I did I would know that I hadn't been thorough. I shoved a blanket and sheet around on the floor and there it was. A long brown wooden object. A rifle.

My mind raced. Whose was it? One of Daddy's old ones? He had promised Mother to get rid of all of them. Kay's? Did it matter? No. Would Kay use it? On someone in anger? In a suicide attempt? *Doesn't matter now. Thing to do is to find out if it is loaded.*

Not having held a rifle since Daddy took me target shooting when I was thirteen, I was nervous about not making a mistake and having it go off. I remembered to look for the safety lock and see if it was on or not. It looked like it was off. *Now to open the chamber.* I slid back the pin. To my relief it looked empty. I remembered to stick my finger far inside to make sure there wasn't one bullet left in the chamber. There wasn't. I sighed. *So far so good.*

*Now what am I going to do with it?* I realized that an empty rifle wasn't the end of it. There might be bullets nearby. I opened the desk drawer and found a half-full box of bullets. *Shit. I must get rid of these fast. But how? Where? Kay could burst in any minute.*

I knew I had to get them far away fast. The best place would be with my cousin Clyde David on the ranch. But I couldn't drive them there because they would still be with me too long and the chances of an encounter with Kay could multiply. And I couldn't leave Mother alone.

The closest place to get rid of them would be a neighbor's house. I scanned my brain for what I could remember about any of the neighbors after all these years. Mother wasn't particularly close with any of them since old friends had died and young people moved in. Then I thought of the house next door. Mother's long-time friend had nice adult sons who often came to stay there now.

I wrapped the rifle in a blanket, pocketed the bullets, and carried them out into the back yard. It was beginning to be dusk now. When I saw a light on next door, I rushed to push open the weather-beaten redwood gate that hadn't been opened for years. It was stuck in the thick Bermuda grass around it, but a hinge was loose, and I reached over the gate and slid the bolt back. It gave.

Quickly I walked up the driveway to their back porch and knocked on the door. A tall man about my age in a baseball cap answered and I told him who I was. He invited me in but I stood on the doorstep and told him my sister had become violent with my mother and we were taking her to court. I had found this rifle and bullets in the house and I wanted them far away. He understood immediately and said he was so sorry to hear about my mother. Yes, he knew what to do with them. He was leaving before dawn to go fishing, then going to a friend's ranch. He would take the rifle with him and give it away to someone. *Thank God.*

I thanked him hurriedly and ran back to make sure Mother was okay. When I got there the locksmith had already changed one of the locks, Mother was chatting with him and heating up the stew she had made for my arrival.

Now I could plop down on the soft white couch under the picture window and catch my breath. As I did so, I bent the edge of a lower blind open and saw an old green station wagon driving slowly by. As it turned our corner, I recognized the driver.

Kay drove off in the opposite direction.

*Shit.* She was stalking the place. Did she know I was there? I began to realize that I could never leave my mother in this house alone. My job now was her. Was this why I had found myself at this time in my life with no job? Being a widow now, I had no relatives in San Diego. Timmy, almost 14 now, was making lasting friends in middle school, but I began wondering if I could find a good job in Corpus Christi. My resume was impressive in a big city, awesome in a small one.

I had already discussed the other possibility with Mother, that of her moving to San Diego. She said she could never leave her church, her friends, and, most importantly, her sister-in-law Lois. My Aunt Lois, whom Daddy had sacrificed his own education for and put through college, was now living in a very nice retirement complex in Corpus. When Daddy was dying, he asked Mother if she would promise to take care of his sister. Of course, she did, and that meant that when Lois's letters became less and less coherent, Mother had driven to San Antonio and arrived unannounced to find the house in disarray and Lois struggling to live alone with what must have been dementia. Mother oversaw Lois's trust using the same officer in Corpus and knew Lois had enough money to move into this luxurious retirement facility. Mother made all the arrangements and now had a schedule of calling Lois every day, taking her out shopping or sightseeing once a week and joining her for lunch in the dining room each Sunday after church.

If Mother could live there too, she could be protected from Kay moving in with her from time to time. I remembered that Mother had said she would love to live there if she had the money.

I called Geri. She said, "I was thinking that if you can't get her to go back with you to California, that this could be the solution. They have security guards there. Of course, it would mean dipping more into the principal of her trust, and it would be harder to project how long she could afford it."

"Okay. But what if Kay tried to stay with her as a 'visitor' and regained control of her?"

"I think the rule there is that you can only have a visitor stay up to three days at a time and they are strict about that. But another problem is that they always have a waiting list of almost a year."

"Maybe if I talked to the Director there about the elder abuse Mother is subjected to if she lives anywhere else."

"The Director is a compassionate woman. She knows your mom and how much she does to take care of Lois. Let me review the costs over there, run some figures and get back to you. Meantime, you have to be in court in two days?"

"Right."

"And your flight back is when?"

"The same day, but I could change that. Timmy called and told me I got a call about a job interview. I need to think about that too."

"You need to do what you can for your mom, Carol, but you can't let all this make you unable to take care of your own life, either."

"Yeah. I know. Thanks. Meantime let's not discuss the housing idea with Mother. She is worried enough about having to see Kay in court, and you know how she worries about not being able to help raise her granddaughter."

"Yes, I do. I'll speak with you later."

"Thanks for everything."

"Bye bye."

I got off the phone in the room that had been my bedroom so many years ago. The room where I had retreated so many times when my father was on a tirade. The room where I woke up screaming from nightmares. I looked around it with new eyes. Yes, the wallpaper I loved so much was still there. The repeated picture of a southern belle under willow trees was faded and looked less romantic now. The white French provincial furniture was all still there too. But, the main feature of the room was gone. The beautiful blue canopy atop my bed had been removed because Kay didn't like it. Now it was a four-poster bed covered by a plain chenille bedspread. My refuge and place of dreaming was gone. No more could I gaze wistfully at the blue fabric dotted with white cotton islets and imagine I was a free spirit.

I looked at the bed and suppressed the urge to lie down and nurse my wounds where I had lain 30 years ago with stomachaches in the mornings. I could see my sweet Mother coming in to my bedside, rubbing my stomach and urging me to try to get up to go to school since "attendance was so important to good grades." If the pain was too bad and I stayed, I could rest for three hours before Daddy would get out of bed and be standing in the doorway.

"If you're too sick to go to school, then I'll have to take you to the doctor. So what's it going to be?"

Trapped between pain and a painful ordeal, I would mentally flip a coin and respond either with "I'm feeling better now," or "I need to see the doctor." After a year of that I either got better with managing pain or I had less pain because he was sick in bed.

When I called Geri back she said she'd had a good conversation with the Director of the retirement facility and that they had a temporary room available for Mother! Geri also said that she thought Mother could afford it, if she stopped supporting her daughter and granddaughter.

Next I had to persuade Mother. Her eyes brightened at the thought of enjoying a safe senior lifestyle with Lois and others she knew from church who lived there. But when she thought about cutting off the money supply, although she admitted it had gotten entirely out of hand, she was worried sick that her child and grandchild would suffer. I, too, felt sad at the thought of their being in abject poverty. I reminded myself that Mother had done more than enough, and that in the end it hadn't helped. A chronic situation, untreated, grows like cancer.

I myself had learned that the hard way. Patrick's fibs grew into lies, his overspending grew into debts, his debtors became angry, he lost jobs, he increased his drug use until he was totally erratic and unpredictable. After four years of this I woke up to the self-realization that his behavior jeopardized our family's stability. Logically, though it tore my heart out, I had to kick him out and file for divorce. And our four-year-old old son couldn't understand why I was so mean.

Mother knew all about this. She also had not forgotten how much Frank had jeopardized her well-being. So, logically, she agreed. Emotionally she felt ashamed and guilty. Better that, than continued abuse, as the situation would become more and more toxic, if not dangerous.

"I think I should try it, I mean move there. And the decision is not irreversible. I can always stay a year or so and then make another change."

I didn't argue with that. It was the best that she could do.

We needed a safe haven that I could settle Mother into before I got on the airplane. She agreed to let me call the Director and make the commitment. That was a big breakthrough.

I stressed to the Director that having security staff there wasn't enough. The staff at the lobby and those who checked on Mother would have to be informed of the terms of the TRO, know Kay was not to be allowed inside, and be willing to call the police if necessary. Thankfully, she agreed. That made four women knowledgeable in domestic violence and elder abuse who were now providing a support system for L'Aleen. Four powerful advocates: her attorney, her trust officer, her housing director, and her younger daughter.

I felt a burden lifting from my shoulders.

Mother looked lighter too. She began to talk about attending travel seminars, book clubs, scrabble games, and holiday parties there. She could even take up swimming again. I was heartened at the rebirth that was forthcoming.

As we arrived at the courthouse, I was on the lookout for Kay. I kept my arm linked to Mother's, ready for anything. No sign of Kay as we crossed the parking lot or in the elevator. I peeked in the courtroom door. Our attorney came out and greeted us. I was wearing my red power suit for the occasion. I knew I might need to get the judge's attention, even though they would not be calling witnesses, since there were none. I wore a tomato red straight skirt topped by a matching jacket with a neat tailored high collar. She was decked out in a subdued but powerful blue pantsuit.

"The judge will hear our case next. Of course he's seen the Temporary Restraining Order and the petition to make it permanent. This judge is tough, but savvy about domestic violence."

"Is Kay in there?"

"No, I haven't seen her yet."

The hall was crowded. Just then I saw a tall woman with bleach blonde scraggly hair sweep through, and slip inside the door. I shuddered.

I hadn't seen her in several years. It was shocking how she had lost her beautiful jet-black hair and slim figure. The skin on her face was an unhealthy yellowish color. She was large, determined, and menacing.

The trembling in Mother's left hand increased as she was helped into a chair next to her attorney. Her Parkinson's disease symptoms were not severe, but viewing her from two rows back in the courtroom I was aware that she was weak and a little unsteady. It wasn't right that she had to be here. Kay should be taking care of her, not victimizing her.

The clerk read off the case information. The judge asked who was representing the two parties. Mother's attorney gave her name. Kay said she didn't have an attorney and was representing herself. Then the judge asked Mother to state her name. He asked her where she lived.

Her voice was weak as she answered his questions.

He leaned forward.

"How long have you lived at this address?"

"Your honor, I think...it's been forty two. Uh," she cleared her throat.

"Mrs. Council, I am not able to hear you clearly. Could you and your attorney come up closer and stand before the bench?"

I got nervous. Mother was showing strain. I knew she couldn't stand up very long because the Parkinson's had made her legs stiff. I wanted to go up there and hold her other arm, but I knew enough about courtroom scenes to know that no one ever goes into the arena without being called there.

Mother was stoic and dignified. But when she nodded and walked to the point indicated, it was because the judge told her to. Not because she was determined. We had coached her to drop her usual diplomatic, long-winded, apologetic style of speech, but I was not at all sure she would tell the judge the whole truth, and if she got winded, she might cave in. She had to walk past the desk where Kay sat on her way, and that unnerved her. As the judge looked at his documents, Mother seemed to look around for something to hold onto. I almost leapt out of my chair, but was quickly relieved when a court attendant got the judge's attention and assent to bring her a chair quickly. She heaved and sighed, then smiled and nodded "Thank you" to the attendant.

"Mrs. Council, are you aware that you are requesting a Restraining Order against your daughter, Kay Council, in order to protect you from abuse?"

"Yes, I suppose I am, although I wouldn't want it misunderstood."

"Misunderstood? How so?"

"Well, I think sometimes people do things that they don't mean to do, and, that, it might not be right to..."

*Oh, no. The sinking feeling came into the pit of my stomach.*

"Are you saying you aren't sure now that you want a Restraining Order?"

Mother looked at Jeanne. Her look meant, "I can't talk or I'll cry."

The judge was poker-faced as he began to speak. "I am going to say some words about elder abuse before we proceed. Domestic violence is violence or the threat of violence done by a spouse, boyfriend, or other member of the family, often residing in the same home. The reasoning behind what is done is not relevant to this court. One person uses their power over another person in a manner that is threatening or harmful. In the case of elder abuse it is usually an adult child who takes advantage of the vulnerability of an elderly parent or person. The very fact that the person is elderly means that they have less real or perceived power than a younger person. Do you understand this?"

"Yes, I think that is clear."

"All right. The law exists to protect you."

"Did your daughter, Kay Council, on Monday the 23rd of last month, take hold of your arms in such a way as to cause the bruises in this photograph?"

Mother stifled a sob, whispered "Yes."

And did the defendant, Kay Council, on that day grab your chin in such a way as to cause the bruises in this photograph?"

"She was trying..."

"Answer yes or no."

"Yes."

I sighed a huge sigh of relief.

"That's all. You may return to your seat."

"The court calls the defendant, Kay Council."

Kay picked up a yellow legal pad, stood up and approached the judge.

"You may begin."

"I will show the court how Mrs. Council has exaggerated the truth. She is an old lady who is very forgetful. Oh, she looks like a sweet old lady, but she is deceitful and loves to play the role of the martyr. She's been doing that all my life and nobody in our family sees it but me. I know the truth. Everyone else is in denial about it. I do my best to take care of her, but I am handicapped and I have a daughter who is handicapped too. We are the ones who need special attention, not her. I don't need to be hauled into court because of her whining when no one will hire me because they didn't diagnose me with Attention Deficit Disorder until four years ago!!!!" Her voice became high, shrill.

*Why doesn't the judge stop her? Poor Mother! No, let her keep talking, she'll hang herself.*

*No, no, the sarcasm building,* "You," she pointed her finger at Mother. "You can't act like goody two shoes...."

The gavel came down.

"That's enough."

"But I haven't finished."

"You are finished when I say you are finished."

Kay was beet-red, puffed up, but managed to hold her tongue.

"I am going to ask you just one question."

"On Monday the 23rd, did you touch your Mother in such a way as to cause the bruises in these two photographs?"

She grabbed the photos, tossed them down, swung around in Mother's direction and yelled, "You know you bruise easily."

The judge shouted. "That's enough!" as he motioned to the bailiff to escort Kay back to her table.

"The request for a restraining order against Kay Council is hereby granted. Violation of these terms will result in arrest..."

The room got noisy. Kay scraped her chair, rustled her papers, turned back and glared at me.

"Court is adjourned."

I stood up and pushed my way against the crowd and toward Mother's side.

Mother looked rattled. She was alone now while Jeanne was gathering papers from the clerk. I looked for Kay again and couldn't spot her. When I saw the bailiff dashing away, I realized he was going after Kay, but Kay was faster than him and dashed out the double doors into the crowd waiting for the elevators.

The bailiff slowly escorted Mother and me toward a guard at the door.

"The guard will make sure that you make it to your car safely."

So, they really did get the picture.

What was she capable of doing right here in the courthouse? I shuddered to think. Once in the hall, we were all tense. There was no sign of Kay and we were stuck waiting for an elevator. Finally the elevator doors opened. It was full of people needing to come out. I could feel Kay's eyes on me from somewhere unknown. The guard, a tall black man, looked straight ahead; he wasn't even looking out for Kay. An opening appeared in the group coming out of the elevator and I pushed Mother toward it.

Suddenly a cry rang out echoing through the halls "You know she bruises easily!"

When the elevator doors closed behind us I was trembling. I checked every head, tall or short, for Kay's angry face. We had made it. She was not there.

As we entered the first floor lobby, there was more open space and I could see that she was not in the lobby. What about outside the doors?

"How long have you lived in Corpus Christi?" Mother asked the guard kindly.

"I've been here six years now. Before that I worked in McAllen."

"Oh, yes I know McAllen. I grew up in Premont."

"Well, you probably know Falfurrias. I have a cousin there now."

We went through the glass doors of the lobby out into the blinding sunshine of a huge parking lot. I did a 180-degree scan of the area but couldn't identify anything but a sea of cars. Mother's car seemed miles away.

"It's a fine sunny day out here," he said as he smiled down on my mother.

I wished he could stay with us forever.

Finally we were at the car and he was opening the door for Mother. I had the car keys ready and jammed them into the lock, slid in the driver's side, locked the door, and check the rearview mirror. No one in sight.

"Thank you, and have a nice day," Mother nodded to him.

"Thank you, ma'am. You have a nice lunch now."

I thanked him, dug through my purse for the bottle of Valium, and downed one.

Instantly I began to breathe easier. My stomach eased and I could hear our breaths as we both exhaled deeply at the same time.

I had no words in me.

It was not over yet. I had to get us out of that parking lot and make sure we weren't being followed. *Where to go?* There was still much to do, and my plane was leaving in about two hours.

"Let's go to the WhataBurger and get some lunch," I said, falling back on my old ways of relaxing at a drive-in burger stand.

"Good. I could use a Dr. Pepper."

"Me too."

We drove to the WhataBurger near the Bay Front. As we unwrapped hot toasted buns, French fries, catsup and mustard packages, things seemed familiar, but surreal. I was still wired. But there had been no sight of Kay. The guard must have scared her off.

"Mother, I have some good news."

Her eyebrow went up, meaning "How is that possible?'"

"They have a room for you at Faith Center. I know you weren't on the waiting list, but they found a temporary room near the staff lounge that you can use and they've put you on the waiting list for a one-bedroom apartment."

"Really? Well, that's nice but I don't think I could afford it, maybe sometime in the future."

"Mother?"

"Yes?"

"I can't leave town and leave you alone in that house. We have all discussed it. Geri says you can afford it. Jeanne says you won't be safe at home and you deserve to finally have a nice lifestyle with senior friends. Plus, you'll be near Lois."

"You, know, I did promise your dad, before he died, that I would take good care of Lois. If I were to live there I could do so much more for her. Little things, like mending, that she can't manage."

She turned from me and looked far away. "I know I can't see Kay and Laurie for a long time."

"Mother, that's right. I'm going to give the staff a copy of the Restraining Order when we get there. The Director already knows about it and will instruct the staff that Kay is not to be allowed inside the lobby."

"They know?"

"Yes. They needed to know the truth."

"I guess so."

"So, I packed your suitcase and medicines. I also put in the four new pantsuits we bought you with the matching jewelry. Everything is in the trunk. Geri said for you to make up a list of anything else you need from home or the store and she will bring it to you tomorrow. She has a set of keys to the house. You have to promise me you won't ever go back there alone, Mother. Or everything we have done this week can be undone in a second."

"Carol, what time is it now?"

"Oh! It's 1:45."

"You better take me there now or you'll miss your plane."

"Right. But do you promise?"

"I think you know what you are doing better than I may. You've handled everything so well, Carol I trust you and Geri and Jeanne, so, yes, I won't go back to Stirman Street alone. In fact, I don't think I'll go anywhere for a while. There's a beauty shop there and I'll ask Geri to bring my portable files, mail, and paperwork I need to catch up on badly."

"Mother? Can you promise you won't let Kay into your new place?"

"That's harder. I don't want to make a scene there. I'll try."

"Don't hang out in the lobby since that is the way she'd have to come in. And if they call to say you have a visitor, be ready to say 'no.' Think it through, rehearse it, and be ready for it."

We were already pulling into the entrance to the building now. I glanced at my watch just as an airport shuttle bus arrived. A nurse in a flowered uniform and a pretty woman in a suit came out to greet Mother and take her things inside. I shook her hand, gave her the car keys and thanked her.

Mother kissed me quickly.

"You had better get going. Give that wonderful grandson of mine a hug."

I nodded, climbed into the van, waved goodbye through the back window to the woman I loved most in the world.

A few weeks after I returned from Texas, I picked up the mail and found a long cheery letter from Mother about how much she was enjoying the social activities in her new community, and Catherine Orr's draft from our interview. The title was intriguing:

"Representing Women: Disciplining Feminism: Activism, Professionalism, and Women's Studies." In the opening paragraph of the December 1996 draft she stated her purpose: "I want to know how women claimed to be knowers and what it is they claim to know through the enterprise of women's studies… First, I discuss the specific geographical, historical, and cultural context of women's studies in San Diego. Then I consider how the women who began as a rap group and became the Ad-Hoc Committee on Women's Studies conceived of themselves as builders of a curriculum around their gendered identities. I follow this trajectory through a major split in the program's first semester that was based on who could claim to authentically represent 'the women' of the women's movement. To conclude the chapter, I analyze the history of San Diego State to demonstrate the significance of women's emergence as subjects of knowledge within the context of women's studies." I was impressed.

I devoured it at once, and, to this day I often re-read it.

Looking back at it now, I'm again filled with the sense of satisfaction that came when I finished reading the last page of her work. Finally a sense of closure grew within me. She had made my wish come true. Someone had finally told the true story — seeing it not from one side or another, but analyzing the events to gain perspective on a multifaceted historical time period. I felt vindicated and proud that the Women's Movement had created women like Catherine Orr to record the history we made.

The effect of Catherine Orr's dissertation (which I highly recommend Women's Studies students to read) the impact was two-fold. One, it relieved me of the feeling that I needed to write that book. Two, being freed up from the historical version may have been what I needed to be able to write my memoirs — this book.

At the same time I wondered if my mother was safe. Temporary Restraining Orders, though used a lot by feminist social workers, were often still ineffective against men, or, in our case, a woman. The next time I saw Mother, it would be years later through a window of a prison.

# 39
# MY FATHER: A VOICE FROM THE THIRTIES

"You might say you led a colorful life back in the thirties," said a woman's voice at the beginning of the tape. *Who was that?*

"Talk about the trip up north and the musicians you met."

"Well," came the long drawling of the beginning of a tale of the old Texan. "I don't know that you would rightly call it colorful, or even particularly interesting. It was the Depression, after all, and that was a terrible time for everyone, though it was particularly bad in west Texas and Oklahoma during the Dust Bowl storms that preceded it. Your mother's family came across in the famous Land Rush, you know. They staked out a bunch of acres and managed to survive quite well. That's where some of the oil and natural gas rights your mother has still come from today — from the Jones side of the family. Course mine come from the Voight side of my family, primarily from the investments your great uncle Charles managed from his little place in Luling."

I could feel the woman growing impatient.

"But you have heard all that before, haven't you now?"

Here the tape got noisy. Listening to the scratchy sounds, I pictured the tape recorder being moved closer to him as I heard a thump on the table. He would be sitting at the head of our lovely oval dining room table that I remembered was finished in distressed pecan wood.

The nearby window air conditioner made its familiar dull roar. Daddy, too tall for any regular chair, would be sitting in his favorite armchair, with his legs stretched out and crossed, his head leaning back, his arms raised, folded back with fingers interlocked. He looked like a tall, old Texan. Pinkish sunspots dotted his light yellowish skin, and darker brown "age spots" dotted his now fleshy face, hiding entirely the Frank Sinatra look of his youth. Only his grayish-blue eyes, should they twinkle, could draw your mind back to the image of his youth. The space above his eyebrows and his balding head had smooth, relatively unblemished skin, the result of multiple skin peels and surgeries for skin cancer. Of course he always felt better, more handsome wearing a wide brimmed hat, but, in keeping with Southern tradition, he would always take it off just inside the doorway. So I pictured him not wearing a hat during this interview.

"Well, all right, I suppose. Those were the days of the great musicians — ones we have never seen since. Some of them, like Al Jolson, Cab Calloway, Louis Armstrong, of course, got their starts in the south — especially in New Orleans — and traveled up north once they had enough money to make it up there by riding the rails and buying an occasional bus ticket in hopes of putting together a band and getting better known.

"They had had enough of playing for pennies in Jackson Square or on street corners. Of course, they had their own little bands that played on Saturday nights at jute joint on the bayou or, on occasion, at some little dive in the French Quarter. But their dreams were to make a recording, or better yet, to audition at the Cotton Club in New York City. The radio, of course, had been around since World War One, when Marconi sent the first trans-Atlantic message from Italy to the U.S., but only people who had electricity could hear the radio, and in my youth only fifteen percent of the homes in the country had it.

"If you lived in a small town, as most people did, there might only be one radio in town, say at the General Store or the café. People would walk in and sit up real close to the radio to hear a broadcast by Edward R. Murrow or a song performed by Ella Fitzgerald.

"You, see, this was the beginning of the era of sound. People who could afford a Victrola like your great aunts, owned a few 78-RPM records they'd play over and over again. A Victrola was a wind-up record box like the one we had at the Lodge in the hill country outside of San Anton. You remember that?"

"Sure, I remember winding it back up after the music ran down," Kay answered. "You were always playing 'I Give To You As You Give To Me.'" At this point he began to hum the melody.

"Yeah, that was one of Cole Porter's greatest. He was a master. Up there with Gershwin and Irving Berlin. One of my all time favorites was 'D'Lovely,' and another one I loved to play was a famous one called 'In the still of the Night.' But, that was later, and they were a different class of people — wealthy white men with ties to Rockefeller and Hollywood.

"No, after the big Stock Market Crash of 1929, I was more interested in the new music of colored people, 'blacks' as we say now, who were having jam sessions in New York and Chicago."

Kay asked, "When did you decide to go to New York?" with a drawl not as strong as Daddy's.

"I found myself with no job after a good stint with the radio station in San Antonio. Well, I knew I could probably go back to work at the telephone company — where I still had some good friends, but I was itching to see the big cities, and hear the great musicians. I had helped to put my sister, your Aunt Lois, through college, and she had been teaching for two years, so I found myself with a little money saved up and no obligations. My mom, you called her 'Big Bambah,' was in poor health, as she had been ever since my Dad died, but she was happy enough living with her sisters, so I didn't have to worry about her too much anymore.

"So, to make a long story short, it seemed like the right time to strike out and see the world. 'Course it wasn't the right time 'cuz it was Depression, but I did it anyway."

I stopped the tape here, and went for Jim Beam and Cokes.

"Trevor," I exclaimed, as I mixed our drinks, "this sounds like me, when I took off for Texas in 1967 to come out to California. You know what I mean. I did it anyway. No money, no support from my family. Did his family denounce him for it like he did me?"

"Really interesting, isn't it? There is definitely an echo here of your own life. But, there is a big difference too. You were a girl, his little girl, and he would never have expected you to run off at nineteen. The Women's Movement had barely begun. But let's get back to the tape. This is really fascinating. Your father's voice gives me a real feeling for his personality. There is so much that is conveyed through the voice," said Trevor, the sound mixer.

I realized his listening to the tape was a double pleasure — one because he was interested in me, the other because he was a professional in sound. His training at the UCLA Graduate School of Film and years of recording documentary interviews, movies, and television series meant he was actually hearing things that I could not. And, of course, I was responding mainly to this male voice as my daddy's. Someone I held a grudge against for not loving me unconditionally.

"Ready?"

I nodded and plopped down beside him on a cushion on the floor next to the little tape recorder while he pushed the "Start" button.

"Took the Greyhound bus from San Antonio to Saint Louis, where I got a hotel room and stayed a few nights. I met some fellas there who had been to New York and gave me names of friends to look up when I got there. I had a mighty good time seeing the sights of the city. Eventually I hooked up with a couple that gave me a ride to their home in Southern Illinois. Then I hitchhiked to Chicago, hung around there for a couple of days, caught the train to New York. My, that sure was a glorious ride. Trains were luxurious in those days. Plush upholstered armchairs, shiny chrome everywhere, a club car, and dining car, with white linen tablecloths and, of course, polite and smiling black porters bowing and treating you like royalty. That was one of the few jobs men who were descendents of former slaves could get then.

"I'd chat with the porters when they weren't busy, offer them a cigarette and hear stories of all the places they'd seen, the nightclubs to go to, and the families they had at home. We had wonderful times, swapping stories and laughing. A couple of them invited me to their homes, if I ever found myself in their neck of the woods.

"By the time I said goodbye to all my porter friends and found myself in that fabulous Grand Central Station, I had a pocketful of notes and maps to guide me to a room at the YMCA, a good lunch counter, a friend at a newsstand, and a good shoeshine man. I also had a letter to hand carry to Mr. Bo Jangles."

"Wait, you mean *the* Bo Jangles? You're not kidding? I have a record with Bob Dylan singing a song about Bo Jangles!"

"Oh, yes, and could he ever dance. I spent many a night watching him."

"How did you get in?"

"That note got me backstage at a club down the street from the Cotton Club. I watched the second half of the performance from behind the curtain. Bo Jangles danced like his legs were made out of spaghetti. He'd jump for joy, whoop, holler, and laugh like a Leprechaun. When they finished the applause they nearly tore the roof down, and people were dancing in the aisles on their way out the door.

"I waited for Bo Jangles to leave the stage, but he sat back down with the band members. Someone passed around a flask of whiskey, and they began to jam. I spied a little stool in the darkest corner of the stage, and made myself at home.

"'Who's that white boy back there? Hey mister, come on out of there. Yeah, that's right, come on over here. How long you were setting there? I seen you earlier tapping your feet, so I nose you can walk on over here.'

"'Give him a chair, boys,' said Mr. Bo Jangles. 'Yeah, we won't bite you.'

"So I took a seat right there with the band.

"'What's your name?'

"'Frank.'

"'Say that again?'

"'My name is Frank Council.'

"'Weeeoooooooo! Listen to that drawl, boys. What part of Texas are you from?'

"I laughed and they laughed at me. I didn't know I had such a discernible drawl. Now every word that came out of mouth sounded hilarious, and we were all belly laughing.

"'Okay, Frank, now you're gonna hear some real music.'

"They began to jam. More instruments arrived; girlfriends and wives with babies came up onstage, joining in. I couldn't play an instrument or sing, but I could feel the music. So I clapped my hands, stomped my feet, and felt more at home that I had since I was a child. And it was like that almost every night.

"Soon I was sleeping on a cot backstage or staying in different band members' apartments. I found the note to Bo Jangles in my wallet one day. I never needed to give it to him. Some folks just don't require introductions. In the daytime I'd leave Harlem and walk uptown. I'd stroll around Carnegie Hall and pick up a standing room only ticket for a matinee. And save money by eating hot dogs or a bowl of chili. Of course, I was looking for work, preferably at a radio station, but they weren't hiring — nobody was hiring during the Depression.

"But the music, well, it was nothing short of fabulous. I saw Cab Calloway, Ella Fitzgerald, and other greats whose names I can't think of right now. We'll, I'm getting a little tired now. Why don't we call it a night?"

Kay responded with, "All right. Those were some good tales."

There was a pause in the tape.

Kay's voice, stronger now, teased, "Tell us about the blonde in the Cadillac."

"The what? Oh, yeah."

He cleared his throat.

"Well, let's see, when I began to run out of money and I could feel winter coming on, I knew I shouldn't put off going back south, but I didn't have enough to buy a bus ticket, so I had to hitchhike. I made it a little past Detroit with rides from truckers and farmers, but then it got tough. I walked all afternoon stopping to sit on my suitcase to rest and be ready to put my thumb out. It was getting a little cloudy and cold as it got closer to sundown, so I put on my overcoat and turned up the collar.

"For a hitchhiker I looked pretty smart, wearing that double breasted herringbone coat and brown felt hat I bought at Macy's bargain basement. I should be able to get a ride. The problem was there were no vehicles on the highway now. I hadn't seen a single car in six hours, and what was worse was that I hadn't see a highway sign listing any towns up ahead. I considered turning back, but I knew if I had to walk all the way, I couldn't make it back until later at night." His voice trailed off.

"So, what did you do then?"

I wondered why someone who hated her father would want to interview him. Had she changed her mind about him over the years? Or was she coldly curious? Her voice was neutral.

"Well, the sun was still shining, and I figured I had another hour before dark when I looked back and saw a car coming in the distance at high speed. As it came closer, the sun struck it. It's shiny white and brand new, something rare in those days. I supposed it would pass a hitchhiker by, so when it slowed down and I saw a blonde driving a white Cadillac, hell, I was almost speechless.

"She pulled up slowly, sizing up my overcoat, hat, suitcase, and examining my face.

"'Where are you headed,' she asked?

"'Back south to Texas, ma'am, but I'd be grateful for a ride just to the next town for the night.'

"'I'm headed to El Paso. I'd be happy to take you to the next city where I'm going to spend the night. I want to get in another hundred miles today. Maybe you could help with the driving.'

"She got out of the Cadillac convertible, stepped lightly in her high heels, and opened the trunk. I slung my lone suitcase inside amidst stacks of white boxes.

"'I'm getting cold. Maybe I should put the roof up,' she said as she slipped into the driver's seat and slid her scarf off of her beautifully golden, coiffed hair.

"I thought she was a vision.

"'I'm a cosmetics saleswoman at the moment, so I'm delivering those boxes on my way out to Hollywood.'

"She was friendly, easy to talk to and asked me about my family and my work. I told her stories of my trip to New York City and time passed quickly. When we got onto the next city, she drove downtown to the YMCA.

"'Do you have money for a room here?'

"'Yes, I surely do.'

"'Okay, I'm going to get a room at a hotel. I'll pick you up tomorrow morning, say at 8:00 o'clock? How does that sound?'

"'Sounds just fine to me. I'm mighty grateful.'

"And that's the way it went day after day. If there weren't a YMCA, I'd sleep at a boarding house or on a bench at the bus station. Each day we told stories and took turns driving, and listened to big band or country music on her car radio. One day she said, 'You know silent movies are out, and everyone is making talkies in Hollywood. They can't make them fast enough, and they are hiring soundmen. With you background in radio, I bet it wouldn't be hard for you to get a job out there. In fact, I could introduce you to a friend or two that might help you out.'"

Here I stopped the tape, my mouth open, goose bumps crawling up my arms.

"Trevor, did you hear that?"

Trevor smiled, nodded that it was true, although we could barely believe our ears.

"Play it again."

We listened closely to his words again.

Yes she said he could leave his relatives, go to Hollywood and become a sound man — just like Trevor had done.

I had fallen in love with a sound man.

My father almost became a sound man, and I didn't know it until now.

Daddy's voice continued, "This was a lot to swallow. I told her I'd give it some thought.

"She said, 'When we get to Amarillo I have to make a little side trip by myself before I head west to El Paso. You can stay in Amarillo and think about which way you want to go. If you are there when I get back I'll take you to El Paso. If you're not, I'll know you went back to San Antonio.'"

"What did you do?"

"I came back to San Antonio, got a job at the telephone company and married your mother. You know that," he said sadly.

The tape ended.

*         *         *         *         *

The interviewer's voice was definitely Kay's. I hadn't heard it in probably seven years. Now I was drawn back to the last time I had heard it. I remembered her calling me to tell me she was pregnant. At 40 years old, she was not married, did not have a boyfriend. She never wanted one again either, and still did not have a real job. When I pointed these things out to her, and suggested it would be a hard life for the child, she grew livid.

"What do you know about a hard life? You've always had it easy. You lived in a commune, before you married Patrick. You've always had a support system around you. I'm the black sheep of the family. I've always been alone and I want it that way. Fuck family. The good 'ol traditional nuclear family hasn't done a thing for me, and I knew it never would. I'm a successful businesswoman now and I can goddamn well bring up a baby if I want to, you act so high and mighty."

"What is your business?" I challenged.

"I have properties I manage and I own several trailers."

"Oh, really. I hadn't heard. That's nice. How many trailers do you have?"

"I have three trailers but I'm going to have four."

I pictured mobile homes in a mobile home park. *Not bad.*

"Well, that's good, where are they, in Austin?"

"One of them is down south of Alice at a friend's farm. I've got another in Bayside, and I'm towing one out to the hill country as soon as I get the permission from the old woman that has a ranch out there."

The scene in my mind shifted. Trailer trash. Tiny trailers lightweight enough for Kay to pull behind her car. This was insanity.

Kay gave up custody of two-year-old Travers to his dad when she divorced him in her early twenties. She knew she couldn't be a good mother then, and now, practically destitute, she wanted a baby. It was clearly for selfish reasons. She wanted a toy, a friend, and someone who would support her in old age. Her behavior with Travers when he was in college in Chicago was consistent with that theory. He was finishing a Journalism degree at the Art Institute of Chicago and was on his way towards writing his first book, later published under the title *Execution Texas*, when Kay called him. She demanded that he drop out, and come take care of her in Arkansas or Georgia — some place where living was cheaper. He told her absolutely not. He had his own life to live and he didn't want contact with her anymore. He had his phone number changed to protect him from further harassment.

# 40
# LOST MOTHER

The letter I opened from Mother had a new address. She explained that Kay had "shown her the financial benefits of living in a studio," and had left Trinity Towers! She said she sometimes walked to the grocery store. She was in her eighties, walking to the grocery store in the scorching, muggy heat of Corpus Christi, lugging back bags, and still putting the best face on it. Everything I had done had unraveled. I called her. It was a fait accompli. I could do nothing. She was taking care of her granddaughter again. The two of them were having a party eating watermelon on the lawn.

in Rockport where Kay had rented an old house. She had broken her hip. I flew to see her. It was hopeless. Kay lived a half-mile away and threatened to take her and her checkbook home.

Back in San Diego, I called the hospital. The nurse said Kay came in the day after I left and took Mother away against the protests of the doctor and the director of the hospital. Kay was screaming that she could do whatever she wanted to do and Mother was smiling meekly, unable to say "No" to her daughter. She needed five more weeks of therapy to be able to walk again.

I had no phone number and no address for Kay or Mother. Months passed. Finally a postcard arrived from Mississippi. Mother said she was "enjoying the scenery their vacation." *But, how was she?* She did not mention a walker or a wheelchair. They were traveling in a van with Laurie, now 11 years old. I pictured Mother lying down in the back of it while they sat up front. Another postcard from Tennessee said they went to Graceland, but she did not actually say she went inside. They were camping and occasionally getting a motel. Where in the hell were they going?

Kay was on the run. She had taken Mother out of the hospital against the doctor's orders. Without notice I had flown in and visited Mother in the hospital. Most likely Kay thought I would go to the authorities and have her convicted of elder abuse.

Kay crossed state lines to avoid the arm of the law and to disappear. I was afraid I would never see my mother again. My mother, who had always been there for me, was gone and taken away, and I could not be there for her.

The nurse at the hospital gave me the name of a friend of Kay's. When I called her she said she used to baby-sit Laurie, and she knew Mother lived in an apartment upstairs and Laurie carried her meals to her there. I began to feel sick. The woman said, "I know you must feel terrible. Your Mother is such a wonderful person. Kay just left her up there. I came to take her to church, but it was too dangerous to try to help her down the outside staircase. Nobody should live like that. I told Kay the social workers who would come from the hospital to follow up on Mother's condition would not approve of her living situation. She said she was going to turn the front porch into a room for her and it was none of their business anyway. Then one weekend I saw fliers on telephone poles about a garage sale. When I went by the house, I saw a sign that said "Yard Sale". I got out and looked. There were you mother's costume jewelry, hats, silver teaspoons, teacups. Even the linens your Grandmother embroidered! I felt horrible but there was nothing I could do except to ask to see your Mother. She said she was sleeping. I cried when I left."

No address. No phone. An agonizing year later, I received a letter postmarked general delivery "Ithaca, New York." Mother said they had gone there because Kay said they had better healthcare in New York.

I used the Internet to research Ithaca. Mother said they had a duplex near the college. Isolating two possible addresses, I phoned the Ithaca police. They found two possible duplexes and spoke to the owners. One said the woman with the old lady and young girl had left last week. I sent letters to the P.O. box begging for a phone number. I had lost my mother.

More months passed. Trevor and I wondered how long they would stay in the cold of New York or when they might head south for a warmer climate. The Trust Officer called and reported withdrawals of $2,000 or $3,000 each month. Kay had gotten Power of Attorney and maybe even changed the will.

There were no clues worth flying to Ithaca for. They had moved on. Then a postcard from Montana said it was beautiful, but it was hard on Kay pushing the wheelchair and changing diapers.

One night three years after Kay kidnapped Mother, the phone rang. It was Mother. She sounded cheerful. They had just installed a phone and she was calling from somewhere in Northern California. She described a red Victorian farmhouse with two porches and a vegetable garden in the front yard. Kay must be listening to her, monitoring her words.

"Mother I need a phone number."

"Yes, the weather is very nice here. Kay planted all pumpkins and made a straw scarecrow in the garden."

She was giving me clues. I grabbed a pencil.

"Are you in Eureka?"

"We sometimes take a scenic drive from Ferndale to McKinleyville. The countryside here is beautiful. There is not another house in sight. Not a lot of trees, but there are a few big old ones like those we used to see near Aransas Pass when you were a girl."

"Mother, I need an address," I pressed.

"Uh, huh."

I heard pots and pans banging in the kitchen, then Mother said, "Grizzly."

"Grizzly? Are there grizzly bears there?"

"I don't think so," she answered, then added, "Might need a nursing home."

"Okay. I understand."

Kay's voice in the background hissed, "Don't start talking about expensive nursing homes! It's time to get off the phone."

"I'll write a letter and ask Kay to mail it," said Mother, then the phone went dead.

The long letter Mother sent on pretty stationery had four numbers written in between the purple and yellow pansies: 8473. Not enough for a phone number. Maybe an address? In the middle of a long sentence, she wrote "help" in parenthesis. Kay hadn't spotted it. A second letter came days later. In the margin, I saw "Grizzly Road" in small letters. I rushed to get on the internet and try Map Quest for the three towns she had cited. Nothing. Nothing. Then bingo! There it was. Grizzly Bluff Road, a long road about three miles outside of Ferndale. My mind rushed as I searched up and down the road for other houses. There were parcels, a few scattered barns, silos, and other farm buildings. Then this had to be it. An isolated red house on a corner. I could see it, touch it, smell it. I was going to try save my mother. Memorial Day weekend was four days away. Mother's letter mentioned an upcoming "vacation." Were they leaving again? I had a four-day holiday from my fundraising job at a private school.

My friend Carlos, the janitor, knew of my mother's

situation and had offered to help if he could. I called him and said I'd pay him $500 to fly with me up there to search for her. I couldn't do it alone. It might be dangerous.

"Your sister is crazy and your mom needs help. Make the reservations now!"

Was I really going to leave my son and go fight my sister?

Many years back I didn't have enough courage to save the black people in the back of the church that Sunday. I became stronger when I fought political battles with the University officials, but I had been intimidated and failed that terrible night at the Women's Studies board meeting. I wondered if I possessed the courage that was needed now.

**Mother**

# 41
# COURAGE

Once on the airplane, I wondered if Kay had a gun. Could I get the sheriff to come out if I found the house? Probably not. I knew domestic violence and elder abuse protocol well. My efforts to talk to someone in that county about helping me had failed. It was the usual reason. "We can't do anything if we don't have proof that something has happened."

Maybe something would *happen* now.

The next morning I rented a green Taurus and we headed out to find Grizzly Road. Carlos said he would drive because I was too nervous. The seaside city of Arcata, with its fast food stores and brand name shops, was not notable. I knew that Kay had a Post Office box there, and hoped I didn't have to go hunting around there for Mother. As we took the turnoff to the historic village of Ferndale, the countryside charmed us. Rich fertile earth, planted with neat rows of crops separated by boundaries of cypress trees.

Before we knew it, we were driving down the main street of Ferndale. A tiny town about five blocks long, sporting historic buildings, gift shops, candle shops, a boutique and a couple of cafes. Then we were out of town! We circled around a residential area to get more of a feeling for the place. Well-manicured, adorable houses of varying vintages lined streets shaded by 100-year-old trees. Consulting the map, we left town and found Grizzly Bluff Road.

We didn't know which way to turn. There were no houses, no addresses. It was a farm road. We decided to go west toward the ocean first. After five or six miles we had found nothing but pastures, farm equipment and an old tree-covered cemetery up a hillside road. The smell of the ocean and shadows of forests of redwood trees meant we must have been going the wrong way. We turned around and headed the other way. The road became flat and straight, matching Mother's description. We slowed to examine a small one-story house and three or four modern ranch houses, which didn't fit the description. None of them had addresses. I told Carlos it must be the wrong road. He kept driving silently. He sped up, passing a plain farmhouse and outbuildings. Looking over my shoulder, I saw something tall in the garden.

"A scarecrow!"

Peering back I made out the lines of a two-story house. A big box-shaped place. No towers, no frills.

"It has a Victorian porch!"

Carlos said we should keep driving and circle back. I held my breath. Mother could be in there! We drove back at the average speed. It was a dark red house with Victorian-style posts and railings on two porches, an outbuilding, and a van parked on a gravel driveway. The house was run down with paint peeling. I put on a baseball cap and slumped down in the seat.

Carlos said, "I'm going to turn the corner and let you out. Just stand on the side of the road. I saw a back road where I can get a better view behind that row of trees over there."

"What?"

"Don't worry. I won't do anything without you. I'll be back in five minutes."

I handed him the binoculars I was glad I had thought to bring. He smiled and drove off, leaving me perspiring on the shoulder of the road for what seemed like an eternity. Shaking and clutching my cell phone, I knew Carlos was thinking straight. A short Latino in jeans would barely be noticed in these fields, but a tall, red-haired woman would certainly draw attention.

*But what if a car came by to ask if I needed help? What if Kay drove up?*

Five minutes passed with no cars in sight.

Then the green Taurus came around the curve in the road, and I jumped inside.

"I think I saw her. She left in a white minivan by herself."

"What did she look like?"

"Tall, big, with orange frizzy long hair."

"That's her!"

"I'm taking you into town to wait at a café while I go back alone. There's a Mexican woman living in the house out back. I'm going to try to talk to her."

"Good." I longed for the safety of the café and an opportunity to gather my wits. He let me out, and I felt coolness flowing over me as I sat down at the window table and ordered two iced teas and two tuna sandwiches to go. I realized we hadn't eaten all day. My stomach was weak. I gobbled my sandwich, peering out at the cute Victorian gift shop on the main street, and relaxed a bit more. Fifteen minutes later the Taurus drove up and Carlos waved for me to get in.

"We've got our chance. I spoke to the Mexican woman in

Spanish. She didn't want to talk at first — she's pregnant and lonely, I think — then she became friendly when I asked about an old woman. She said she used to see her sometimes sitting in a rocking chair on the front porch, but that she hadn't seen her for a long time."

"*Let's hurry. Kay could come back soon.*"

My adrenaline kicked in. I was ready.

Pulling up to the side of the house, I saw a note taped to the top step of the porch. "Gone on a very long trip. Sorry we missed you." I had just missed them by minutes! Probably the three of them were headed out on a trip down the coast for the Memorial Day weekend. My hopes were dashed.

But the note said "a very long trip." It was meant to discourage anyone from looking further. She knew I was coming! Yes, I was certain. They could be inside. But Carlos said Kay had left. Mother might be inside alone! My mind and heart raced.

Creeping up the porch stairs, I noticed something eerie. Yellowed drawstring shades were pulled down so tightly that they were practically glued to the windows. I tried to peer in two windows but could not see a thing. I remember how Daddy covered his windows completely in black so it would be dark all day. Although it was mid-day, I imagined the whole house shrouded in darkness. *Go one by one to every window and door on all four sides of the house, and count them as you go.*

"Mother, are you in there?" I called at the first window.

*One.*

"Mother, it's Carol." I knocked on the next window.

*Two.*

I completed the search of the door and more windows on that side of the house.

*Three, Four, Five.*

Carlos stayed behind to keep an eye on the driveway where Kay had parked before, while I turned the corner to the front of the house. Stepping through the vegetable patch and passing the scarecrow, I saw in the distance a white car coming in my direction. I froze. The vehicle slowed. It was a white minivan. Did Carlos say "Van"? I walked on, turning my back and stepped onto the front porch as a visitor might. I slowed further. My heart pounded. I turned around and saw two men in the front seat looking at me. The van was just slowing to turn the corner.

*Oh my God, I've got to get inside this house. I tried the doorknob on a door at the end of the front porch. Damn it, it wouldn't budge.*

*Six.*

*Onward.* There were two more windows and the main door on this porch. Checking the windows, I moved towards the door. Taped to a rocking chair was a larger note. "We are all gone on a long trip." Tiptoeing closer, I could see an etched window in the dark wooden door. It had no shade or curtain on it. Getting up my nerve, I leaned in, peering into darkness. I could make out dark hardwood floors, but nothing beyond. As my eyes adjusted, I could see that a tri-fold Chinese scene had been set in front of the wide door. She certainly did not want anyone seeing anything inside that house.

*Seven, Eight, Nine.*

Now I was on the opposite side of the house, out of the main view of the road and out of hearing distance from Carlos. I walked quickly past five more windows, to see what was in back. There were no windows or doors on the back wall of the house. Odd. Like an addition for storage. Mother had said Kay and her survival group were stockpiling supplies to be ready for Armageddon when the millennium would come on January 1st, 2000. I felt creepy. I started to retrace my steps towards window number 10, but I felt eyes on me now. Turning back, I saw movement in the grove of trees by the little house out back. Someone was watching me. I guessed it was the pregnant girl Carlos had met.

"Mother are you there?" I demanded at the 10th window. No answer.

"Mother, it's Carol" I pleaded at the 11th. Silence.

At the 12th window, I stopped; I thought I heard something. A tapping sound, first, then a soft, raspy "Carol, is that you?"

"Mother, it's me!"

"Oh, Carol."

"Are you alone?"

"Kay went to town."

"And where is Laurie?"

"At a friend's house spending the night."

"Can you come to the front door?"

"Kay keeps the room locked."

"You're locked in?"

"I think so. She took my walker away."

I dialed the sheriff while I told Mother she could come

home with me to live in San Diego.

"I'm locked in this room. She took my walker. I can't move," Mother said.

I relayed this to the officer, who said he would come out. In the meantime, Carlos had joined me. Mother's voice sounded stronger, closer. I put away the phone, looked up and saw the yellow shade move slightly. A fingernail was working at it. I was going to see Mother's face. I pictured her curly brown hairdo and smiling red lips. Then one bony finger lifted the edge of the shade and she pressed her fingertip on the glass. My forefinger reached up and touched hers. We couldn't see each other, but we were now connected.

A sheriff's deputy arrived. After he interviewed me and assessed the situation, he said he couldn't do anything unless "something happened." The shade inched back to reveal the face of an old woman with straight white hair hanging down below her shoulders. *My God.* This skeleton was my mother. I stifled my horror. She beamed at me and I tried to give her a good smile back. "Mommy!" I said.

She nodded her head and said, "You sure look good."

My heart was pounding triple time. I was going to get her out of there even if I had to fight Kay.

The deputy leaned his head in to speak to Mother and asked me to step back.

"Mrs. Council, are you hurt?"

"No, I'm fine, thank you."

"Are you locked in a room?"

"Yes."

"Do you have food and water?"

"Yes, I have both. Kay left me a sandwich for supper."

"Mrs. Council, would you like to stay here or go live with Carol?"

"What? Well, I..."

"You need to make the decision. Nobody can make it for you. Neither can your daughters. It's your right. Do you understand?"

*Mother, don't waffle now*, I begged silently. *Don't say you are all right. Please don't let me lose you again.*

"I could go live with Carol in San Diego?"

"Yes."

"I want to go with Carol."

Tears streamed down my cheeks.

The officer called back to the Sheriff's Office, while I returned to the window.

Mother looked uncomfortable suddenly. "I have to go the bathroom, a 'BM'." She disappeared. How was she going to do that without a walker?

"I still can't go inside. It's Sunday. I can't get a search warrant. And I can't do anything unless I have evidence that she is in danger or something has happened here."

In that moment I saw my mother falling on the floor. I *wished* it.

There was a crashing sound.

"Mother?"

"I fell down."

"That's it, I'm going in!" said the officer. As he ran, he called for backup. I followed fast. He stopped at the smaller front door, pulled out a club, and smashed in its window. Reaching in to unlock the door handle, he pushed the door open and nodded to me that it was okay for me to follow. His gun drawn, we entered a dark, litter-strewn parlor. I had to stop to let my eyes adjust to the dark. That is when I felt Kay's presence. The Chinese screen was too flat to hide anyone. I looked up. A staircase with a half wall led upstairs. Was she behind it? Or in a room up there. I froze. Silence.

I ran forward after the cop. He was moving boxes and nodded for me to help. They were cardboard boxes, mostly empty, piled high in front of the bedroom door. Tearing them down he tried the doorknob. As I decided to go around the corner to look for another door, I heard Mother tell him it was locked from inside. Turning the corner I almost ran into a giant-sized table. It was actually a large wooden cable spool turned on its end. Then I saw a door tied up with ropes. The rope stretched out to a doorknob on the partially open bathroom door. The knot was loose. Coming behind me the officer saw the situation, snapped a photo and kindly nodded to me that I should be the one to free my mother. Careful not to hurt her, I got down on my hands and knees and cracked the door open slowly. My mother was lying on her side, smiling up at me.

"I didn't break any bones, Carol. The heater broke my fall." Curling up next to her I hugged her tightly; her head was resting on the bottom drawer of a chest. Carlos was inside now, with another officer who was taking photographs of the smashed door and the rooms inside. The two officers came in, carefully picked her up, and set her on the bed. She sat there immobilized, watching everyone. She sat there stoically, as in the church pew that Sunday when the deacons had acted to remove the black visitors from the Baptist sanctuary. I had seen that expression on her face all my life. Immobilized. She had to let other people make the decisions for her. So female. My mother, educated, but powerless. I was no longer a girl in pink frozen by her side. I was a woman in red full of passion, pulse, and power. In my pocket, I fingered the red and white women's button. My liberation, my identity, had been squelched by the San Diego sisterhood. But the fire of feminism, the fire of the Longest Revolution, was powering me now. The journey had led me here to face my demons. Another sister, my blood sister, was my ultimate antagonist.

Next to the bed was a pile of diapers, wet wipes, and a small trash can with a tightly knotted plastic bag in it. On a wooden chair was a small plate with a half a bologna sandwich on it and a glass with a quarter inch of water in it. The camera zoomed in on the scene. More photos were taken.

"She said she'd be back after supper."

"What time is suppertime here?"

She shrugged her shoulders.

"Let's get moving. Mother, what do you need? Do you have a suitcase?

"Up there."

I swung it down from a closet shelf, set it on the floor by her bed, and threw in the diapers, asking "What else?"

"A pair of pants. I've been in these pajamas for three weeks. And a couple of blouses."

I grabbed them, a robe, and a pair of shoes.

"Medicines."

"They are all in the bathroom or kitchen."

I turned to the second deputy, "Go get all the bottles with her name on it."

"Valuables?" asked Carlos.

Mother handed me a small Kleenex box. "I put my jewelry in the bottom. I didn't think Kay would ever look there."

I threw it in the suitcase.

"My files are over there."

I dumped a box of file folders in.

"Let's go. That's all we can take."

Carlos said he had pulled the car up as close as

possible, but it would take all three men to carry her out to the porch and down the stairs. There she was, my big baby, being placed gently in the back seat.

The first officer said, "You go on. I'm putting a note on the front door saying I smashed the door in because she fell, with my name and a case number on it. She doesn't need to know anything else now. The charges will probably be false imprisonment, endangerment, and neglect. Here's my card. Go!"

I nodded, jumped into the passenger seat, and the car lurched forward, scraping the gravel driveway and skidding on the pavement. There were no other cars in sight. As we sped toward the airport, I looked over my shoulder. The two patrol cars drove off in the other direction.

# 42
# DEATH OR REBIRTH

The acute care facility that Mother entered focused on anemia. She couldn't walk. She wanted to badly. Her own mother was still walking at 104 years of age. She had never expected to end up like this at 86. She couldn't sit on the bed without falling over, but she kept trying. She showed me where Kay had pulled out fistfuls of her hair and pinched her arms so many times the wound could not heel. When Kay got too annoyed helping her on and off the toilet, she took away her walker. Mother was left in a locked room with diapers and a trash can next to her bed. She hadn't used her muscles in months. Tremors from Parkinson's prevented her from controlling her movements. The doctor adjusted her medications and sent in a psychologist, to whom she was gracious but too embarrassed to tell the truth.

Eight months later, at a senior's apartment we rented near our house, I sat on the couch. Mother said she had a surprise for me. Her eyes twinkled as she shifted her position in the motorized wheelchair, which had become her legs.

"Look." She reached out to drag a walker in front of her. With great effort, Mother slowly pulled herself up. She wavered, trembled and then gave up the battle. Mother plopped down to her armchair like an autumn leaf falling in the slightest October wind. The room became awkwardly silent.

Her eyes slowly turned to me with a look of resignation. She was immobilized. The sparkle in her eyes disappeared. I kept on smiling, but I thought she'd never walk again. I felt like the last three years had robbed her of that wonderful gift. My sister had won.

I took a deep breath and sighed, betraying my lack of confidence... Perhaps Mother noticed that I, too, had given up.

Yet, I still countered, "Mother, try it just one more time..."

She again reached out to the walker in front of her, taking a big breath, and pulled herself halfway up, then grunted and pushed herself all the way up. Gritting her teeth, she straightened to almost a standing position.

One heavy foot slid forward, then the other. I watched in disbelief. As I watched her walk, I thought of all the things I had tried to do for women and how often I had failed. Somehow, seeing her determined slow progress to her destination made me again realize the strength of a person's efforts. I followed her with joy as she walked — counting aloud the seven steps to the kitchen. They say all great endeavors begin with just a few simple actions. Her seven difficult steps crystallized the nobility of her spirit in my heart. The world seemed transformed. To another's eyes, it would probably mean nothing, an ancient lady's weak effort against the winds of time and obvious destiny.

Yet, to me, it meant everything. Even though it was only a few steps taken by a woman near death, a woman who helped me take my first steps.

In fact, that moment reached right up there with the day the Centaur for Women's Studies took seven steps and led the parade across San Diego State University.

# EPILOGUE

The San Diego State Women's Studies Department grew stronger each year, developing a national and international reputation for excellence in its curriculum and faculty. Today there are over 700 Women's Studies university programs across the world, and women's classes are held in Beijing, Vienna, Mexico City and many other cities, while women's consciousness raising groups have mobilized in Afghanistan despite the oppression of the Taliban.

Women and men around the world draw on Women's Studies to further advance the Longest Revolution. Their efforts will ultimately lead to the empowerment and equality of women everywhere. In our hearts we all know there will be world peace when women are free and equal in all nations on Earth.

To all the young readers who come to this page, I would like to part with one last thought: As a youth I had unlimited curiosity and enthusiasm, but little self-esteem or belief in my abilities. I was forever embarrassed by my Texas accent. If you, as a young person, reach inside and grasp your potential, which YOU ALL HAVE, you can, with others, change the world.

Good-night to ya'all, and ya'll come back now, you hear?

# REFERENCES

Cisler, Lucinda, *Women: A Bibliography,* New York, Lucinda Cisler Publisher, 1970.

De Beauvoir, Simone, *The Second Sex*, 1948, English Translation by H.M. Parshley, New York, Vintage Books, 1989.

Firestone, Shulamith, *The Dialectic of Sex,* New York, Morrow, 1970.

Freeman, Jo (Joreen), "Trashing," *Ms Magazine*, April, 1971.

Freidan, Betty, *The Feminine Mystique*, New York, Norton, 1963.

Howe, Florence, ed., "Female Studies II," Pittsburgh, KNOW, Inc., 1970.

Love, Barbara, ed., *Feminists Who Changed America: 1963-1975*, Urbana and Chicago, University of Illinois Press, 2007.

Millett, Kate, *Sexual Politics,* London, Virago, 1970.

Mitchell, Juliet, "The Longest Revolution," 1966 article in *The New Left Review*, revised and printed as Chapter 4 of her book *Women's Estate,* Penguin, 1971.

Mor, Barbara, ed., *Rainbow Snake: A Women's Poetry Anthology,* San Diego, Center for Women's Studies and Services, 1971.

Morgan, Robin, "Goodbye to All That," article, 1970.

Morgan, Robin, ed., *Sisterhood is Powerful: An Anthology of Writings from the Women's Liberation Movement*, New York, Vintage, 1970.

Nower, Joyce, *Year of the Fires,* San Diego, Center for Women's Studies and Services, 1983.

Orr, Catherine, "Representing Women/Disciplining Feminism: Activism, Professionalism, and Women's Studies," Thesis (Ph.D.), University of Wisconsin, Minnesota, chapters on origins of Women's Studies at San Diego State University, 1998, archived in SDSU Library, Special Collections.

Rosen, Ruth, *The World Split Open*, New York, Viking Press, 2000.

Wollstonecraft, Mary, *A Vindication of the Rights of Women,* London, printed for J. Johnson, St. Paul's Church Tarb, 1792.

**The Ghost of the Centaur for Women rides on in our dreams of unity and freedom. We will never forget her quest for our true destiny.**